Software Testing

Ron Patton

800 E. 96th St., Indianapolis, Indiana, 46240 USA

Software Testing
Copyright © 2001 by Sams Publishing

International Standard Book Number: 0-672-31983-7

Library of Congress Catalog Card Number: 00-102897

Printed in the United States of America

First Printing: November 2000

06 05 04   9 8 7 6

Trademarks

Warning and Disclaimer

Bulk Sales

Sams Publishing offers excellent discounts on this book when ordered in quantity for bulk purchases or special sales. For more information, please contact

U.S. Corporate and Government Sales
1-800-382-3419
corpsales@pearsontechgroup.com

For sales outside of the U.S., please contact

International Sales
1-317-428-3341
international@pearsontechgroup.com

ASSOCIATE PUBLISHER
Bradley L. Jones

ACQUISITIONS EDITOR
Neil Rowe

DEVELOPMENT EDITOR
Susan Shaw Dunn

MANAGING EDITOR
Charlotte Clapp

PROJECT EDITOR
Dawn Pearson

COPY EDITOR
Kim Cofer

INDEXER
Eric Schroeder

PROOFREADER
Daniel Ponder

TECHNICAL EDITOR
Gwen Heib

TEAM COORDINATOR
Meggo Barthlow

INTERIOR DESIGNER
Anne Jones

COVER DESIGNER
Anne Jones

LAYOUT TECHNICIANS
Ayanna Lacey
Heather Hiatt Miller
Stacey Richwine-DeRome

Contents at a Glance

Contents

PART IV   Supplementing Your Testing   217

14   Automated Testing and Test Tools   219

15   Bug Bashes and Beta Testing   241

About the Author

Ron Patton lives and works in Washington state as a software consultant. His software test experience is wide and varied, from mission-critical systems to painting programs for kids. Ron graduated from Penn State in 1984 with a B.S. degree in computer science. He began his career at Texas Instruments as a quality assurance engineer, testing embedded systems and user interface software for industrial automation equipment. In 1992 he joined Microsoft as a software test lead in the Systems Group for Multimedia Viewer, the authoring tool and multimedia display engine used by Encarta, Cinemania, and Bookshelf. He moved on to become the software test manager of the Kids Product Unit, shipping CD-ROM titles such as Creative Writer, Fine Artist, 3D Movie Maker, and the Magic School Bus series. Most recently, he was the software test manager of the Microsoft Hardware Group responsible for the software shipped with the mouse, keyboard, gaming, telephony, and ActiMates product lines.

Ron's most memorable project was ActiMates Barney, for which he test managed both the hardware and software efforts. "Microsoft actually paid my team and me to shake, bake, freeze, thaw, pull, drop, tumble, dunk, and shock dozens of prototype Barney dolls until we reduced them to piles of electronic rubble and purple fuzz," he recalls. "You can't get much more test satisfaction than that."

If you have comments or suggestions for this book, or if you find a bug in it that you want to report, you can send Ron an email at test@valart.com.

Dedication

To my best friend and wife, Valerie, who sacrificed a summer patiently waiting for me to finish this book. Hey Val, we can go out now!

Acknowledgments

Many thanks go to Sams Publishing and the editors and staff who produced this book. A special thanks goes to Neil Rowe, Susan Dunn, Dawn Pearson, and Gwen Heib who helped me through my first big-time writing effort and turned my idea for this book into a reality. A thank you also goes to Danny Faught who provided great input as an expert reviewer.

To my parents, Walter and Eleanore, for allowing me to quit my accordion lessons and buying me a TRS-80 Model I computer back in 1977. To my sister, Saundra, for keeping my parents busy with her baton competitions so I could hide in my room and learn to program. To Ruth Voland, my computer science teacher at Mohawk High School, for dragging me to all those science fairs and giving me extra time on the school's ASR 33 teletypes. To Mark Ferrell, who taught me electronics and kept me out of trouble as a teenager. To Alan Backus and Galen Freemon of TI for allowing me the freedom to explore software test automation. To all my past co-workers and employees for teaching me more than I could have ever learned myself about software testing. And, to my wonderful wife, Valerie, for saying, "Go ahead, send it in, see what happens" when, in 1991, I posed the question of sending my résumé to a little company called Microsoft in far-away Seattle. Each of you made a contribution to this book. Thank you!

Tell Us What You Think!

As the reader of this book, *you* are our most important critic and commentator. We value your opinion and want to know what we're doing right, what we could do better, what areas you'd like to see us publish in, and any other words of wisdom you're willing to pass our way.

As an associate publisher for Sams, I welcome your comments. You can email or write me directly to let me know what you did or didn't like about this book—as well as what we can do to make our books stronger.

Please note that I cannot help you with technical problems related to the topic of this book, and that due to the high volume of mail I receive, I might not be able to reply to every message.

When you write, please be sure to include this book's title and author as well as your name and phone or fax number. I will carefully review your comments and share them with the author and editors who worked on the book.

Email: feedback@samspublishing.com

Mail: Michael Stephens
        Associate Publisher
        Sams Publishing
        800 E. 96th Street
        Indianapolis, IN 46240 USA

Introduction

It seems as though each day there's yet another news story about a computer software problem: a bank reporting incorrect account balances, a Mars lander lost in space, a grocery store scanner charging too much for bananas, and the infamous Y2K bug.

Why does this happen? Can't computer programmers figure out ways to make software just plain work? Unfortunately, no. As software gets more complex, gains more features, and is more interconnected, it becomes more and more difficult to create a glitch-free program. Despite how good the programmers are and how much care is taken, there will always be software problems.

That's where software testing comes in. We've all found those little *Inspector 12* tags in our new clothes. Well, software has *Inspector 12*s, too. Many large software companies are so committed to quality they have one or more testers for each programmer. These jobs span the software spectrum from computer games to factory automation to business applications.

This book, *Software Testing*, will introduce you to the basics of software testing, teaching you not just the fundamental technical skills but also the supporting skills necessary to become a successful software tester. You will learn how to immediately find problems in any computer program, how to plan an effective test approach, how to clearly report your findings, and how to tell when your software is ready for release.

Who Should Use This Book?

This book is aimed at three different groups of people:

- Students or computer hobbyists interested in software testing as a full-time job, internship, or co-op. Read this book before your interview or before your first day on the job to really impress your new boss.

- Career changers wanting to move from their field of expertise into the software industry. There are lots of opportunities for non-software experts to apply their knowledge to software testing. For example, a flight instructor could test a flight simulator game, an accountant could test tax preparation software, or a teacher could test a new child education program.

- Programmers, software project managers, and other people who make up a software development team who want to improve their knowledge and understanding of what software testing is all about.

What This Book Will Do for You

In this book you will learn something about nearly every aspect of software testing:

- How software testing fits into the software development process
- Basic and advanced software testing techniques
- Applying testing skills to common testing tasks
- Improving test efficiency with automation
- Planning and documenting your test effort
- Effectively reporting the problems you find
- Measuring your test effort and your product's progress
- Knowing the difference between testing and quality assurance
- Finding a job as a software tester

Software Necessary to Use This Book

The methods presented in this book are generic and can be applied to testing any type of computer software. But, to make the examples familiar and usable by most people, they are based on simple programs such as Calculator, Notepad, and WordPad included with Windows 95/98 and Windows NT/2000.

Even if you don't have a PC running Windows, you will likely have similar programs available on your computer that you can easily adapt to the text. Be creative! Creativity is one trait of a good software tester.

> **NOTE**
>
> The examples used throughout this book of various applications, software bugs, and software test tools are in no way intended as an endorsement or a disparagement of the software. They're simply used to demonstrate the concepts of software testing.

How This Book Is Organized

This book is designed to lead you through the essential knowledge and skills necessary to become a good software tester. Software testing is not about banging on the keyboard hoping you'll eventually crash the computer. A great deal of science and engineering is behind it, lots of discipline and planning, and there can be some fun, too—as you'll soon see.

Part I: The Big Picture

The chapters in Part I lay the foundation for this book by showing you how software products are developed and how software testing fits into the overall development process. You'll see the importance of software testing and gain an appreciation for the magnitude of the job.

- Chapter 1, "Software Testing Background," helps you understand exactly what a software bug is, how serious they can be, and why they occur. You'll learn what your ultimate goal is as a software tester and what traits will help make you a good one.

- Chapter 2, "The Software Development Process," gives you an overview of how a software product is created in the corporate world. You'll learn what components typically go into software, what types of people contribute to it, and the different process models that can be used.

- Chapter 3, "The Realities of Software Testing," brings a reality check to how software is developed. You'll see why no matter how hard you try, software can never be perfect. You'll also learn a few fundamental terms and concepts used throughout the rest of this book.

Part II: Testing Fundamentals

The chapters in Part II teach you the fundamental approaches to software testing. The work of testing software is divided into four basic areas, and you see the techniques used for each one:

- Chapter 4, "Examining the Specification," teaches you how to find bugs by carefully inspecting the documentation that describes what the software is intended to do.

- Chapter 5, "Testing the Software with Blinders On," teaches you the techniques to use for testing software without having access to the code or even knowing how to program. This is the most common type of testing.

- Chapter 6, "Examining the Code," shows you how to perform detailed analysis of the program's source code to find bugs. You'll learn that you don't have to be an expert programmer to use these techniques.

- Chapter 7, "Testing the Software with X-Ray Glasses," teaches you how you can improve your testing by leveraging information you gain by reviewing the code or being able to see it execute while you run your tests.

Part III: Applying Your Testing Skills

The chapters in Part III take the techniques that you learned in Part II and apply them to some real-world scenarios that you'll encounter as a software tester:

- Chapter 8, "Configuration Testing," teaches you how to organize and perform software testing on different hardware configurations and platforms.

- Chapter 9, "Compatibility Testing," teaches you how to test for issues with different software applications and operating systems interacting with each other.

- Chapter 10, "Foreign-Language Testing," shows you that a whole world of software is out there and that it's important to test for the special problems that can arise when software is translated into other languages.

- Chapter 11, "Usability Testing," teaches you how to apply your testing skills when checking a software application's user interface and how to assure that your software is accessible to the disabled.

- Chapter 12, "Testing the Documentation," explains how to examine the software's documentation such as help files, user manuals, even the marketing material, for bugs.

- Chapter 13, "Web Site Testing," takes everything you've learned so far and applies it to a present-day situation. You'll see how something as simple as testing a Web site can encompass nearly all aspects of software testing.

Part IV: Supplementing Your Testing

The chapters in Part IV show you how to improve your test coverage and capability by leveraging both technology and people to perform your testing more efficiently and effectively:

- Chapter 14, "Automated Testing and Test Tools," explains how you can use computers and software to test other software. You'll learn several different methods for automating your tests and using tools. You'll also learn why using technology isn't foolproof.

- Chapter 15, "Bug Bashes and Beta Testing," shows you how to use other people to see the software differently and to find bugs that you completely overlooked.

Part V: Working with Test Documentation

The chapters in Part V cover how software testing is documented so that its plans, bugs, and results can be seen and understood by everyone on the project team:

- Chapter 16, "Planning Your Test Effort," shows you what goes into creating a test plan for your project. As a new software tester, you likely won't write a test plan from scratch, but it's important to know what's in one and why.

- Chapter 17, "Writing and Tracking Test Cases," teaches you how to properly document the test cases you develop so that you and other testers can use them.

- Chapter 18, "Reporting What You Find," teaches you how to tell the world when you find a bug, how to isolate the steps necessary to make it recur, and how to describe it so that others will understand and want to fix it.

- Chapter 19, "Measuring Your Success," describes various types of data, charts, and graphs used to gauge both your progress and success at testing and your software project's steps toward release.

Part VI: The Future

The chapters in Part VI explain where the future lies in software testing and set the stage for your career:

- Chapter 20, "Software Quality Assurance," teaches you the big difference between software testing and quality assurance. You'll learn about different software industry goals such as ISO 9000 and the Capabilities Maturity Model and what it takes to achieve them.

- Chapter 21, "Your Career as a Software Tester," gives you that kick in the behind to go out and be a software tester. You'll learn what types of jobs are available and where to look for them. You'll also find many pointers to more information.

Appendix

Each chapter in this book ends with a short quiz where you can try out the testing concepts that you learn. The answers appear in Appendix A, "Answers to Quiz Questions."

Conventions Used in This Book

This book uses several common conventions to help teach software testing topics. Here's a summary of those typographical conventions:

- New terms are emphasized in *italics* the first time they are used.
- Commands and computer output appear in a special monospaced font.
- Words you type appear in a **monospaced bold** font.

In addition to typographical conventions, the following special elements are included to set off different types of information to make them easily recognizable.

NOTE

Special notes augment the material you read in each chapter. These notes clarify concepts and procedures.

TIP

You'll find various tips that offer shortcuts and solutions to common problems.

REMINDER

Reminders refer to concepts discussed in previous chapters to help refresh your memory and reinforce important concepts.

The Big Picture

A crash is when your competitor's program dies. When your program dies, it is an "idiosyncrasy." Frequently, crashes are followed with a message like "ID 02." "ID" is an abbreviation for "idiosyncrasy" and the number that follows indicates how many more months of testing the product should have had.

—Guy Kawasaki, "The Macintosh Way"

I love deadlines. I especially like the whooshing sound they make as they go flying by.

—Douglas Adams, author of "The Hitch Hiker's Guide to the Galaxy"

IN THIS PART

Software Testing Background

IN THIS CHAPTER

In 1947, computers were big, room-sized machines operating on mechanical relays and glowing vacuum tubes. The state of the art at the time was the Mark II, a behemoth being built at Harvard University. Technicians were running the new computer through its paces when it suddenly stopped working. They scrambled to figure out why and discovered, stuck between a set of relay contacts deep in the bowels of the computer, a moth. It had apparently flown into the system, attracted by the light and heat, and was zapped by the high voltage when it landed on the relay.

The computer bug was born. Well, okay, it died, but you get the point.

Welcome to the first chapter of *Software Testing*. In this chapter, you'll learn about the history of software bugs and software testing.

Highlights of this chapter include

- How software bugs impact our lives
- What bugs are and why they occur
- Who software testers are and what they do

Infamous Software Error Case Studies

It's easy to take software for granted and not really appreciate how much it has infiltrated our daily lives. Back in 1947, the Mark II computer required legions of programmers to constantly maintain it. The average person never conceived of someday having his own computer in his home. Now there's free software CD-ROMs attached to cereal boxes and more software in our kids' video games than on the space shuttle. What once were techie gadgets, such as pagers and cell phones, have become commonplace. Most of us now can't go a day without logging on to the Internet and checking our email. We rely on overnight packages, long-distance phone service, and cutting-edge medical treatments.

Software is everywhere. However, it's written by people—so it's not perfect, as the following examples show.

Disney's *Lion King*, 1994–1995

In the fall of 1994, the Disney company released its first multimedia CD-ROM game for children, *The Lion King Animated Storybook*. Although many other companies had been marketing children's programs for years, this was Disney's first venture into the market and it was highly promoted and advertised. Sales were huge. It was "the game to buy" for children that holiday season. What happened, however, was a huge debacle. On December 26, the day after Christmas, Disney's customer support phones began to ring, and ring, and ring. Soon the phone support technicians were swamped with calls from angry parents with crying children who couldn't get the software to work. Numerous stories appeared in newspapers and on TV news.

It turns out that Disney failed to properly test the software on the many different PC models available on the market. The software worked on a few systems—likely the ones that the Disney programmers used to create the game—but not on the most common systems that the general public had.

Intel Pentium Floating-Point Division Bug, 1994

Enter the following equation into your PC's calculator:

(4195835 / 3145727) * 3145727 - 4195835

If the answer is zero, your computer is just fine. If you get anything else, you have an old Intel Pentium CPU with a floating-point division bug—a software bug burned into a computer chip and reproduced over and over in the manufacturing process.

On October 30, 1994, Dr. Thomas R. Nicely of Lynchburg (Virginia) College traced an unexpected result from one of his experiments to an incorrect answer by a division problem solved on his Pentium PC. He posted his find on the Internet and soon afterward a firestorm erupted as numerous other people duplicated his problem and found additional situations that resulted in wrong answers. Fortunately, these cases were rare and resulted in wrong answers only for extremely math-intensive, scientific, and engineering calculations. Most people would never encounter them doing their taxes or running their businesses.

What makes this story notable isn't the bug, but the way Intel handled the situation:

- Their software test engineers had found the problem while performing their own tests before the chip was released. Intel's management decided that the problem wasn't severe enough or likely enough to warrant fixing it, or even publicizing it.

- Once the bug was found, Intel attempted to diminish its perceived severity through press releases and public statements.

- When pressured, Intel offered to replace the faulty chips, but only if a user could prove that he was affected by the bug.

There was a public outcry. Internet newsgroups were jammed with irate customers demanding that Intel fix the problem. News stories painted the company as uncaring and incredulous. In the end, Intel apologized for the way it handled the bug and took a charge of over $400 million to cover the costs of replacing bad chips. Intel now reports known problems on its Web site and carefully monitors customer feedback on Internet newsgroups.

NOTE

On August 28th, 2000, shortly before this book went to press, Intel announced a recall of all the 1.13MHz Pentium III processors it had shipped after the chip had been in production for a month. A problem was discovered with the execution of certain instructions that could cause running applications to freeze. Computer manufacturers were creating plans for recalling the PCs already in customers' hands and calculating the costs of replacing the defective chips. As the baseball legend Yogi Berra once said, "This is like *déjà vu* all over again."

NASA Mars Polar Lander, 1999

On December 3, 1999, NASA's Mars Polar Lander disappeared during its landing attempt on the Martian surface. A Failure Review Board investigated the failure and determined that the most likely reason for the malfunction was the unexpected setting of a single data bit. Most alarming was why the problem wasn't caught by internal tests.

In theory, the plan for landing was this: As the lander fell to the surface, it was to deploy a parachute to slow its descent. A few seconds after the chute deployed, the probe's three legs were to snap open and latch into position for landing. When the probe was about 1,800 meters from the surface, it was to release the parachute and ignite its landing thrusters to gently lower it the remaining distance to the ground.

To save money, NASA simplified the mechanism for determining when to shut off the thrusters. In lieu of costly radar used on other spacecraft, they put an inexpensive contact switch on the leg's foot that set a bit in the computer commanding it to shut off the fuel. Simply, the engines would burn until the legs "touched down."

Unfortunately, the Failure Review Board discovered in their tests that in most cases when the legs snapped open for landing, a mechanical vibration also tripped the touch-down switch, setting the fatal bit. It's very probable that, thinking it had landed, the computer turned off the thrusters and the Mars Polar Lander smashed to pieces after falling 1,800 meters to the surface.

The result was catastrophic, but the reason behind it was simple. The lander was tested by multiple teams. One team tested the leg fold-down procedure and another the landing process from that point on. The first team never looked to see if the touch-down bit was set—it wasn't their area; the second team always reset the computer, clearing the bit, before it started its testing. Both pieces worked perfectly individually, but not when put together.

Patriot Missile Defense System, 1991

The U.S. Patriot missile defense system is a scaled-back version of the Strategic Defense Initiative ("Star Wars") program proposed by President Ronald Reagan. It was first put to use in the Gulf War as a defense for Iraqi Scud missiles. Although there were many news stories touting the success of the system, it did fail to defend against several missiles, including one that killed 28 U.S. soldiers in Dhahran, Saudi Arabia. Analysis found that a software bug was the problem. A small timing error in the system's clock accumulated to the point that after 14 hours, the tracking system was no longer accurate. In the Dhahran attack, the system had been operating for more than 100 hours.

The Y2K (Year 2000) Bug, circa 1974

Sometime in the early 1970s a computer programmer—let's suppose his name was Dave—was working on a payroll system for his company. The computer he was using had very little memory for storage, forcing him to conserve every last byte he could. Dave was proud that he could pack his programs more tightly than any of his peers. One method he used was to shorten dates from their 4-digit format, such as 1973, to a 2-digit format, such as 73. Because his payroll program relied heavily on date processing, Dave could save lots of expensive memory space. He briefly considered the problems that might occur when the current year hit 2000 and his program began doing computations on years such as 00 and 01. He knew there would be problems but decided that his program would surely be replaced or updated in 25 years and his immediate tasks were more important than planning for something that far out in time. After all, he had a deadline to meet. In 1995, Dave's program was still being used, Dave was retired, and no one knew how to get into the program to check if it was Y2K compliant, let alone how to fix it.

It's estimated that several hundred billion dollars were spent, worldwide, to replace or update computer programs such as Dave's, to fix potential Year 2000 failures.

What Is a Bug?

You've just read examples of what happens when software fails. It can be inconvenient, as when a computer game doesn't work properly, or it can be catastrophic, resulting in the loss of life. In these instances, it was obvious that the software didn't operate as intended. As a software tester you'll discover that most failures are hardly ever this obvious. Most are simple, subtle failures, with many being so small that it's not always clear which ones are true failures, and which ones aren't.

Terms for Software Failures

Depending on where you're employed as a software tester, you will use different terms to describe what happens when software fails. Here are a few:

Defect	Variance
Fault	Failure
Problem	Inconsistency
Error	Feature
Incident	Bug
Anomaly	

(There's also a list of unmentionable terms, but they're most often used privately among programmers.)

You might be amazed that so many names could be used to describe a software failure. Why so many? It's all really based on the company's culture and the process the company uses to develop its software. If you look up these words in the dictionary, you'll find that they all have slightly different meanings. They also have inferred meanings by how they're used in day-to-day conversation.

For example, *fault*, *failure*, and *defect* tend to imply a condition that's really severe, maybe even dangerous. It doesn't sound right to call an incorrectly colored icon a *fault*. These words also tend to imply blame: "It's his fault that the software failed."

Anomaly, *incident*, and *variance* don't sound quite so negative and infer more unintended operation than an all-out failure. "The president stated that it was a software anomaly that caused the missile to go off course."

Problem, *error*, and *bug* are probably the most generic terms used.

Just Call It What It Is and Get On with It

It's interesting that some companies and product teams will spend hours and hours of precious development time arguing and debating which term to use. A well-known computer company spent weeks in discussion with its engineers before deciding to rename Product Anomaly Reports (PARs) to Product Incident Reports (PIRs). Countless dollars were spent in the process of deciding which term was better. Once the decision was made, all the paperwork, software, forms, and so on had to be updated to reflect the new term. It's unknown if it made any difference to the programmer's or tester's productivity.

So, why bring this topic up? It's important as a software tester to understand the personality behind the product development team you're working with. How they refer to their software problems is a tell-tale sign of how they approach their overall development process. Are they cautious, careful, direct, or just plain blunt?

In this book, all software problems will be called *bugs*. It doesn't matter if it's big, small, intended, unintended, or someone's feelings will be hurt because they create one. There's no reason to dice words. A bug's a bug's a bug.

Software Bug: A Formal Definition

Calling any and all software problems *bugs* may sound simple enough, but doing so hasn't really addressed the issue. Now the word *problem* needs to be defined. To keep from running in circular definitions, there needs to be a definitive description of what a bug is.

First, you need a supporting term: *product specification*. A product specification, sometimes referred to as simply a *spec* or *product spec*, is an agreement among the software development team. It defines the product they are creating, detailing what it will be, how it will act, what it will do, and what it won't do. This agreement can range in form from a simple verbal understanding to a formalized written document. In Chapter 2, "The Software Development Process," you will learn more about software specifications and the development process, but for now, this definition is sufficient.

For the purposes of this book and much of the software industry, a *software bug* occurs when one or more of the following five rules is true:

1. The software doesn't do something that the product specification says it should do.
2. The software does something that the product specification says it shouldn't do.
3. The software does something that the product specification doesn't mention.
4. The software doesn't do something that the product specification doesn't mention but should.
5. The software is difficult to understand, hard to use, slow, or —in the software tester's eyes—will be viewed by the end user as just plain not right.

To better understand each rule, try the following example of applying them to a calculator.

The specification for a calculator probably states that it will perform correct addition, subtraction, multiplication, and division. If you, as the tester, receive the calculator, press the + key, and nothing happens, that's a bug because of Rule #1. If you get the wrong answer, that's also a bug because of Rule #1.

The product spec might state that the calculator should never crash, lock up, or freeze. If you pound on the keys and get the calculator to stop responding to your input, that's a bug because of Rule #2.

Suppose that you receive the calculator for testing and find that besides addition, subtraction, multiplication, and division, it also performs square roots. Nowhere was this ever specified. An ambitious programmer just threw it in because he felt it would be a great feature. This isn't a feature—it's really a bug because of Rule #3.

The fourth rule may read a bit strange with its double negatives, but its purpose is to catch things that were forgotten in the specification. You start testing the calculator and discover when the battery gets weak that you no longer receive correct answers to your calculations. No one ever considered how the calculator should react in this mode. A bad assumption was made that the batteries would always be fully charged. You expected it to keep working until the batteries were completely dead, or at least notify you in some way that they were weak. Correct calculations didn't happen with weak batteries and it wasn't specified what should happen. Rule #4 makes this a bug.

Rule #5 is the catch-all. As a tester you are the first person to really use the software. If you weren't there, it would be the customer using the product for the first time. If you find something that you don't feel is right, for whatever reason, it's a bug. In the case of the calculator, maybe you found that the buttons were too small. Maybe the placement of the = key made it hard to use. Maybe the display was difficult to read under bright lights. All of these are bugs because of Rule #5.

NOTE

Every person who uses a piece of software will have different expectations and opinions as to how it should work. It would be impossible to write software that every user thought was perfect. As a software tester, you should keep this in mind when you apply Rule #5 to your testing. Be thorough, use your best judgment, and be reasonable.

These are greatly simplified examples, so think about how the rules apply to software that you use every day. What is expected, what is unexpected? What do you think was specified and what was forgotten? And, what do you just plain dislike about the software?

This definition of a bug covers a lot of ground but it assures that all problems are identified.

Why Do Bugs Occur?

Now that you know what bugs are, you might be wondering why they occur. What you'll be surprised to find out is that most of them aren't caused by programming errors. Numerous studies have been performed on very small to extremely large projects and the results are always the same. The number one cause of software bugs is the specification (see Figure 1.1).

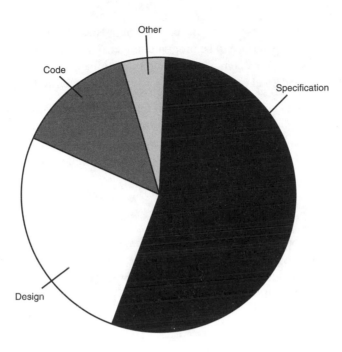

FIGURE 1.1

Bugs are caused for numerous reasons, but the main cause can be traced to the specification.

There are several reasons specifications are the largest bug producer. In many instances a spec simply isn't written. Other reasons may be that the spec isn't thorough enough, it's constantly changing, or it's not communicated well to the entire development team. Planning software is vitally important. If it's not done correctly, bugs will be created.

The next largest source of bugs is the design. This is where the programmers lay out their plan for the software. Compare it to an architect creating the blueprints for a building. Bugs occur here for the same reason they occur in the specification. It's rushed, changed, or not well communicated.

NOTE

There's an old saying, "If you can't say it, you can't do it." This applies perfectly to software development and testing.

Coding errors may be more familiar to you if you're a programmer. Typically, these can be traced to the software's complexity, poor documentation (especially in code that's being updated or revised), schedule pressure, or just plain dumb mistakes. It's important to note that many bugs that appear on the surface to be programming errors can really be traced to specification and design errors. It's quite common to hear a programmer say, "Oh, so that's what it's supposed to do. If somebody had just told me that I wouldn't have written the code that way."

The other category is the catch-all for what's left. Some bugs can be blamed on false positives, conditions that were thought to be bugs but really weren't. There may be duplicate bugs, multiple ones that resulted from the same root cause. Some bugs can also be traced to testing errors. In the end, these bugs usually make up such a small percentage of all bugs found that they aren't worth worrying about.

The Cost of Bugs

As you will learn in Chapter 2, software doesn't just magically appear—there's usually a planned, methodical development process used to create it. From its inception, through the planning, programming, and testing, to its use by the public, there's the potential for bugs to be found. Figure 1.2 shows how the cost of fixing these bugs grows over time.

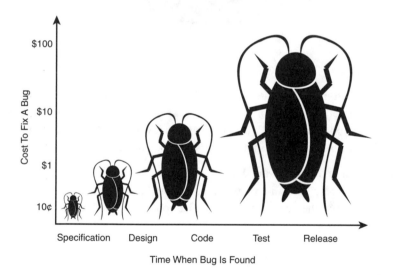

FIGURE 1.2

The cost to fix bugs increases dramatically over time.

The costs are logarithmic—that is, they increase tenfold as time increases. A bug found and fixed during the early stages when the specification is being written might cost next to nothing, or 10 cents in our example. The same bug, if not found until the software is coded and tested, might cost $1 to $10. If a customer finds it, the cost could easily top $100.

As an example of how this works, consider the Disney *Lion King* case discussed earlier. The root cause of the problem was that the software wouldn't work on a very popular PC platform. If, in the early specification stage, someone had researched what PCs were popular and specified that the software needed to be designed and tested to work on those configurations, the cost of that effort would have been almost nothing. If that didn't occur, a backup would have been for the software testers to collect samples of the popular PCs and verify the software on them. They would have found the bug, but it would have been more expensive to fix because the software would have to be debugged, fixed, and retested. The development team could have also sent out a preliminary version of the software to a small group of customers in what's called a *beta test*. Those customers, chosen to represent the larger market, would have likely discovered the problem. As it turned out, however, the bug was completely missed until many thousands of CD-ROMs were created and purchased. Disney ended up paying for telephone customer support, product returns, replacement CD-ROMs, as well as another debug, fix, and test cycle. It's very easy to burn up your entire product's profit if serious bugs make it to the customer.

What Exactly Does a Software Tester Do?

You've now seen examples of really nasty bugs, you know what the definition of a bug is, and you know how costly they can be. By now it should be pretty evident what a tester's goal is:

> *The goal of a software tester is to find bugs.*

You may run across product teams who want their testers to simply confirm that the software works, not to find bugs. Reread the case study about the Mars Polar Lander, and you'll see why this is the wrong approach. If you're only testing things that should work and setting up your tests so they'll pass, you will miss the things that don't work. You will miss the bugs.

If you're missing bugs, you're costing your project and your company money. As a software tester you shouldn't be content at just finding bugs—you should think about how to find them sooner in the development process, thus making them cheaper to fix.

> *The goal of a software tester is to find bugs, and find them as early as possible.*

But, finding bugs, even finding them early, isn't enough. Remember the definition of a bug. You, the software tester, are the customer's eyes, the first one to see the software. You speak for the customer and must demand perfection.

> *The goal of a software tester is to find bugs, find them as early as possible, and make sure they get fixed.*

This final definition is very important. Commit it to memory and refer back to it as you learn the testing techniques discussed throughout the rest of this book.

What Makes a Good Software Tester?

In the movie *Star Trek II: The Wrath of Khan*, Spock says, "As a matter of cosmic history, it has always been easier to destroy than to create." At first glance, it may appear that a software tester's job would be easier than a programmer's. Breaking code and finding bugs must surely be easier than writing the code in the first place. Surprisingly, it's not. The methodical and disciplined approach to software testing that you'll learn in this book requires the same hard work and dedication that programming does. It involves very similar skills, and although a software tester doesn't necessarily need to be a full-fledged programmer, having that knowledge is a great benefit.

Today, most mature companies treat software testing as a technical engineering profession. They recognize that having trained software testers on their project teams and allowing them to apply their trade early in the development process allows them to build better quality software.

Here's a list of traits that most software testers should have:

- **They are explorers.** Software testers aren't afraid to venture into unknown situations. They love to get a new piece of software, install it on their PC, and see what happens.

- **They are troubleshooters.** Software testers are good at figuring out why something doesn't work. They love puzzles.

- **They are relentless.** Software testers keep trying. They may see a bug that quickly vanishes or is difficult to re-create. Rather than dismiss it as a fluke, they will try every way possible to find it.

- **They are creative.** Testing the obvious isn't sufficient for software testers. Their job is to think up creative and even off-the-wall approaches to find bugs.

- **They are (mellowed) perfectionists.** They strive for perfection, but they know when it becomes unattainable and they're OK with getting as close as they can.

- **They exercise good judgment.** Software testers need to make decisions about what they will test, how long it will take, and if the problem they're looking at is really a bug.

- **They are tactful and diplomatic.** Software testers are always the bearers of bad news. They have to tell the programmers that their baby is ugly. Good software testers know how to do so tactfully and professionally and know how to work with programmers who aren't always tactful and diplomatic.

- **They are persuasive.** Bugs that testers find won't always be viewed as severe enough to be fixed. Testers need to be good at making their points clear, demonstrating why the bug does indeed need to be fixed, and following through on making it happen.

Software Testing Is Fun!

A fundamental trait of software testers is that they simply like to break things. They live to find those elusive system crashes. They take great satisfaction in laying to waste the most complex programs. They're often seen jumping up and down in glee, giving each other high-fives, and doing a little dance when they bring a system to its knees. It's the simple joys of life that matter the most.

In addition to these traits, having some education in software programming is a big plus. As you'll see in Chapter 6, "Examining the Code," knowing how software is written can give you a different view of where bugs are found, thus making you a more efficient and effective tester. It can also help you develop the testing tools discussed in Chapter 14, "Automated Testing and Test Tools."

Lastly, if you're an expert in some non-computer field, your knowledge can be invaluable to a software team creating a new product. Software is being written to do just about everything today. Your knowledge of teaching, cooking, airplanes, carpentry, medicine, or whatever would be a tremendous help finding bugs in software for those areas.

Summary

Software testing is a critical job. With the size and complexity of today's software, it's imperative that software testing be performed professionally and effectively. Too much is at risk. We don't need more defective computer chips or lost Mars landers.

In the following chapters of Part I, you'll learn more about the big picture of software development and how software testing fits in. This knowledge is critical to helping you apply the specific test techniques covered in the remainder of this book.

Quiz

These quiz questions are provided for your further understanding. See Appendix A, "Answers to Quiz Questions," for the answers—but don't peek!

1. In the Year 2000 bug example, did Dave do anything wrong?
2. **True or False:** It's important what term your company or team calls a problem in its software.
3. What's wrong with just testing that a program works as expected?
4. How much more does it cost to fix a bug found after the product is released than it does from the very start of the project?

5. What's the goal of a software tester?

6. **True or False:** A good tester relentlessly strives for perfection.

7. Give several reasons why the product specification is usually the largest source of bugs in a software product.

The Software Development Process

CHAPTER

2

IN THIS CHAPTER

To be an effective software tester, it's important to have at least a high-level understanding of the overall process used to develop software. If you write small programs as a student or hobbyist, you'll find that the methods you use are much different from what big companies use to develop software. The creation of a new software product may involve dozens, hundreds, even thousands of team members all playing different roles and working together under tight schedules. The specifics of what these people do, how they interact, and how they make decisions are all part of the software development process.

The goal of this chapter isn't to teach you everything about the software development process—that would take an entire book! The goal is to give you an overview of the all the pieces that go into a software product and a look at a few of the common approaches in use today. With this knowledge you'll have a better understanding of how best to apply the software testing skills you learn in the later chapters of this book.

The highlights of this chapter include

- What major components go into a software product
- What different people and skills contribute to a software product
- How software progresses from an idea to a final product

Product Components

What exactly is a software product? Many of us think of it as simply a program that we install from a floppy disk or CD-ROM that runs on our computer. That's a pretty good description, but in reality, many hidden pieces go into making that software. There are also many pieces that "come in the box" that are often taken for granted or might even be ignored. Although it may be easy to forget about all those parts, as a software tester, you need to be aware of them, because they're all testable pieces and can all have bugs.

What Effort Goes Into a Software Product?

First, look at what effort goes into a software product. Figure 2.1 identifies a few of the abstract pieces that you may not have considered.

So what are all these things, besides the actual code, that get funneled into the software? At first glance they probably seem much less tangible than the program listing a programmer creates. And they definitely aren't something that can be viewed directly from the product's CD-ROM. But, to paraphrase a line from an old spaghetti sauce commercial, "they're in there." At least, they should be.

The term used in the software industry to describe a software product component that's created and passed on to someone else is *deliverable*. The easiest way to explain what all these deliverables are is to organize them into major categories.

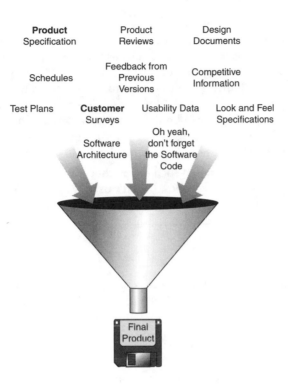

Product
Specification

Product
Reviews

Design
Documents

Schedules

Feedback from
Previous
Versions

Competitive
Information

Test Plans

Customer
Surveys

Usability Data

Look and Feel
Specifications

Oh yeah,
don't forget
the Software
Code

Software
Architecture

Final
Product

FIGURE 2.1

A lot of hidden effort goes into a software product.

Customer Requirements

Software is written to fulfill some need that a person or a group of people has. Let's call them the *customer*. To properly fill that need, the product development team must find out what the customer wants. Some teams simply guess, but most collect detailed information in the form of surveys, feedback from previous versions of the software, competitive product information, magazine reviews, focus groups, and numerous other methods, some formal, some not. All this information is then studied, condensed, and interpreted to decide exactly what features the software product should have.

Put Your Features in Perspective with Focus Groups

A popular means to get direct feedback from potential customers of a software product is to use focus groups. Focus groups are often organized by independent survey companies who set up offices in shopping malls. The surveyors typically walk around the mall with a clipboard and ask passers-by if they want to take part in a study. They'll ask a few questions to qualify you such as "Do you have a PC at home? Do you use software X? How much time do you spend online?" And so on. If you fit their demographic, they'll invite you to return for a few hours to participate with several other people in a focus group. There, you'll be asked more detailed questions about computer software. You may be shown various software boxes and be asked to choose your favorite. Or, you may discuss as a group features you'd like to see in a new product. Best of all, you get paid for your time.

Most focus groups are conducted in such a way that the software company requesting the information is kept anonymous. But, it's usually easy to figure out who they are.

Specifications

The result of the customer requirements studies is really just raw data. It doesn't describe the proposed product, it just confirms whether it should (or shouldn't) be created and what features the customers want. The specifications take all this information plus any unstated but mandatory requirements and truly define what the product will be, what it will do, and how it will look.

The format of specifications varies greatly. Some companies—especially those developing products for the government, aerospace, financial, and medical industries—use a very rigorous process with many checks and balances. The result is a very detailed and thorough specification that's *locked down*, meaning that it can't change except under very extreme conditions. Everyone on the development team knows exactly what they are creating.

There are development teams, usually ones creating software for less-critical applications, who produce specifications on cocktail napkins, if they create them at all. This has the distinct advantage of being very flexible, but there's lots of risk that not everyone is "on the same page." And, what the product finally becomes isn't known until it's released.

Schedules

A key part of a software product is its schedule. As a project grows in size and complexity, with many pieces and many people contributing to the product, it becomes necessary to have some mechanism to track its progress. This could range from simple task lists to Gantt charts (see Figure 2.2) to detailed tracking of every minute task with project management software.

The goals of scheduling are to know which work has been completed, how much work is still left to do, and when it will all be finished.

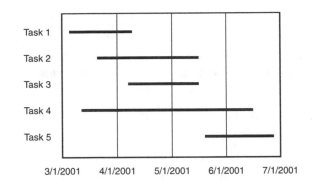

FIGURE 2.2
A Gantt chart is a bar chart that shows a project's tasks against a horizontal timeline.

Software Design Documents

One common misconception is that when a programmer creates a program, he simply sits down and starts writing code. That may happen in some small, informal software shops, but for anything other than the smallest programs, there must be a design process to plan out how the software will be written. Think about this book, which required an outline before the first words were typed, or a building, which has blueprints drawn before the first concrete is poured. The same planning should happen with software.

The documents that programmers create vary greatly depending on the company, the project, and the team, but their purpose is to plan and organize the code that is to be written.

Here is a list of a few common software design documents:

- **Architecture.** A document that describes the overall design of the software, including descriptions of all the major pieces and how they interact with each other.

- **Data Flow Diagram.** A formalized diagram that shows how data moves through a program. It's sometimes referred to as a *bubble chart* because it's drawn by using circles and lines.

- **State Transition Diagram.** Another formalized diagram that breaks the software into basic states, or conditions, and shows the means for moving from one state to the next.

- **Flowchart.** The traditional means for pictorially describing a program's logic. Flowcharting isn't very popular today, but when it's used, writing the program code from a detailed flowchart is a very simple process.

- **Commented Code.** There's an old saying that you may write code once, but it will be read by someone at least 10 times. Properly embedding useful comments in the software code itself is extremely important, so that programmers assigned to maintain the code can more easily figure out what it does and how.

Test Documents

Test documentation is discussed in detail in Chapters 17–19 but is mentioned here because it's integral to what makes up a software product. For the same reasons that programmers must plan and document their work, software testers must as well. It's not unheard of for a software test team to create more deliverables than the programmers.

Here's a list of the more important test deliverables:

- The *test plan* describes the overall method to be used to verify that the software meets the product specification and the customer's needs. It includes the quality objectives, resource needs, schedules, assignments, methods, and so forth.

- *Test cases* list the specific items that will be tested and describe the detailed steps that will be followed to verify the software.

- *Bug reports* describe the problems found as the test cases are followed. These could be done on paper but are often tracked in a database.

- *Metrics*, *statistics*, and *summaries* convey the progress being made as the test work progresses. They take the form of graphs, charts, and written reports.

What Parts Make Up a Software Product?

So far in this chapter you've learned about the effort that goes into creating a software product. It's also important to realize that when the product is ready to be boxed up and shipped out the door, it's not just the code that gets delivered. Numerous supporting parts go along with it (see Figure 2.3). Since all these parts are seen or used by the customer, they need to be tested too.

It's unfortunate, but these components are often overlooked in the testing process. You've surely attempted to use a product's built-in help file and found it to be not so helpful or—worse—just plain wrong. Or, maybe you've checked the system requirements printed on the side of a software box only to find out after you bought it that the software didn't work on your PC. These seem like simple things to test, but no one probably even gave them a second look before the product was OK'd for release. You will.

Later in this book you'll learn about these non-software pieces and how to properly test them. Until then, keep this list in mind as just a sampling of what more there is to a software product than just the code:

Help files	Users manual
Samples and examples	Labels and stickers
Product support info	Icons and art
Error messages	Ads and marketing material
Setup and installation	Readme file

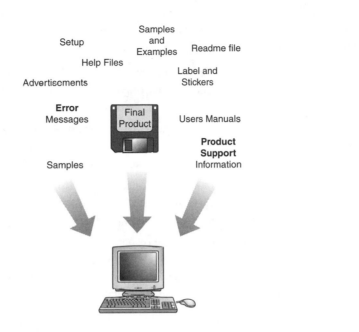

FIGURE 2.3
The software floppy disk or CD-ROM is just one of the many pieces that make up a software product.

Don't Forget to Test Error Messages

Error messages are one of the most overlooked parts of a software product. Programmers, not trained writers, typically write them. They're seldom planned for and are usually hacked in while fixing bugs. It's also very difficult for testers to find and display all of them. Don't let error messages such as these creep into your software:

```
Error: Keyboard not found. Press F1 to continue.

Can't instantiate the video thing.

Windows has found an unknown device and is installing a driver for it.

A Fatal Exception 006 has occurred at 0000:0000007.
```

Software Project Staff

Now that you know what goes into a software product and what ships with one, it's time to learn about all the people who create software. Of course, this varies a great deal based on the company and the project, but for the most part the roles are the same, it's just the titles that are different.

The following lists, in no particular order, the major players and what they do. The most common names are given, but expect variations and additions:

- *Project managers*, *program managers*, or *producers* drive the project from beginning to end. They're usually responsible for writing the product spec, managing the schedule, and making the critical decisions and trade-offs.

- *Architects* or *system engineers* are the technical experts on the product team. They're usually very experienced and therefore are qualified to design the overall systems architecture or design for the software. They work very closely with the programmers.

- *Programmers*, *developers*, or *coders* design, write, and fix bugs in the software. They work closely with the architects and project managers to create the software. Then, they work closely with the project managers and testers to get the bugs fixed.

- *Testers* or *QA (Quality Assurance)* are responsible for finding and reporting problems in the software product. They work very closely with all members of the team as they develop and run their tests, and report the problems they find. Chapter 20, "Software Quality Assurance," thoroughly covers the differences between software testing and software quality assurance tasks.

- *Technical writers*, *user assistance*, *user education*, *manual writers*, or *illustrators* create the paper and online documentation that comes with a software product.

- *Configuration management* or *builder* handles the process of pulling together all the software written by the programmers and all the documentation created by the writers and putting it together into a single package.

As you can see, several groups of people contribute to a software product. On large teams there may be dozens or hundreds working together. To successfully communicate and organize their approach, they need a plan, a method for getting from point A to point B. That's what the next section is about.

Software Development Lifecycle Models

A running joke in the computer industry is that three things should never be seen in the process of being created: laws, sausage, and software. Their creation is so messy and disgusting that it's best to just wait and see the final result. That may or may not be totally true, but with most old sayings, there is a grain of truth behind the words. Some software is developed with the rigor and discipline of a fine craftsman, some software with tightly controlled chaos, and other software is stuck together with duct tape and chewing gum. Usually, in the end, it's apparent to the customer what process was used. The process used to create a software product from its initial conception to its public release is known as the *software development lifecycle model*.

As discussed previously, there are many different methods that can be used for developing software, and no model is necessarily the best for a particular project. There are four frequently used models, with most others just variations of these:

- Big-Bang
- Code-and-Fix
- Waterfall
- Spiral

Each model has its advantages and disadvantages. As a tester, you will likely encounter them all and will need to tailor your test approach to fit the model being used for your current project. Refer to these model descriptions as you read the rest of this book and think about how you would apply the various testing techniques you learn under each of them.

Big-Bang Model

One theory of the creation of the universe is the big-bang theory. It states that billions of years ago, the universe was created in a single huge explosion of nearly infinite energy. Everything that exists is the result of energy and matter lining up to produce this book, floppy disks, and Bill Gates. If the atoms didn't line up just right, these things might all be just quivering masses of goop.

The big-bang model for software development shown in Figure 2.4 follows much the same principle. A huge amount of matter (people and money) is put together, a lot of energy is expended—often violently—and out comes the perfect software product...or it doesn't.

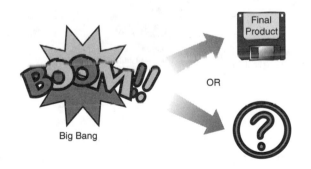

OR

Big Bang

FIGURE 2.4
The big-bang model is by far the simplest method of software development.

The beauty of the big-bang method is that it's simple. There is little if any planning, scheduling, or formal development process. All the effort is spent developing the software and writing the code. It's an ideal process if the product requirements aren't well understood and the final release date is flexible. It's also important to have very flexible customers, too, because they won't know what they're getting until the very end.

Notice that testing isn't shown in Figure 2.4. In most cases, there is little to no formal testing done under the big-bang model. If testing does occur, it's squeezed in just before the product is released. It's a mystery why testing is sometimes inserted into this model, but it's probably to make everyone feel good that some testing was performed.

If you are called in to test a product under the big-bang model, you have both an easy and a difficult task. Because the software is already complete, you have the perfect specification— the product itself. And, because it's impossible to go back and fix things that are broken, your job is really just to report what you find so the customers can be told about the problems.

The downside is that, in the eyes of project management, the product is ready to go, so your work is holding up delivery to the customer. The longer you take to do your job and the more bugs you find, the more contentious the situation will become. Try to stay away from testing in this model.

Code-and-Fix Model

The code-and-fix model shown in Figure 2.5 is usually the one that project teams fall into by default if they don't consciously attempt to use something else. It's a step up, procedurally, from the big-bang model, in that it at least requires some idea of what the product require-ments are.

Typically informal
Product Specification

Code, Fix,
Repeat Until?

Final
Product

FIGURE 2.5
The code-and-fix model repeats until someone gives up.

A wise man once said, "There's never time to do it right, but there's always time to do it over." That pretty much sums up this model. A team using this approach usually starts with a rough idea of what they want, does some simple design, and then proceeds into a long repeating cycle of coding, testing, and fixing bugs. At some point they decide that enough is enough and release the product.

As there's very little overhead for planning and documenting, a project team can show results immediately. For this reason, the code-and-fix model works very well for small projects intended to be created quickly and then thrown out shortly after they're done, such as prototypes and demos. Even so, code-and-fix has been used on many large and well-known software products. If your word processor or spreadsheet software has lots of little bugs or it just doesn't seem quite finished, it was likely created with the code-and-fix model.

Like the big-bang model, testing isn't specifically called out in the code-and-fix model but does play a significant role between the coding and the fixing.

As a tester on a code-and-fix project, you need to be aware that you, along with the programmers, will be in a constant state of cycling. As often as every day you'll be given new or updated releases of the software and will set off to test it. You'll run your tests, report the bugs, and then get a new software release. You may not have finished testing the previous release when the new one arrives, and the new one may have new or changed features. Eventually, you'll get a chance to test most of the features, find fewer and fewer bugs, and then someone (or the schedule) will decide that it's time to release the product.

You will most likely encounter the code-and-fix model during your work as a software tester. It's a good introduction to software development and will help you appreciate the more formal methods.

Waterfall Model

The waterfall method is usually the first one taught in programming school. It's been around forever. It's simple, elegant, and makes sense. And, it can work well on the right project. Figure 2.6 shows the steps involved in this model.

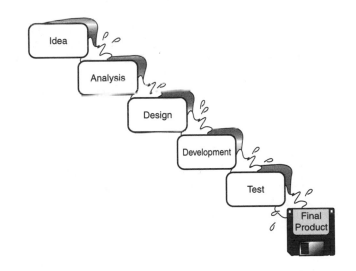

FIGURE 2.6

The software development process flows from one step to the next in the waterfall model.

A project using the waterfall model moves down a series of steps starting from an initial idea to a final product. At the end of each step, the project team holds a review to determine if they're ready to move to the next step. If the project isn't ready to progress, it stays at that level until it's ready.

Notice three important things about the waterfall method:

- There's a large emphasis on specifying what the product will be. Note that the development or coding phase is only a single block!

- The steps are discrete; there's no overlap.

- There's no way to back up. As soon as you're on a step, you need to complete the tasks for that step and then move on—you can't go back.[1]

This may sound very limiting, and it is, but it works well for projects with a well-understood product definition and a disciplined development staff. The goal is to work out all the unknowns and nail down all the details before the first line of code is written. The drawback is that in today's fast moving culture, with products being developed on Internet time, by the time a software product is so carefully thought out and defined, the original reason for its being may have changed.

From a testing perspective, the waterfall model offers one huge advantage over the other models presented so far. Everything is carefully and thoroughly specified. By the time the software is delivered to the test group, every detail has been decided on, written down, and turned into software. From that, the test group can create an accurate plan and schedule. They know exactly what they're testing, and there's no question about whether something is a feature or a bug.

But, with this advantage, comes a large disadvantage. Because testing occurs only at the end, a fundamental problem could creep in early on and not be detected until days before the scheduled product release. Remember from Chapter 1, "Software Testing Background," how the cost of bugs increases over time? What's needed is a model that folds the testing tasks in earlier to find problems before they become too costly.

Spiral Model

It's not quite utopia, but the spiral model (see Figure 2.7) goes a long way in addressing many of the problems inherent with the other models while adding a few of its own nice touches.

---

[1] *Variations of the waterfall model loosen the rules a bit, allowing some overlap of the steps and the ability to back up one step if necessary.*

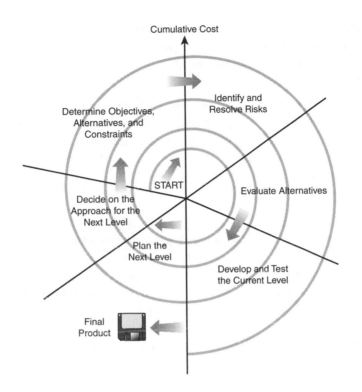

FIGURE 2.7

The spiral model starts small and gradually expands as the project becomes better defined and gains stability.

The spiral model was introduced by Barry Boehm in 1986 in his Association for Computing Machinery (ACM) paper, "A Spiral Model of Software Development and Enhancement." It's used fairly often and has proven to be an effective approach to developing software.

The general idea behind the spiral model is that you don't define everything in detail at the very beginning. You start small, define your important features, try them out, get feedback from your customers, and then move on to the next level. You repeat this until you have your final product.

Each time around the spiral involves six steps:

1. Determine objectives, alternatives, and constraints.
2. Identify and resolve risks.
3. Evaluate alternatives.
4. Develop and test the current level.
5. Plan the next level.
6. Decide on the approach for the next level.

Built into the spiral model is a bit of waterfall (the steps of analysis, design, develop, test), a bit of code-and-fix (each time around the spiral), and a bit of big-bang (look at it from the outside). Couple this with the lower costs of finding problems early, and you have a pretty good development model.

If you're a tester, you'll like this model. You'll get a chance to influence the product early by being involved in the preliminary design phases. You'll see where the project has come from and where it's going. And, at the very end of the project, you won't feel as rushed to perform all your testing at the last minute. You've been testing all along, so the last push should only be a validation that everything is OK.

Summary

You now have an understanding of how software products are created—both what goes into them and the processes used to put them together. As you can see, there's no definitive approach. The four models presented here are just examples. There are many others and lots of variations of these. Each company, each project, and each team will choose what works for them. Sometimes they will choose right, sometimes they will choose wrong. Your job as a software tester is to work the best you can in the development model you're in, applying the testing skills you learn in the rest of this book to create the best software possible.

Quiz

These quiz questions are provided for your further understanding. See Appendix A, "Answers to Quiz Questions," for the answers—but don't peek!

1. Name several tasks that should be performed before a programmer starts writing the first line of code.

2. What disadvantage is there to having a formal, locked-down specification?

3. What is the best feature of the big-bang model of software development?

4. When using the code-and-fix model, how do you know when the software is ready to release?

5. Why can the waterfall method be difficult to use?

6. Why would a software tester like the spiral model better than the others?

The Realities of Software Testing

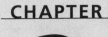

IN THIS CHAPTER

In Chapters 1 and 2, you learned about the basics of software testing and the software development process. The information presented in these chapters offered a very high-level and arguably idealistic view of how software projects might be run. Unfortunately, in the real world you will never see a project flawlessly follow the spiral model of development. You will never be given a thoroughly detailed specification that perfectly meets the customer's needs. It just doesn't happen. But, to be an effective software tester, you need to understand what the ideal process is so that you have something to aim for.

The goal of this chapter is to temper that idealism with a reality check from a software tester's perspective. It will help you see that, in practice, trade-offs and concessions must be made throughout the development cycle. Many of those trade-offs are directly related to the software test effort. The bugs you find and the problems you prevent all significantly affect the project. After reading this chapter, you'll have a much clearer picture of the roles, the impact, and the responsibilities that software testing has and you'll hopefully appreciate the behind-the-scenes decisions that must be made to create a software product.

The highlights of this chapter include

- Why software can never be perfect
- Why software testing isn't just a technical problem
- The terms commonly used by software testers

Testing Axioms

This first section of this chapter is a list of axioms, or truisms. Think of them as the "rules of the road" or the "facts of life" for software testing and software development. Each of them is a little tidbit of knowledge that helps put some aspect of the overall process into perspective.

It's Impossible to Test a Program Completely

As a new tester, you might believe that you can approach a piece of software, fully test it, find all the bugs, and assure that the software is perfect. Unfortunately, this isn't possible, even with the simplest programs, due to four key reasons:

- The number of possible inputs is very large.
- The number of possible outputs is very large.
- The number of paths through the software is very large.
- The software specification is subjective. You might say that a bug is in the eye of the beholder.

Multiply all these "very large" possibilities together and you get a set of test conditions that's too large to attempt. If you don't believe it, consider the example shown in Figure 3.1, the Microsoft Windows Calculator.

FIGURE 3.1

Even a simple program such as the Windows Calculator is too complex to completely test.

Assume that you are assigned to test the Windows Calculator. You decide to start with addition. You try 1+0=. You get an answer of 1. That's correct. Then you try 1+1=. You get 2. How far do you go? The calculator accepts a 32-digit number, so you must try all the possibilities up to

1+99999999999999999999999999999999=

Once you complete that series, you can move on to 2+0=, 2+1=, 2+2=, and so on. Eventually you'll get to

99999999999999999999999999999999+99999999999999999999999999999999=

Next you should try all the decimal values: 1.0+0.1, 1.0+0.2, and so on.

Once you verify that regular numbers sum properly, you need to attempt illegal inputs to assure that they're properly handled. Remember, you're not limited to clicking the numbers onscreen—you can press keys on your computer keyboard, too. Good values to try might be 1+a, z+1, 1a1+2b2,.... There are literally billions upon billions of these.

Edited inputs must also be tested. The Windows Calculator allows the Backspace and Delete keys, so you should try them. 1<backspace>2+2 should equal 4. Everything you've tested so far must be retested by pressing the Backspace key for each entry, for each two entries, and so on.

If you or your heirs manage to complete all these cases, you can then move on to adding three numbers, then four numbers,....

There are so many possible entries that you could never complete them, even if you used a super computer to feed in the numbers. And that's only for addition. You still have subtraction, multiplication, division, square root, percentage, and inverse to cover.

The point of this example is to demonstrate that it's impossible to completely test a program, even software as simple as a calculator. If you decide to eliminate any of the test conditions because you feel they're redundant or unnecessary, or just to save time, you've decided not to test the program completely.

Software Testing Is a Risk-Based Exercise

If you decide not to test every possible test scenario, you've chosen to take on risk. In the calculator example, what if you choose not to test that 1024+1024=2048? It's possible the programmer accidentally left in a bug for that situation. If you don't test it, a customer will still use it, and he or she will discover the bug. It'll be a costly bug, too, since it wasn't found until the software was in the customer's hands.

This may all sound pretty scary. You can't test everything, and if you don't, you will likely miss bugs. The product has to be released, so you will need to stop testing, but if you stop too soon, there will still be areas untested. What do you do?

One key concept that software testers need to learn is how to reduce the huge domain of possible tests into a manageable set, and how to make wise risk-based decisions on what's important to test and what's not.

Figure 3.2 shows the relationship between the amount of testing performed and the number of bugs found. If you attempt to test everything, the costs go up dramatically and the number of missed bugs declines to the point that it's no longer cost effective to continue. If you cut the testing short or make poor decisions of what to test, the costs are low but you'll miss a lot of bugs. The goal is to hit that optimal amount of testing so that you don't test too much or too little.

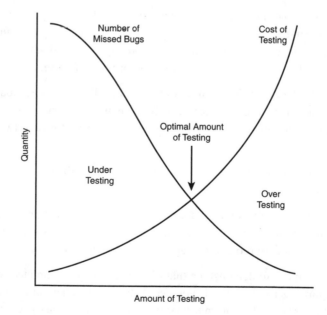

FIGURE 3.2

Every software project has an optimal test effort.

You will learn how to design and select test scenarios that minimize risk and optimize your testing in Chapters 4 through 7.

Testing Can't Show That Bugs Don't Exist

Think about this for a moment. You're an exterminator charged with examining a house for bugs. You inspect the house and find evidence of bugs—maybe live bugs, dead bugs, or nests. You can safely say that the house has bugs.

You visit another house. This time you find no evidence of bugs. You look in all the obvious places and see no signs of an infestation. Maybe you find a few dead bugs or old nests but you see nothing that tells you that live bugs exist. Can you absolutely, positively state that the house is bug free? Nope. All you can conclude is that in your search you didn't find any live bugs. Unless you completely dismantled the house down to the foundation, you can't be sure that you didn't simply just miss them.

Software testing works exactly as the exterminator does. It can show that bugs exist, but it can't show that bugs don't exist. You can perform your tests, find and report bugs, but at no point can you guarantee that there are no longer any bugs to find. You can only continue your testing and possibly find more.

The More Bugs You Find, the More Bugs There Are

There are even more similarities between real bugs and software bugs. Both types tend to come in groups. If you see one, odds are there will be more nearby.

Frequently, a tester will go for long spells without finding a bug. He'll then find one bug, then quickly another and another. There are several reasons for this:

- **Programmers have bad days.** Like all of us, programmers can have off days. Code written one day may be perfect; code written another may be sloppy. One bug can be a tell-tale sign that there are more nearby.

- **Programmers often make the same mistake.** Everyone has habits. A programmer who is prone to a certain error will often repeat it.

- **Some bugs are really just the tip of the iceberg.** Very often the software's design or architecture has a fundamental problem. A tester will find several bugs that at first may seem unrelated but eventually are discovered to have one primary serious cause.

It's important to note that the inverse of this "bugs follow bugs" idea is true, as well. If you fail to find bugs no matter how hard you try, it may very well be that the software was cleanly written and that there are indeed few if any bugs to be found.

The Pesticide Paradox

In 1990, Boris Beizer, in his book *Software Testing Techniques*, Second Edition, coined the term *pesticide paradox* to describe the phenomenon that the more you test software, the more immune it becomes to your tests. The same thing happens to insects with pesticides (see Figure 3.3). If you keep applying the same pesticide, the insects eventually build up resistance and the pesticide no longer works.

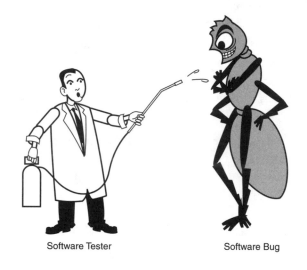

Software Tester   Software Bug

FIGURE 3.3
Software undergoing the same repetitive tests eventually builds up resistance to them.

Remember the spiral model of software development described in Chapter 2? The test process repeats each time around the loop. With each iteration, the software testers receive the software for testing and run their tests. Eventually, after several passes, all the bugs that those tests would find are exposed. Continuing to run them won't reveal anything new.

To overcome the pesticide paradox, software testers must continually write new and different tests to exercise different parts of the program and find more bugs.

Not All the Bugs You Find Will Be Fixed

One of the sad realities of software testing is that even after all your hard work, not every bug you find will be fixed. Now, don't be disappointed—this doesn't mean that you've failed in achieving your goal as a software tester, nor does it mean that you or your team will release a poor quality product. It does mean, however, that you'll need to rely on a couple of those traits of a software tester listed in Chapter 1—exercising good judgment and knowing when perfection isn't reasonably attainable. You and your team will need to make trade-offs, risk-based decisions for each and every bug, deciding which ones will be fixed and which ones won't.

There are several reasons why you might choose not to fix a bug:

- **There's not enough time.** In every project there are always too many software features, too few people to code and test them, and not enough room left in the schedule to finish. If you're working on a tax preparation program, April 15 isn't going to move—you must have your software ready in time.

- **It's really not a bug.** Maybe you've heard the phrase, "It's not a bug, it's a feature!" It's not uncommon for misunderstandings, test errors, or spec changes to result in would-be bugs being dismissed as features.

- **It's too risky to fix.** Unfortunately, this is all too often true. Software is fragile, inter-twined, and sometimes like spaghetti. You might make a bug fix that causes other bugs to appear. Under the pressure to release a product under a tight schedule, it might be too risky to change the software. It may be better to leave in the known bug to avoid the risk of creating new, unknown ones.

- **It's just not worth it.** This may sound harsh, but it's reality. Bugs that would occur infrequently or bugs that appear in little-used features may be dismissed. Bugs that have work-arounds, ways that a user can prevent or avoid the bug, are often not fixed. It all comes down to a business decision based on risk.

The decision-making process usually involves the software testers, the project managers, and the programmers. Each carries a unique perspective on the bugs and has his own information and opinions as to why they should or shouldn't be fixed. In Chapter 18, "Reporting What You Find," you'll learn more about reporting bugs and getting your voice heard.

What Happens When You Make the Wrong Decision?

Remember the Intel Pentium bug described in Chapter 1? The Intel test engineers found this bug before the chip was released, but the product team decided that it was such a small, rare bug that it wasn't worth fixing. They were under a tight sched-ule and decided to meet their current deadline and fix the bug in later releases of the chip. Unfortunately, the bug was discovered and the rest, they say, is history.

When a Bug's a Bug Is Difficult to Say

If there's a problem in the software but no one ever discovers it—not programmers, not testers, and not even a single customer—is it a bug?

Get a group of software testers in a room and ask them this question. You'll be in for a lively discussion. Everyone has their own opinion and can be pretty vocal about it. The problem is that there's no definitive answer. The answer is based on what you and your development team decide works best for you.

For the purposes of this book, refer back to the rules to define a bug from Chapter 1:

1. The software doesn't do something that the product specification says it should do.
2. The software does something that the product specification says it shouldn't do.
3. The software does something that the product specification doesn't mention.
4. The software doesn't do something that the product specification doesn't mention but should.
5. The software is difficult to understand, hard to use, slow, or—in the software tester's eyes—will be viewed by the end user as just plain not right.

Following these rules helps clarify the dilemma by making a bug a bug only if it's observed. To claim that the software does or doesn't do "something" implies that the software was run and that "something" or the lack of "something" was witnessed. Since you can't report on what you didn't see, you can't claim that a bug exists if you didn't see it.

Here's another way to think of it. It's not uncommon for two people to have completely different opinions on the quality of a software product. One may say that the program is incredibly buggy and the other may say that it's perfect. How can both be right? The answer is that one has used the product in a way that reveals lots of bugs. The other hasn't.

> **NOTE**
>
> For the purposes of this book, a bug is a bug only if it's observed. Bugs that haven't been found yet are simply undiscovered bugs.

If this is as clear as mud, don't worry. Discuss it with your peers in software testing and find out what they think. Listen to others' opinions, test their ideas, and form your own definition. Remember the old question, "If a tree falls in the forest and there's no one there to hear it, does it make a sound?"

Product Specifications Are Never Final

Software developers have a problem. The industry is moving so fast that last year's cutting-edge products are obsolete this year. At the same time, software is getting larger and gaining more features and complexity, resulting in longer and longer development schedules. These two opposing forces result in conflict, and the result is a constantly changing product specification.

There's no other way to respond to the rapid changes. Assume that your product had a locked-down, final, absolutely-can't-change-it product spec. You're halfway through the planned two-year development cycle, and your main competitor releases a product very similar to yours but with several desirable features that your product doesn't have. Do you continue with your spec as is and release an inferior product in another year? Or, does your team regroup, rethink the product's features, rewrite the product spec, and work on a revised product? In most cases, wise business dictates the latter.

As a software tester, you must assume that the spec will change. Features will be added that you didn't plan to test. Features will be changed or even deleted that you had already tested and reported bugs on. It will happen. You'll learn techniques for being flexible in your test planning and test execution in the remainder of this book.

Software Testers Aren't the Most Popular Members of a Project Team

Remember the goal of a software tester?

> *The goal of a software tester is to find bugs, find them as early as possible, and make sure they get fixed.*

Your job is to inspect and critique your peer's work, find problems with it, and publicize what you've found. Ouch! You won't win a popularity contest doing this job.

Here are a couple of tips to keep the peace with your fellow teammates:

- **Find bugs early.** That's your job, of course, but work hard at doing this. It's much less of an impact and much more appreciated if you find a serious bug three months before, rather than one day before, a product's scheduled release.

- **Temper your enthusiasm.** Okay, you really love your job. You get really excited when you find a terrible bug. But, if you bounce into a programmer's cubicle with a huge grin on your face and tell her that you just found the nastiest bug of your career and it's in her code, she won't be happy.

- **Don't always report bad news.** If you find a piece of code surprisingly bug free, tell the world. Pop into a programmer's cubicle occasionally just to chat. If all you ever do is report bad news, people will see you coming and will run and hide.

Software Testing Is a Disciplined Technical Profession

It used to be that software testing was an afterthought. Software products were small and not very complicated. The number of people with computers using software was limited. And, the few programmers on a project team could take turns debugging each others' code. Bugs weren't that much of a problem. The ones that did occur were easily fixed without much cost or disruption. If software testers were used, they were frequently untrained and brought into the project late to do some "ad-hoc banging on the code to see what they might find." Times have changed.

Look at the software help-wanted ads and you'll see numerous listings for software testers. The software industry has progressed to the point where professional software testers are mandatory. It's now too costly to build bad software.

To be fair, not every company is on board yet. Many computer game and small-time developers still use a fairly loose software development model—usually big-bang or code-and-fix. But most software is now developed with a disciplined approach that has software testers as core, vital members of their staff.

This is great news if you're interested in software testing. It can now be a career choice—a job that requires training and discipline, and allows for advancement.

Software Testing Terms and Definitions

This chapter wraps up the first section of this book with a list of software testing terms and their definitions. These terms describe fundamental concepts regarding the software development process and software testing. Because they're often confused or used inappropriately, they're defined here as pairs to help you understand their true meanings and the differences between them.

Precision and Accuracy

As a software tester, it's important to know the difference between *precision* and *accuracy*. Suppose that you're testing a calculator. Should you test that the answers it returns are precise or accurate? Both? If the project schedule forced you to make a risk-based decision to focus on only one of these, which one would you choose?

What if the software you're testing is a simulation game such as baseball or a flight simulator? Should you primarily test its precision or its accuracy?

Figure 3.4 helps to graphically describe these two terms. The goal of this dart game is to hit the bull's-eye in the center of the board. The darts on the board in the upper left are neither precise nor accurate. They aren't closely grouped and not even close to the center of the target.

The board on the upper right shows darts that are precise but not accurate. They are closely grouped, so the thrower has precision, but he's not very accurate because the darts didn't even hit the board.

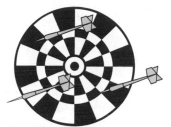

Neither Accurate nor Precise   Precise, but not Accurate

Accurate, but not Precise   Accurate and Precise

FIGURE 3.4
Darts on a dartboard demonstrate the difference between precision and accuracy.

The board on the lower left is an example of accuracy but poor precision. The darts are very close to the center, so the thrower is getting close to what he's aiming at, but because they aren't closely positioned, the precision is off.

The board in the lower right is a perfect match of precision and accuracy. The darts are closely grouped and on target.

Whether the software you test needs to be precise or accurate depends much on what the product is and ultimately what the development team is aiming at (excuse the pun). A software calculator likely demands that both are achieved—a right answer is a right answer. But, it may be decided that calculations will only be accurate and precise to the fifth decimal place. After that, the precision can vary. As long as the testers are aware of that specification, they can tailor their testing to confirm it.

Verification and Validation

Verification and *validation* are often used interchangeably but have different definitions. These differences are important to software testing.

Verification is the process confirming that something—software—meets its specification. *Validation* is the process confirming that it meets the user's requirements. These may sound very similar, but an explanation of the Hubble space telescope problems will help show the difference.

In April 1990, the Hubble space telescope was launched into orbit around the Earth. As a reflective telescope, Hubble uses a large mirror as its primary means to magnify the objects it's aiming at. The construction of the mirror was a huge undertaking requiring extreme precision and accuracy. Testing of the mirror was difficult since the telescope was designed for use in space and couldn't be positioned or even viewed through while it was still on Earth. For this reason, the only means to test it was to carefully measure all its attributes and compare the measurements with what was specified. This testing was performed and Hubble was declared fit for launch.

Unfortunately, soon after it was put into operation, the images it returned were found to be out of focus. An investigation discovered that the mirror was improperly manufactured. The mirror was ground according to the specification, but the specification was wrong. The mirror was extremely *precise*, but it wasn't *accurate*. Testing had confirmed that the mirror met the spec—*verification*—but it didn't confirm that it met the original requirement—*validation*.

In 1993, a space shuttle mission repaired the Hubble telescope by installing a "corrective lens" to refocus the image generated by the improperly manufactured mirror.

Although this is a not a software example, verification and validation apply equally well to software testing. Never assume that the specification is correct. If you verify the spec and validate the final product, you help avoid problems such as the one that hit the Hubble telescope.

Quality and Reliability

Merriam-Webster's Collegiate Dictionary defines *quality* as "a degree of excellence" or "superiority in kind." If a software product is of high quality, it will meet the customer's needs. The customer will feel that the product is excellent and superior to his other choices.

Software testers often fall into the trap of believing that quality and reliability are the same thing. They feel that if they can test a program until it's stable, dependable, and reliable, they are assuring a high-quality product. Unfortunately, that isn't necessarily true. Reliability is just one aspect of quality.

A software user's idea of quality may include the breadth of features, the ability of the product to run on his old PC, the software company's phone support availability, or even the color of the box. Reliability, or how often the product crashes or trashes his data, may be important, but not always.

To ensure that a program is of high quality and is reliable, a software tester must both verify and validate throughout the product development process.

Testing and Quality Assurance (QA)

The last pair of definitions is *testing* and *quality assurance* (sometimes shortened to *QA*). These two terms are the ones most often used to describe either the group or the process that's verifying and validating the software. In Chapter 20, "Software Quality Assurance," you'll learn more about software quality assurance, but for now, consider these definitions:

- The goal of a software tester is to find bugs, find them as early as possible, and make sure they get fixed.

- A software quality assurance person's main responsibility is to create and enforce standards and methods to improve the development process and to prevent bugs from ever occurring.

Of course, there is overlap. Some testers will do a few QA tasks and some QA-ers will perform a bit of testing. The two jobs and their tasks are intertwined. What's important is that you know what your primary job responsibilities are and communicate that information to the rest of the development team. Confusion among the team members about who's testing and who's not has caused lots of process pain in many projects.

Summary

Sausages, laws, and software—watching them being made can be pretty messy. Hopefully the previous three chapters haven't scared you off.

Many software testers have come into a project not knowing what was happening around them, how decisions were being made, or what procedure they should be following. It's impossible to be effective that way. With the information you've learned so far about software testing and the software development process, you'll have a head start when you begin testing for the first time. You'll know what your role should be, or at least know what questions to ask to find your place in the big picture.

For now, all the process stuff is out of the way, and the next chapter of this book begins a new section that will introduce you to the basic techniques of software testing.

Quiz

These quiz questions are provided for your further understanding. See Appendix A, "Answers to Quiz Questions," for the answers—but don't peek!

3

THE REALITIES OF
SOFTWARE
TESTING

1. Given that it's impossible to test a program completely, what information do you think should be considered when deciding whether it's time to stop testing?

2. Start the Windows Calculator. Type **5,000-5=** (the comma is important). Look at the result. Is this a bug? Why or why not?

3. If you were testing a simulation game such as a flight simulator or a city simulator, what do you think would be more important to test—its accuracy or its precision?

4. Is it possible to have a high-quality and low-reliability product? What might an example be?

5. Why is it impossible to test a program completely?

6. If you were testing a feature of your software on Monday and finding a new bug every hour, at what rate would you expect to find bugs on Tuesday?

Testing Fundamentals

PART II

Go out looking for one thing, and that's all you'll ever find.

—Old prospector's saying

The most exciting phrase to hear in science, the one that heralds the most discoveries, is not "Eureka!" but "That's funny..."

—Isaac Asimov, science and science-fiction author

IN THIS PART

Examining the Specification

IN THIS CHAPTER

This chapter will introduce you to your first real hands-on testing—but it may not be what you expect. You won't be installing or running software and you won't be pounding on the keyboard hoping for a crash. In this chapter, you'll learn how to test the product's specification to find bugs before they make it into the software.

Testing the product spec isn't something that all software testers have the luxury of doing. Sometimes you might come into a project midway through the development cycle after the specification is written and the coding started. If that's the case, don't worry—you can still use the techniques presented here to test the final specification.

If you're fortunate enough to be involved on the project early and have access to a preliminary specification, this chapter is for you. Finding bugs at this stage can potentially save your project huge amounts of time and money.

Highlights of this chapter include

- What is black-box and white-box testing
- How static and dynamic testing differ
- What high-level techniques can be used for reviewing a product specification
- What specific problems you should look for when reviewing a product specification in detail

Getting Started

Think back to the four development models presented in Chapter 2, "The Software Development Process": big-bang, code-and-fix, waterfall, and spiral. In each model, except big-bang, the development team creates a product specification, sometimes called a *requirements document*, to define what the software will become.

Typically, the product specification is a written document using words and pictures to describe the intended product. An excerpt from the Windows Calculator (see Figure 4.1) product spec might read something like this:

> The Edit menu will have two selections: Copy and Paste. These can be chosen by one of three methods: pointing and clicking with the mouse, using access-keys (Alt+C for Copy and Alt+P for Paste), or using the standard Windows shortcut keys of Ctrl+C for Copy and Ctrl+V for Paste.

> The Copy function will copy the current entry displayed in the number text box into the Windows Clipboard. The Paste function will paste the value stored in the Windows Clipboard into the number text box.

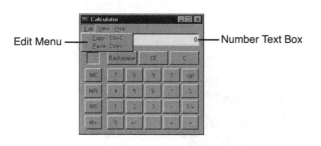

Edit Menu ——

—— Number Text Box

CHAPTER 4

FIGURE 4.1
The standard Windows Calculator displaying the drop-down Edit menu.

As you can see, it took quite a few words just to describe the operation of two menu items in a simple calculator program. A thoroughly detailed spec for the entire application could be a hundred pages long.

It may seem like overkill to create a meticulous document for such simple software. Why not just let a programmer write a calculator program on his own? The problem is that you would have no idea what you'd eventually get. The programmer's idea of what it should look like, what functionality it should have, and how the user would use it could be completely different from yours. The only way to assure that the end product is what the customer required—and to properly plan the test effort—is to thoroughly describe the product in a specification.

The other advantage of having a detailed spec, and the basis of this chapter, is that as a tester you'll also have a document as a testable item. You can use it to find bugs before the first line of code is written.

Black-Box and White-Box Testing

Two terms that software testers use to describe how they approach their testing are *black-box testing* and *white-box testing*. Figure 4.2 shows the difference between the two approaches. In black box testing, the tester only knows what the software is supposed to do—he can't look in the box to see how it operates. If he types in a certain input, he gets a certain output. He doesn't know how or why it happens, just that it does.

Think about the Windows Calculator shown in Figure 4.1. If you type **3.14159** and press the sqrt button, you get 1.772453102341. With black-box testing, it doesn't matter what gyrations the software goes through to compute the square root of pi. It just does it. As a software tester, you can verify the result on another "certified" calculator and determine if the Windows Calculator is functioning correctly.

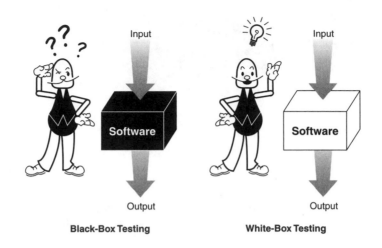

Black-Box Testing   White-Box Testing

FIGURE 4.2
With black-box testing, the software tester doesn't know the details of how the software works.

In white-box testing (sometimes called *clear-box testing*), the software tester has access to the program's code and can examine it for clues to help him with his testing—he can see inside the box. Based on what he sees, the tester may determine that certain numbers are more or less likely to fail and can tailor his testing based on that information.

NOTE

There is a risk to white-box testing. It's very easy to become biased and fail to objectively test the software because you might tailor the tests to match the code's operation.

Static and Dynamic Testing

Two other terms used to describe how software is tested are *static testing* and *dynamic testing*. Static testing refers to testing something that's not running—examining and reviewing it. Dynamic testing is what you would normally think of as testing—running and using the software.

The best analogy for these terms is the process you go through when checking out a used car. Kicking the tires, checking the paint, and looking under the hood are static testing techniques. Starting it up, listening to the engine, and driving down the road are dynamic testing techniques.

Static Black-Box Testing: Testing the Specification

Testing the specification is static black-box testing. The specification is a document, not an executing program, so it's considered static. It's also something that was created using data from many sources—usability studies, focus groups, marketing input, and so on. You don't necessarily need to know how or why that information was obtained or the details of the process used to obtain it, just that it's been boiled down into a product specification. You can then take that document, perform static black-box testing, and carefully examine it for bugs.

Earlier you saw an example of a product specification for the Windows Calculator. This example used a standard written document with a picture to describe the software's operation. Although this is the most common method for writing a spec, there are lots of variations. Your development team may emphasize diagrams over words or it may use a self-documenting computer language such as Ada. Whatever their choice, you can still apply all the techniques presented in this chapter. You will have to tailor them to the spec format you have, but the ideas are still the same.

What do you do if your project doesn't have a spec? Maybe your team is using the big-bang model or a loose code-and-fix model. As a tester, this is a difficult position. Your goal is to find bugs early—ideally finding them before the software is coded—but if your product doesn't have a spec, this may seem impossible to do. Although the spec may not be written down, someone, or several people, know what they're trying to build. It may be the developer, a project manager, or a marketer. Use them as the walking, talking, product spec and apply the same techniques for evaluating this "mental" specification as though it was written on paper. You can even take this a step further by recording the information you gather and circulating it for review. Tell your project team, "This is what I plan to test and submit bugs against." You'll be amazed at how many details they'll immediately fill in.

> **NOTE**
>
> You can test a specification with static black-box techniques no matter what the format of the specification. It can be a written or graphical document or a combination of both. You can even test an unwritten specification by questioning the people who are designing and writing the software.

Performing a High-Level Review of the Specification

Defining a software product is a difficult process. The spec must deal with many unknowns, take a multitude of changing inputs, and attempt to pull them all together into a document that describes a new product. The process is an inexact science and is prone to having problems.

The first step in testing the specification isn't to jump in and look for specific bugs. The first step is to stand back and view it from a high level. Examine the spec for large fundamental problems, oversights, and omissions. You might consider this more research than testing, but ultimately the research is a means to better understand what the software should do. If you have a better understanding of the whys and hows behind the spec, you'll be much better at examining it in detail.

Pretend to Be the Customer

The easiest thing for a tester to do when he first receives a specification for review is to pretend to be the customer. Do some research about who the customers will be. Talk to your marketing or sales people to get hints on what they know about the end user. If the product is an internal software project, find out who will be using it and talk to them.

It's important to understand the customer's expectations. Remember that the definition of *quality* means "meeting the customer's needs." As a tester, you must understand those needs to test that the software meets them. To do this effectively doesn't mean that you must be an expert in the field of nuclear physics if you're testing software for a power plant, or that you must be a professional pilot if you're testing a flight simulator. But, gaining some familiarity with the field the software applies to would be a great help.

Above all else, assume nothing. If you review a portion of the spec and don't understand it, don't assume that it's correct and go on. Eventually, you'll have to use this specification to design your software tests, so you'll eventually have to understand it. There's no better time to learn than now. If you find bugs along the way (and you will), all the better.

Research Existing Standards and Guidelines

Back in the days before Microsoft Windows and the Apple Macintosh, nearly every software product had a different user interface. There were different colors, different menu structures, unlimited ways to open a file, and myriad cryptic commands to get the same tasks done. Moving from one software product to another required complete retraining.

Thankfully, there has been an effort to standardize the hardware and the software. There has also been extensive research done on how people use computers. The result is that we now have products reasonably similar in their look and feel that have been designed with ergonomics in mind. You may argue that the adopted standards and guidelines aren't perfect, that there may be better ways to get certain tasks done, but efficiency has greatly improved because of this commonality.

Chapter 11, "Usability Testing," will cover this topic in more detail, but for now you should think about what standards and guidelines might apply to your product.

> **NOTE**
>
> The difference between standards and guidelines is a matter of degree. A standard is much more firm than a guideline. Standards should be strictly adhered to. Guidelines are optional but should be followed.

Here are several examples of standards and guidelines to consider. This list isn't definitive. You should research what might apply to your software:

- **Corporate Terminology and Conventions.** If this software is tailored for a specific company, it should adopt the common terms and conventions used by the employees of that company.

- **Industry Requirements.** The medical, pharmaceutical, industrial, and financial industries have very strict standards that their software must follow.

- **Government Standards.** The government, especially the military, has strict standards.

- **Graphical User Interface (GUI).** If your software runs under Microsoft Windows or Apple Macintosh operating systems, there are published standards and guidelines for how the software should look and feel to a user.

- **Hardware and Networking Standards.** Low-level software and hardware interface standards must be adhered to, to assure compatibility across systems.

As a tester, your job isn't to define what guidelines and standards should be applied to your software. That job lies with the project manager or whoever is writing the specification. You do, however, need to perform your own investigation to "test" that the correct standards are being used and that none are overlooked. You also have to be aware of these standards and test against them when you verify and validate the software. Consider them as part of the specification.

Review and Test Similar Software

One of the best methods for understanding what your product will become is to research similar software. This could be a competitor's product or something similar to what your team is creating. It's likely that the project manager or others who are specifying your product have already done this, so it should be relatively easy to get access to what products they used in their research. The software likely won't be an exact match (that's why you're creating new software, right?), but it should help you think about test situations and test approaches. It should also flag potential problems that may not have been considered.

Some things to look for when reviewing competitive products include

- **Scale.** Will your software be smaller or larger? Will that size make a difference in your testing?
- **Complexity.** Will your software be more or less complex? Will this impact your testing?
- **Testability.** Will you have the resources, time, and expertise to test software such as this?
- **Quality/Reliability.** Is this software representative of the overall quality planned for your software? Will your software be more or less reliable?

There's no substitute for hands-on experience, so do whatever you can to get a hold of similar software, use it, bang on it, and put it through its paces. You'll gain a lot of experience that will help you when you review your specification in detail.

Low-Level Specification Test Techniques

After you complete the high-level review of the product specification, you'll have a better understanding of what your product is and what external influences affect its design. Armed with this information, you can move on to testing the specification at a lower level. The remainder of this chapter explains the specifics for doing this.[1]

Specification Attributes Checklist

A good, well-thought-out product specification, with "all its t's crossed and its i's dotted," has eight important attributes:

- **Complete.** Is anything missing or forgotten? Is it thorough? Does it include everything necessary to make it stand alone?
- **Accurate.** Is the proposed solution correct? Does it properly define the goal? Are there any errors?
- **Precise, Unambiguous, and Clear.** Is the description exact and not vague? Is there a single interpretation? Is it easy to read and understandable?
- **Consistent.** Is the description of the feature written so that it doesn't conflict with itself or other items in the specification?
- **Relevant.** Is the statement necessary to specify the feature? Is it extra information that should be left out? Is the feature traceable to an original customer need?

---

[1] *The checklists are adapted from pp.294-295 and 303-308 of the* Handbook of Walkthroughs, Inspections, and Technical Reviews, *3rd Edition Copyright 1990, 1982 by D.P. Freedman and G.M. Weinberg. Used by permission of Dorset House Publishing (*www.dorsethouse.com*). All rights reserved.*

- **Feasible.** Can the feature be implemented with the available personnel, tools, and resources within the specified budget and schedule?
- **Code-free.** Does the specification stick with defining the product and not the underlying software design, architecture, and code?
- **Testable.** Can the feature be tested? Is enough information provided that a tester could create tests to verify its operation?

When you're testing a product spec, reading its text, or examining its figures, carefully consider each of these traits. Ask yourself if the words and pictures you're reviewing have these attributes. If they don't, you've found a bug that needs to be addressed.

Specification Terminology Checklist

A complement to the previous attributes list is a list of problem words to look for while reviewing a specification. The appearance of these words often signifies that a feature isn't yet completely thought out—it likely falls under one of the preceding attributes. Look for these words in the specification and carefully review how they're used in context. The spec may go on to clarify or elaborate on them, or it may leave them ambiguous—in which case, you've found a bug.

- **Always, Every, All, None, Never.** If you see words such as these that denote something as certain or absolute, make sure that it is, indeed, certain. Put on your tester's hat and think of cases that violate them.
- **Certainly, Therefore, Clearly, Obviously, Evidently.** These words tend to persuade you into accepting something as a given. Don't fall into the trap.
- **Some, Sometimes, Often, Usually, Ordinarily, Customarily, Most, Mostly.** These words are too vague. It's impossible to test a feature that operates "sometimes."
- **Etc., And So Forth, And So On, Such As.** Lists that finish with words such as these aren't testable. Lists need to be absolute or explained so that there's no confusion as to how the series is generated and what appears next in the list.
- **Good, Fast, Cheap, Efficient, Small, Stable.** These are unquantifiable terms. They aren't testable. If they appear in a specification, they must be further defined to explain exactly what they mean.
- **Handled, Processed, Rejected, Skipped, Eliminated.** These terms can hide large amounts of functionality that need to be specified.
- **If...Then...(but missing Else).** Look for statements that have "If...Then" clauses but don't have a matching "Else." Ask yourself what will happen if the "if" doesn't happen.

4

EXAMINING THE SPECIFICATION

Summary

After completing this chapter, you may have decided that testing a specification is a very subjective process. High-level review techniques will flush out oversights and omissions, and low-level techniques help assure that all the details are defined. But, these techniques aren't really step-by-step processes to follow, for two reasons:

- This is an introductory book whose aim is to get you rapidly up the testing curve. The material presented here will do just that. Armed with the information presented in this chapter, you will make a big dent in any software spec you're given to test.

- The format of specifications can vary widely. You'll be able to apply the techniques from this chapter whether you're pulling the spec out of someone's brain, looking at a high-level diagram, or parsing through sentences. You will find bugs.

If you're interested in pursuing more advanced techniques for reviewing specifications, do some research on the work of Michael Fagan. While at IBM, Mr. Fagan pioneered a detailed and methodical approach called *software inspections* that many companies use, especially companies creating mission-critical software, to formally review their software specifications and code. You can find more information on his Web site: `www.mfagan.com`.

Quiz

These quiz questions are provided for your further understanding. See Appendix A, "Answers to Quiz Questions," for the answers—but don't peek!

1. Can a software tester perform white-box testing on a specification?

2. Cite a few example of Mac or Windows standards or guidelines.

3. Explain what's wrong with this specification statement: When the user selects the Compact Memory option, the program will compress the mailing list data as small as possible using a Huffman-sparse-matrix approach.

4. Explain what a tester should worry about with this line from a spec: The software will allow up to 100 million simultaneous connections, although no more than 1 million will normally be used.

Testing the Software with Blinders On

IN THIS CHAPTER

Okay, now for the good stuff! This chapter covers what most people imagine when they think of software testing. It's time to crack your knuckles, sit in front of your computer, and start looking for bugs.

As a new software tester, this may be the first job you're assigned to do. If you're interviewing for a software test position, you will no doubt be asked how you'd approach testing a new software program or a new program's features.

It's very easy to jump right in, start pounding on keys, and hope that something breaks. Such an approach might work for a little while. If the software is still under development, it's very easy to get lucky and find a few bugs right away. Unfortunately, those easy pickings will quickly disappear and you'll need a more structured and targeted approach to continue finding bugs and to be a successful software tester.

This chapter describes the most common and effective techniques for testing software. It doesn't matter what kind of program you're testing—the same techniques will work whether it's a custom accounting package for your company, an industrial automation program, or a mass-market shoot-'em-up computer game.

You also don't need to be a programmer to use these techniques. Although they're all based on fundamental programming concepts, they don't require you to write code. A few techniques have some background information that explains why they're effective, but any code samples are short and written in BASIC to easily demonstrate the point. If you're into programming and want to learn more low-level test techniques, after you finish reading this chapter, move on to Chapter 6, "Examining the Code," and 7, "Testing the Software with X-Ray Glasses," the white-box testing chapters.

Topics covered in this chapter include

- What is dynamic black-box testing?
- How to reduce the number of test cases by equivalence partitioning
- How to identify troublesome boundary conditions
- Good data values to use to induce bugs
- How to test software states and state transitions
- How to use repetition, stress, and high loads to locate bugs
- A few secret places where bugs hide

Dynamic Black-Box Testing: Testing the Software While Blindfolded

Testing software without having an insight into the details of underlying code is *dynamic black-box* testing. It's *dynamic* because the program is running—you're using it as a customer would. And, it's *black-box* because you're testing it without knowing exactly how it works—with blinders on. You're entering inputs, receiving outputs, and checking the results. Another name commonly used for dynamic black-box testing is *behavioral testing* because you're testing how the software actually behaves when it's used.

To do this effectively requires some definition of what the software does—namely, a requirements document or product specification. You don't need to be told what happens inside the software "box"—you just need to know that inputting A outputs B or that performing operation C results in D. A good product spec will provide you with these details.

Once you know the ins and outs of the software you're about to test, your next step is to start defining the *test cases*. Test cases are the specific inputs that you'll try and the procedures that you'll follow when you test the software. Figure 5.1 shows an example of several cases that you might use for testing the addition function of the Windows Calculator.

```
Addition Test Cases for Windows Calculator

0+0       should equal 0
0+1       should equal 1
254+1     should equal 255
255+1     should equal 256
256+1     should equal 257
1022+1 should equal 1023
1023+1 should equal 1024
1024+1 should equal 1025
. . .
. . .
```

FIGURE 5.1
Test cases show the different inputs and the steps to test a program.

NOTE

Selecting test cases is the single most important task that software testers do. Improper selection can result in testing too much, testing too little, or testing the wrong things. Intelligently weighing the risks and reducing the infinite possibilities to a manageable effective set is where the magic is.

The rest of this chapter and much of the rest of the book will teach you how to strategically select good test cases. Chapter 17, "Writing and Tracking Test Cases," discusses the specific techniques for writing and managing test cases.

Use Exploratory Testing If You Don't Have a Spec

A professional, mature software development process will have a detailed specification for the software. If you're stuck in a big-bang model or a sloppy code-and-fix model, you may not have a software spec to base your tests on. That's not an ideal situation for a software tester, but you can use a workable solution known as *exploratory testing*.

You need to treat the software as the specification. Methodically explore the software feature by feature. Take notes of what the software does, map out the features, and apply some of the static black-box techniques you learned in Chapter 3, "The Realities of Software Testing." Analyze the software as though *it* is the specification. Then apply the dynamic black-box techniques from this chapter.

You won't be able to test the software as thoroughly as you would if you had a spec—you won't necessarily know if a feature is missing, for example. But, you will be able to systematically test it. In this situation, finding any bugs would be a positive thing.

Test-to-Pass and Test-to-Fail

There are two fundamental approaches to testing software: *test-to-pass* and *test-to-fail*. When you test-to-pass, you really assure only that the software minimally works. You don't push its capabilities. You don't see what you can do to break it. You treat it with kid gloves, applying the simplest and most straightforward test cases.

You may be thinking that if your goal is to find bugs, why would you test-to-pass? Wouldn't you want to find bugs by any means possible? The answer is no, not initially.

Think about an analogy with a newly designed car (see Figure 5.2). You're assigned to test the very first prototype that has just rolled off the assembly line and has never been driven. You probably wouldn't get in, start it up, head for the test track, and run it wide open at full speed as hard as you could. You'd probably crash and die. With a new car, there'd be all kinds of bugs that would reveal themselves at low speed under normal driving conditions. Maybe the tires aren't the right size, or the brakes are inadequate, or the engine red lines too early. You could discover these problems and have them fixed before getting on the track and pushing the limits.

Test-to-pass

Test-to-fail

FIGURE 5.2
Use test-to-pass to reveal bugs before you test-to-fail.

NOTE

When designing and running your test cases, always run the test-to-pass cases first. It's important to see if the software fundamentally works before you throw the kitchen sink at it. You might be surprised how many bugs you find just using the software normally.

After you assure yourself that the software does what it's specified to do in ordinary circumstances, it's time to put on your sneaky, conniving, devious hat and attempt to find bugs by trying things that should force them out. Designing and running test cases with the sole purpose of breaking the software is called testing-to-fail or *error-forcing*. You'll learn later in this chapter that test-to-fail cases often don't appear intimidating. They often look like test-to-pass cases, but they're strategically chosen to probe for common weaknesses in the software.

Error Messages: Test-to-Pass or Test-to-Fail

A common class of test cases is one that attempts to force error messages. You know the ones—like saving a file to a floppy disk but not having one inserted in the drive. These cases actually straddle the line between test-to-pass and test-to-fail. The specification probably states that certain input conditions should result in an error message. That seems pretty clear as a test-to-pass case. But, you're also forcing an error, so it could be viewed as test-to-fail. In the end, it's probably both.

> Don't worry about the distinction. What's important is to try to force the error messages that are specified and to invent test cases to force errors that were never considered. You'll likely end up finding both test-to-pass and test-to-fail bugs.

Equivalence Partitioning

Selecting test cases is the single most important task that software testers do and *equivalence partitioning*, sometimes called *equivalence classing*, is the means by which they do it. Equivalence partitioning is the process of methodically reducing the huge (infinite) set of possible test cases into a much smaller, but still equally effective, set.

Remember the Windows Calculator example from Chapter 3? It's impossible to test all the cases of adding two numbers together. Equivalence partitioning provides a systematic means for selecting the values that matter and ignoring the ones that don't.

For example, without knowing anything more about equivalence partitioning, would you think that if you tested 1+1, 1+2, 1+3, and 1+4 that you'd need to test 1+5 and 1+6? Do you think you could safely assume that they'd work?

How about 1+9999999999999999999999999999999 (the maximum number you can type in)? Is this test case maybe a little different than the others, maybe in a different class, a different equivalence partition? If you had the choice, would you include it or 1+13?

See, you're already starting to think like a software tester!

REMINDER

> An equivalence class or equivalence partition is a set of test cases that tests the same thing or reveals the same bug.

What is the difference between 1+9999999999999999999999999999999 and 1+13? In the case of 1+13, it looks like a standard simple addition, a lot like 1+5 or 1+392. However, 1+999... is way out there, on the edge. If you enter the largest possible number and then add 1 to it, something bad might happen—possibly a bug. This extreme case is in a unique partition, a different one from the normal partition of regular numbers.

When looking for equivalence partitions, think about ways to group similar inputs, similar outputs, and similar operation of the software. These groups are your equivalence partitions.

Look at a few examples:

- In the case of adding two numbers together, there seemed to be a distinct difference between testing 1+13 and 1+99999999999999999999999999999999. Call it a gut feeling, but one seemed to be normal addition and the other seemed to be risky. That gut feeling is right. A program would have to handle the addition of 1 to a maxed-out number differently than the addition of two small numbers. It would need to handle an overflow condition. These two cases, because the software most likely operates on them differently, are in different equivalence partitions.

  If you have some programming experience, you might be thinking of several more "special" numbers that could cause the software to operate differently. If you're not a programmer, don't worry—you'll learn the techniques very shortly and be able to apply them without having to understand the code in detail.

- Figure 5.3 shows the Calculator's Edit menu selected to display the copy and paste commands. There are five ways to perform each function. For copy, you click the Copy menu item, type c or C, or press Ctrl+c or Ctrl+Shift+c. Each input path copies the current number into the Clipboard—they perform the same output and produce the same result.

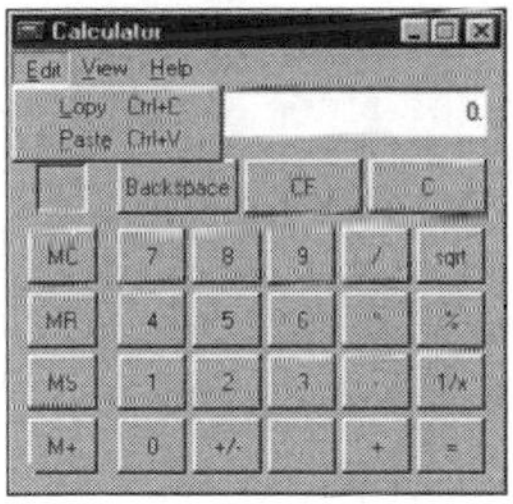

FIGURE 5.3
The multiple ways to invoke the copy function all have the same result.

If your job is to test the copy command, you could partition these five input paths down to three: Clicking the command on the menu, typing a c, or pressing Ctrl+c. As you grow more confident with the software's quality and know that the copy function, no matter how it's enabled, is working properly, you might even partition these down into a single partition, maybe Ctrl+c.

- As a third example, consider the possibilities for entering a filename in the standard Save As dialog box (see Figure 5.4).

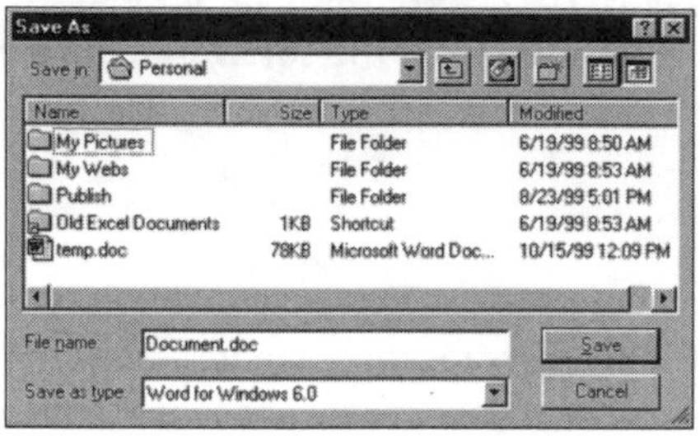

FIGURE 5.4

The File Name text box in the Save As dialog box illustrates several equivalence partition possibilities.

A Windows filename can contain any characters except \ / : * ? " < > and |.Filenames can have from 1 to 255 characters. If you're creating test cases for filenames, you will have equivalence partitions for valid characters, invalid characters, valid length names, names that are too short, and names that are too long.

Remember, the goal of equivalence partitioning is to reduce the set of possible test cases into a smaller, manageable set that still adequately tests the software. You're taking on risk because you're choosing not to test everything, so you need to be careful how you choose your classes.

NOTE

If you do equivalence partitioning too far in your effort to reduce the number of test cases, you risk eliminating tests that could reveal bugs. If you're new to testing, always get someone with more experience to review your proposed classes.

A final point about equivalence partitioning is that it can be subjective. It's science but it's also art. Two testers who test a complex program may arrive at two different sets of partitions. That's okay as long as the partitions are reviewed and everyone agrees that they acceptably cover the software being tested.

Data Testing

The simplest view of software is to divide its world into two parts: the data (or its domain) and the program. The data is the keyboard input, mouse clicks, disk files, printouts, and so on. The program is the executable flow, transitions, logic, and computations. A common approach to software testing is to divide up the test work along the same lines.

When you perform software testing on the data, you're checking that information the user inputs, results that he receives, and any interim results internal to the software are handled correctly.

Examples of data would be

- The words you type into a word processor
- The numbers entered into a spreadsheet
- The number of shots you have remaining in your space game
- The picture printed by your photo software
- The backup files stored on your floppy disk
- The data being sent by your modem over the phone lines

The amount of data handled by even the simplest programs can be overwhelming. Remember all the possibilities for simple addition on a calculator? Consider a word processor, a missile guidance system, or a stock trading program. The trick (if you can call it that) to making any of these testable is to intelligently reduce the test cases by equivalence partitioning based on a few key concepts: boundary conditions, sub-boundary conditions, nulls, and bad data.

Boundary Conditions

The best way to describe *boundary condition* testing is shown in Figure 5.5. If you can safely and confidently walk along the edge of a cliff without falling off, you can almost certainly walk in the middle of a field. If software can operate on the edge of its capabilities, it will almost certainly operate well under normal conditions.

Boundary conditions are special because programming, by its nature, is susceptible to problems at its edges. Software is very binary—something is either true or it isn't. If an operation is performed on a range of numbers, odds are the programmer got it right for the vast majority of the numbers in the middle, but maybe made a mistake at the edges. Listing 5.1 shows how a boundary condition problem can make its way into a very simple program.

LISTING 5.1 A Simple BASIC Program Demonstrating a Boundary Condition Bug

```
1: Rem Create a 10 element integer array
2: Rem Initialize each element to -1
3: Dim data(10) As Integer
4: Dim i As Integer
5: For i = 1 To 10
6:    data(i) = -1
7:    Next i
8: End
```

FIGURE 5.5
A software boundary is much like the edge of a cliff.

The purpose of this code is to create a 10-element array and initialize each element of the array to –1. It looks fairly simple. An array (data) of 10 integers and a counter (i) are created. A For loop runs from 1 to 10, and each element of the array from 1 to 10 is assigned a value of –1. Where's the boundary problem?

In most BASIC scripts, when an array is dimensioned with a stated range—in this case, Dim data(10) as Integer—the first element created is 0, not 1. This program actually creates a data array of 11 elements from data(0) to data(10). The program loops from 1 to 10 and initializes those values of the array to –1, but since the first element of our array is data(0), it doesn't get initialized. When the program completes, the array values look like this:

data(0) = 0	data(6) = –1
data(1) = –1	data(7) = –1
data(2) = –1	data(8) = –1
data(3) = –1	data(9) = –1
data(4) = –1	data(10) = –1
data(5) = –1	

Notice that data(0)'s value is 0, not –1. If the same programmer later forgot about, or a different programmer wasn't aware of how this data array was initialized, he might use the first element of the array, data(0), thinking it was set to –1. Problems such as this are very common and, in large complex software, can result in very nasty bugs.

Types of Boundary Conditions

Now it's time to open your mind and really think about what constitutes a boundary. Beginning testers often don't realize how many boundaries a given set of data can have. Usually there are a few obvious ones, but if you dig deeper you'll find the more obscure, interesting, and often bug-prone boundaries.

> **NOTE**
>
> Boundary conditions are those situations at the edge of the planned operational limits of the software.

When you're presented with a software test problem that involves identifying boundaries, look for the following types:

Numeric	Speed
Character	Location
Position	Size
Quantity	

And, think about the following characteristics of those types:

First/Last	Min/Max
Start/Finish	Over/Under
Empty/Full	Shortest/Longest
Slowest/Fastest	Soonest/Latest
Largest/Smallest	Highest/Lowest
Next-To/Farthest-From	

These are not by any means definitive lists. They cover many of the possible boundary conditions, but each software testing problem is different and may involve very different data with very unique boundaries.

> **TIP**
>
> If you have a choice of what data you're going to include in your equivalence partition, choose data that lies on the boundary.

Testing the Boundary Edges

What you've learned so far is that you need to create equivalence partitions of the different data sets that your software operates on. Since software is susceptible to bugs at the boundaries, if you're choosing what data to include in your equivalence partition, you'll find more bugs if you choose data from the boundaries.

But testing the data points just at the edge of the boundary line isn't usually sufficient. As the words to the "Hokey Pokey" imply ("Put your right hand in, put your right hand out, put your right hand in, and you shake it all about…"), it's a good idea to test on both sides of the boundary—to shake things up a bit.

You'll find the most bugs if you create two equivalence partitions. The first should contain data that you would expect to work properly—values that are the last one or two valid points inside the boundary. The second partition should contain data that you would expect to cause an error—the one or two invalid points outside the boundary.

> **TIP**
>
> When presented with a boundary condition, always test the valid data just inside the boundary, test the last possible valid data, and test the invalid data just outside the boundary.

Testing outside the boundary is usually as simple as adding one, or a bit more, to the maximum value and subtracting one, or a bit more, from the minimum value. For example:

- First–1/Last+1
- Start–1/Finish+1
- Less than Empty/More than Full
- Even Slower/Even Faster
- Largest+1/Smallest–1
- Min–1/Max+1
- Just Over/Just Under

- Even Shorter/Longer
- Even Sooner/Later
- Highest+1/Lowest−1

Look at a few examples so you can start thinking about all the boundary possibilities:

- If a text entry field allows 1 to 255 characters, try entering 1 character and 255 characters as the valid partition. You might also try 254 characters as a valid choice. Enter 0 and 256 characters as the invalid partitions.

- If a program reads and writes to a floppy disk, try saving a file that's very small, maybe with one entry. Save a file that's very large—just at the limit for what a floppy holds. Also try saving an empty file and a file that's too large to fit on the disk.

- If a program allows you to print multiple pages onto a single page, try printing just one (the standard case) and try printing the most pages that it allows. If you can, try printing zero pages and one more than it allows.

- Maybe the software has a data-entry field for a 9-digit ZIP code. Try 00000-0000, the simplest and smallest. Try entering 99999-9999 as the largest. Try entering one more or one less digit than what's allowed.

- If you're testing a flight simulator, try flying right at ground level and at the maximum allowed height for your plane. Try flying below ground level and below sea level as well as into outer space.

Since you can't test everything, performing equivalence partitioning around boundary conditions, such as in these examples, to create your test cases is critical. It's the most effective way to reduce the amount of testing you need to perform.

> **NOTE**
>
> It's vitally important that you continually look for boundaries in every piece of software you work with. The more you look, the more boundaries you'll discover, and the more bugs you'll find.

Sub-Boundary Conditions

The normal boundary conditions just discussed are the most obvious to find. They're the ones defined in the specification or evident when using the software. Some boundaries, though, that are internal to the software aren't necessarily apparent to an end user but still need to be checked by the software tester. These are known as *sub-boundary conditions* or *internal boundary conditions*.

These boundaries don't require that you be a programmer or that you be able to read the raw code that you're testing, but they do require a bit of general knowledge about how software works. Two examples are powers-of-two and the ASCII table. The software that you're testing can have many others, so you should talk with your team's programmers to see if they can offer suggestions for other sub-boundary conditions that you should check.

Powers-of-Two

Computers and software are based on binary numbers—*bits* representing 0s and 1s, *bytes* made up of 8 bits, *words* made up of 4 bytes, and so on. Table 5.1 shows the common powers-of-two units and their equivalent values.

TABLE 5.1   Software Powers-of-Two

Term	Range or Value
Bit	0 or 1
Nibble	0–15
Byte	0–255
Word	0–65,535 or 0–4,294,967,295
Kilo	1,024
Mega	1,048,576
Giga	1,073,741,824
Tera	1,099,511,627,776

The ranges and values shown in Table 5.1 are critical values to treat as boundary conditions. You likely won't see them specified in a requirements document unless the software presents the same range to the user. Often, though, they're used internally by the software and are invisible, unless of course they create a situation for a bug.

An Example of Powers-of-Two

An example of how powers-of-two come into play is with communications software. Bandwidth, or the transfer capacity of your information, is always limited. There's always a need to send and receive information faster than what's possible. For this reason, software engineers try to pack as much data into communications strings as they can.

One way they do this is to compress the information into the smallest units possible, send the most common information in these small units, and then expand to the next size units as necessary.

> Suppose that a communications protocol supports 256 commands. The software could send the most common 15 commands encoded into a small nibble of data. For the 16th through 256th commands, the software could then switch over to send the commands encoded into the longer bytes.
>
> The software user knows only that he can issue 256 commands; he doesn't know that the software is performing special calculations and different operations on the nibble/byte boundary.

When you create your equivalence partitions, consider whether powers-of-two boundary conditions need to be included in your partition. For example, if your software accepts a range of numbers from 1 to 1000, you know to include in your valid partition 1 and 1000, maybe 2 and 999. To cover any possible powers-of-two sub-boundaries, also include the nibble boundaries of 14, 15, and 16, and the byte boundaries of 254, 255, and 256.

ASCII Table

Another common sub-boundary condition is the ASCII character table. Table 5.2 is a partial listing of the ASCII table.

TABLE 5.2   A Partial ASCII Table of Values

Character	ASCII Value	Character	ASCII Value
Null	0	B	66
Space	32	Y	89
/	47	Z	90
0	48	[	91
1	49	`	96
2	50	a	97
9	57	b	98
:	58	y	121
@	64	z	122
A	65	{	123

Notice that Table 5.2 is not a nice, contiguous list. 0 through 9 are assigned to ASCII values 48 through 57. The slash character, /, falls before 0. The colon, :, comes after 9. The uppercase letters A through Z go from 65 to 90. The lowercase letters span 97 to 122. All these cases represent sub-boundary conditions.

If you're testing software that performs text entry or text conversion, you'd be very wise to reference a copy of the ASCII table and consider its boundary conditions when you define what values to include in your data partitions. For example, if you are testing a text box that accepts only the characters A–Z and a–z, you should include in your invalid partition the values just below and above those in the ASCII table—@, [, ', and {.

ASCII and Unicode

Although ASCII is still very popular as the common means for software to represent character data, it's being replaced by a new standard called Unicode. Unicode was developed by the Unicode Consortium in 1991 to solve ASCII's problem of not being able to represent all characters in all written languages.

ASCII, using only 8 bits, can represent only 256 different characters. Unicode, which uses 16 bits, can represent 65,536 characters. To date, more than 39,000 characters have been assigned, with more than 21,000 being used for Chinese ideographs.

Default, Empty, Blank, Null, Zero, and None

Another source of bugs that may seem obvious is when the software requests an entry—say, in a text box—but rather than type the correct information, the user types nothing. He may just press Enter. This situation is often overlooked in the specification or forgotten by the programmer but is a case that typically happens in real life.

Well-behaved software will handle this situation. It will usually default to the lowest valid boundary limit or to some reasonable value in the middle of the valid partition, or return an error.

The Windows Paint Attributes dialog box (see Figure 5.6) normally places default values in the Width and Height text fields. If the user accidentally or purposely deletes them so that the fields are blank and then clicks OK, what happens?

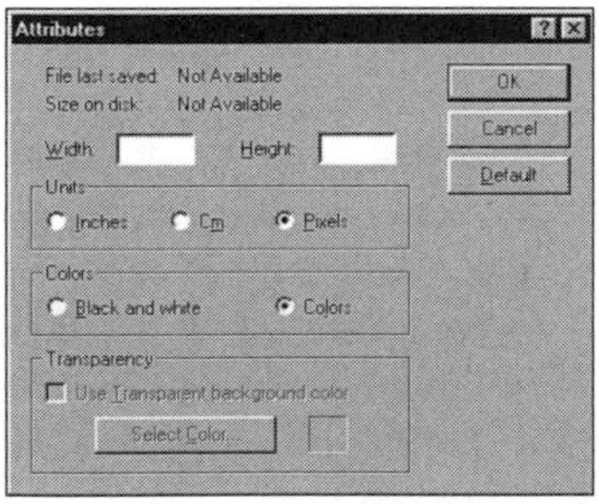

FIGURE 5.6
The Windows Paint Attributes dialog box with the Width and Height text fields blanked out.

Ideally, the software would handle this by defaulting to some valid width and height. If it did not do that, some error should be returned, which is exactly what you get (see Figure 5.7). The error isn't the most descriptive one ever written, but that's another topic.

FIGURE 5.7
The error message returned if Enter is pressed with the Width and Height text fields blanked out.

> **TIP**
>
> Always consider creating an equivalence partition that handles the default, empty, blank, null, zero, or none conditions.

You should create a separate equivalence partition for these values rather than lump them into the valid cases or the invalid cases because the software usually handles them differently. It's likely that in this default case, a different software path is followed than if the user typed 0 or –1 as invalid values. Since you expect different operation of the software, they should be in their own partition.

Invalid, Wrong, Incorrect, and Garbage Data

The final type of data testing is garbage data. This is where you test-to-fail. You've already proven that the software works as it should by testing-to-pass with boundary testing, sub-boundary testing, and default testing. Now it's time to throw the trash at it.

Software testing purists might argue that this isn't necessary, that if you've tested everything discussed so far you've proven the software will work. In the real word, however, there's nothing wrong with seeing if the software will handle whatever a user can do to it.

If you consider that packaged software today can sell hundreds of millions of copies, it's conceivable that some percentage of the users will use the software incorrectly. If that results in a crash or data loss, users won't blame themselves—they will blame the software. If the software doesn't do what they expect, it has a bug. Period.

So, with invalid, wrong, incorrect, and garbage data testing, have some fun. If the software wants numbers, give it letters. If it accepts only positive numbers, enter negative numbers. If it's date sensitive, see if it'll work correctly on the year 3000. Pretend to have "fat fingers" and press multiple keys at a time.

There are no real rules for this testing other than to try to break the software. Be creative. Be devious. Have fun.

State Testing

So far what you've been testing is the data—the numbers, words, inputs, and outputs of the software. The other side of software testing is to verify the program's logic flow through its various states. A *software state* is a condition or mode that the software is currently in. Consider Figures 5.8 and 5.9.

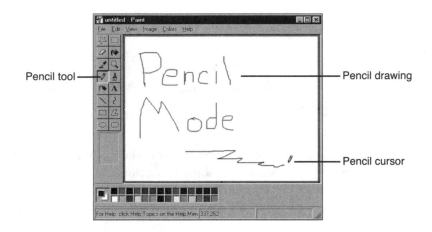

Pencil tool — Pencil drawing — Pencil cursor

FIGURE 5.8
The Windows Paint program in the pencil drawing state.

Airbrush tool — Airbrush drawing — Airbrush sizes — Airbrush cursor

FIGURE 5.9
The Windows Paint program in the airbrushing state.

Figure 5.8 shows the Windows Paint program in the pencil drawing state. This is the initial state in which the software starts. Notice that the pencil tool is selected, the cursor looks like a pencil, and a fine line is used to draw onscreen. Figure 5.9 shows the same program in the airbrush state. In this state, the airbrush tool is selected, airbrush sizes are provided, the cursor looks like a spray-paint can, and drawing results in a spray-paint look.

Take a closer look at all the available options that Paint provides—all the tools, menu items, colors, and so on. Whenever you select one of these and make the software change its look, its menus, or its operation, you're changing its state. The software follows a path through the code, toggles some bits, sets some variables, loads some data, and arrives at a new state of being.

> **NOTE**
>
> A software tester must test a program's states and the transitions between them.

Testing the Software's Logic Flow

Remember the example in Chapter 3 that showed the infinite data possibilities for testing the Windows Calculator? You learned earlier in this chapter that to make the testing manageable, you must reduce the data possibilities by creating equivalence partitions of only the most vital numbers.

Testing the software's states and logic flow has the same problems. It's usually possible to visit all the states (after all, if you can't get to them, why have them?). The difficulty is that except for the simplest programs, it's often impossible to traverse all paths to all states. The complexity of the software, especially due to the richness of today's user interfaces, provides so many choices and options that the number of paths grows exponentially.

The problem is similar to the well-known traveling salesman problem: Given a fixed number of cities and the distance between each pair of them, find the shortest route to visit all of them once, returning to your starting point. If there were only five cities, you could do some quick math and discover that there are 120 different routes. Traversing each of them and finding the shortest route to all wouldn't be that difficult or take that much time. If you increase that to hundreds or thousands of cities—or, in our case, hundreds or thousands of software states—you soon have a difficult-to-solve problem.

The solution for software testing is to apply equivalence partition techniques to the selection of the states and paths, assuming some risk because you will choose not to test all of them, but reducing that risk by making intelligent choices.

Creating a State Transition Map

The first step is to create your own state transition map of the software. Such a map may be provided as part of the product specification. If it is, you should statically test it as described in Chapter 4, "Examining the Specification." If you don't have a state map, you'll need to create one.

There are several different diagramming techniques for state transition diagrams. Figure 5.10 shows two examples. One uses boxes and arrows and the other uses circles (bubbles) and arrows. The technique you use to draw your map isn't important as long as you and the other members of your project team can read and understand it.

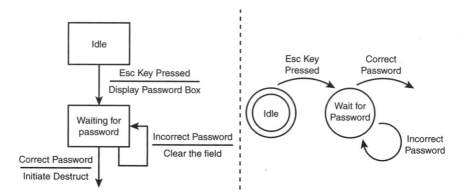

FIGURE 5.10
State transition diagrams can be drawn by using different techniques.

NOTE

State transition diagrams can become quite large. Many development teams cover their office walls with the printouts. If you expect that your diagrams will become that complex, look for commercial software that helps you draw and manage them.

A state transition map should show the following items:

- **Each unique state that the software can be in.** A good rule of thumb is that if you're unsure whether something is a separate state, it probably is. You can always collapse it into another state if you find out later that it isn't.

- **The input or condition that takes it from one state to the next.** This might be a key press, a menu selection, a sensor input, a telephone ring, and so on. A state can't be exited without some reason. The specific reason is what you're looking for here.

- **Set conditions and produced output when a state is entered or exited.** This would include a menu and buttons being displayed, a flag being set, a printout occurring, a calculation being performed, and so on. It's anything and everything that happens on the transition from one state to the next.

> **NOTE**
>
> Because you are performing black-box testing, you don't need to know what low-level variables are being set in the code. Create your map from the user's view of the software.

Reducing the Number of States and Transitions to Test

Creating a map for a large software product is a huge undertaking. Hopefully, you'll be testing only a portion of the overall software so that making the map is a more reasonable task. Once you complete the map, you'll be able to stand back and see all the states and all the ways to and from those states. If you've done your job right, it'll be a scary picture!

If you had infinite time, you would want to test every path through the software—not just each line connecting two states, but each set of lines, back to front, round and round. As in the traveling salesman problem, it would be impossible to hit them all.

Just as you learned with equivalence partitioning for data, you need to reduce the huge set of possibilities to a set of test cases of workable size. There are five ways to do this.

- Visit each state at least once. It doesn't matter how you get there, but each state needs to be tested.

- Test the state-to-state transitions that look like the most common or popular. This sounds subjective, and it is, but it should be based on the knowledge you gained when you performed static black-box analysis (in Chapter 3) of the product specification. Some user scenarios will be more frequently used than others. You want those to work!

- Test the least common paths between states. It's likely that these paths were overlooked by the product designers and the programmers. You may be the first one to try them.

- Test all the error states and returning from the error states. Many times error conditions are difficult to create. Very often programmers write the code to handle specific errors but can't test the code themselves. There are often cases when errors aren't properly handled, when the error messages are incorrect, or when the software doesn't recover properly when the error is fixed.

- Test random state transitions. If you have a printed state map, throw darts at it and try to move from dart to dart. If you have time to do more, read Chapter 14, "Automated Testing and Test Tools," for information on how to automate your random state transition testing.

What to Specifically Test

After you identify the specific states and state transitions that you want to test, you can begin defining your test cases.

Testing states and state transitions involves checking all the *state variables*—the static conditions, information, values, functionality, and so on that are associated with being in that state or moving to and from that state. Figure 5.11 shows an example of Windows Paint in the startup state.

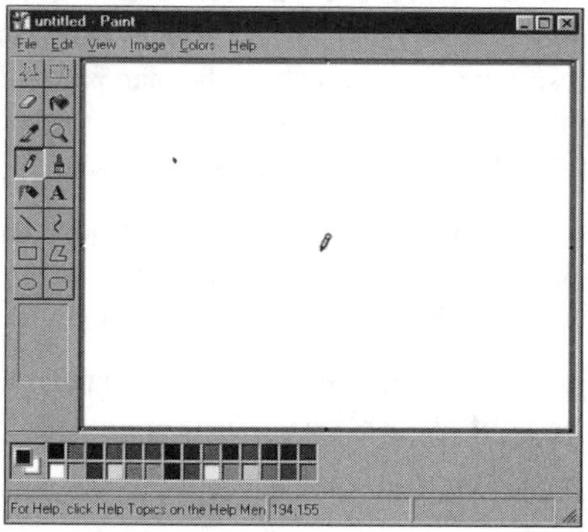

FIGURE 5.11

The Windows Paint opening screen in the startup state.

Here's a partial list of the state variables that define Paint's startup state:

- The window looks as shown in Figure 5.11.
- The window size is set to what it was the last time Paint was used.
- The drawing area is blank.
- The tool box, color box, and status bar are displayed.
- The pencil tool is selected. All the others are not.
- The default colors are black foreground on a white background.
- The document name is untitled.

There are many, many more state variables to consider for Paint, but these should give you an idea of what's involved in defining a state. Keep in mind that the same process of identifying state conditions is used whether the state is something visible such as a window or a dialog box, or invisible such as one that's part of a communications program or a financial package.

It's a good idea to discuss your assumptions about the states and state transitions with your team's spec writers and programmers. They can offer insights into states that happen behind the scenes that you may not have considered.

The Dirty Document Flag

State variables can be invisible but very important. A common example is the dirty document flag.

When a document is loaded into an editor, such as a word processor or painting program, an internal state variable called the *dirty document flag* is cleared and the software is in the "clean" state. The software stays in this state as long as no changes are made to the document. It can be viewed and scrolled and the state stays the same. As soon as something is typed or the document is modified in some way, the software changes state to the "dirty" state.

If an attempt is made to close or exit the software in the clean state, it shuts down normally. If the document is dirty, users will get a message asking if they want to save their work before quitting.

Some software is so sophisticated that if an edit is made that dirties the document and then the edit is undone to restore the document to its original condition, the software is returned to the clean state. Exiting the program will occur without a prompt to save the document.

Testing States to Fail

Everything discussed so far regarding state testing has been about testing-to-pass. You're reviewing the software, sketching out the states, trying many valid possibilities, and making sure the states and state transitions work. The flip side to this, just as in data testing, is to find test cases that test the software to fail. Examples of such cases are race conditions, repetition, stress, and load.

Race Conditions and Bad Timing

Most operating systems today, whether for personal computers or for specialized equipment, can do multitasking. *Multitasking* means that an operating system is designed to run separate processes concurrently. These processes can be separate programs such as a spreadsheet and email. Or they can be part of the same program such as printing in the background while allowing new words to be typed into a word processor.

Designing a multitasking operating system isn't a trivial exercise, and designing applications software to take advantage of multitasking is a difficult task. In a truly multitasking environment, the software can't take anything for granted. It must handle being interrupted at any moment, be able to run concurrently with everything else on the system, and share resources such as memory, disk, communications, and other hardware.

The results of all this are race condition problems. These are when two or more events line up just right and confuse software that didn't expect to be interrupted in the middle of its operation. In other words, it's bad timing. The term *race condition* comes from just what you'd think—multiple processes racing to a finish line, not knowing which will get there first.

> **NOTE**
>
> Race condition testing is difficult to plan for, but you can get a good start by looking at each state in your state transition map and thinking about what outside influences might interrupt that state. Consider what the state might do if the data it uses isn't ready or is changing when it's needed. What if two or more of the connecting arcs or lines occur at exactly the same time?

Here are a few examples of situations that might expose race conditions:

- Saving and loading the same document at the same time with two different programs
- Sharing the same printer, communications port, or other peripheral
- Pressing keys or sending mouse clicks while the software is loading or changing states
- Shutting down or starting up two or more instances of the software at the same time
- Using different programs to simultaneously access a common database

These may sound like harsh tests, but they aren't. Software must be robust enough handle these situations. Years ago they may have been out of the ordinary but today, users expect their software to work properly under these conditions.

Repetition, Stress, and Load

Three other test-to-fail state tests are repetition, stress, and load. These tests target state handling problems where the programmer didn't consider what might happen in the worst-case scenarios.

Repetition testing involves doing the same operation over and over. This could be as simple as starting up and shutting down the program over and over. It could also mean repeatedly saving and loading data or repeatedly selecting the same operation. You might find a bug after only a couple repetitions or it might take thousands of attempts to reveal a problem.

The main reason for doing repetition testing is to look for *memory leaks*. A common software problem happens when computer memory is allocated to perform a certain operation but isn't completely freed when the operation completes. The result is that eventually the program uses up memory that it depends on to work reliably. If you've ever used a program that works fine when you first start it up, but then becomes slower and slower or starts to behave erratically over time, it's likely due to a memory leak bug. Repetition testing will flush these problems out.

Stress testing is running the software under less-than-ideal conditions—low memory, low disk space, slow CPUs, slow modems, and so on. Look at your software and determine what external resources and dependencies it has. Stress testing is simply limiting them to their bare minimum. Your goal is to starve the software. Does this sound like boundary condition testing? It is.

Load testing is the opposite of stress testing. With stress testing, you starve the software; with load testing, you feed it all that it can handle. Operate the software with the largest possible data files. If the software operates on peripherals such as printers or communications ports, connect as many as you can. If you're testing an Internet server that can handle thousands of simultaneous connections, do it. Max out the software's capabilities. Load it down.

Don't forget about time as a load testing variable. With most software, it's important for it to run over long periods. Some software should be able to run forever without being restarted.

NOTE

There's no reason that you can't combine repetition, stress, and load, running all the tests at the same time.

There are two important considerations with repetition, stress, and load testing:

- Your team's programmers and project managers may not be completely receptive to your efforts to break the software this way. You'll probably hear them complain that no customer will use the system this way or stress it to the point that you are. The short answer is that yes, they will. Your job is to make sure that the software does work in these situations and to report bugs if it doesn't. Chapter 18, "Reporting What You Find," discusses how to best report your bugs to make sure that they're taken seriously and are fixed.

- Opening and closing your program a million times is probably not possible if you're doing it by hand. Likewise, finding a few thousand people to connect to your Internet server might be difficult to organize. Chapter 14 covers test automation and will give you ideas on how to perform testing such as this without requiring people to do the dirty work.

Other Black-Box Test Techniques

The remaining categories of black-box test techniques aren't standalone methods as much as they are variations of the data testing and state testing that has already been described. If you've done thorough equivalence partitioning of your program's data, created a detailed state map, and developed test cases from these, you'll find most software bugs that a user would find.

What's left are techniques for finding the stragglers, the ones that, if they were real living bugs, might appear to have a mind of their own, going their own way. Finding them might appear a bit subjective and not necessarily based on reason, but if you want to flush out every last bug, you'll have to be a bit creative.

Behave Like a Dumb User

The politically correct term might be *inexperienced user* or *new user*, but in reality, they're all the same thing. Put a person who's unfamiliar with the software in front of your program and they'll do and try things that you never imagined. They'll enter data that you never thought of. They'll change their mind in mid-stream, back up, and do something different. They'll surf through your Web site, clicking things that shouldn't be clicked. They'll discover bugs that you completely missed.

It can be frustrating, as a tester, to watch someone who has no experience in testing spend five minutes using a piece of software and crash it. How do they do it? They weren't operating on any rules or making any assumptions.

When you're designing your test cases or looking at the software for the first time, try to think like a dumb user. Throw out any preconceived ideas you had about how the software should work. If you can, bring in a friend who isn't working on the project to brainstorm ideas with you. Assume nothing. Adding these test cases to your designed library of test cases will create a very comprehensive set.

Look for Bugs Where You've Already Found Them

There are two reasons to look for bugs in the areas where you've already found them:

- As you learned in Chapter 3, the more bugs you find, the more bugs there are. If you discover that you're finding lots of bugs at the upper boundary conditions across various features, it would be wise to emphasize testing these upper boundaries on all features. Of course you're going to test these anyway, but you might want to throw in a few special cases to make sure the problem isn't pervasive.

- Many programmers tend to fix only the specific bug you report. No more, no less. If you report a bug that starting, stopping, and restarting a program 255 times results in a crash, that's what the programmer will fix. There may have been a memory leak that caused the problem and the programmer found and fixed it. When you get the software back to retest, make sure you rerun the same test for 256 times and beyond. There could very well be yet another memory leak somewhere out there.

Follow Experience, Intuition, and Hunches

There's no better way to improve as a software tester than to gain experience. There's no better learning tool than just doing it, and there's no better lesson than getting that first phone call from a customer who found a bug in the software you just finished testing.

Experience and intuition can't be taught. They must be gained over time. You can apply all the techniques you've learned so far and still miss important bugs. It's the nature of the business. As you progress through your career, learning to test different types and sizes of products, you'll pick up little tips and tricks that steer you toward those tough-to-find bugs. You'll be able to start testing a new piece of software and quickly find bugs that your peers would have missed.

Take notes of what works and what doesn't. Try different approaches. If you think something looks suspicious, take a closer look. Go with your hunches until you prove them false.

Experience is the name every one gives to their mistakes.

—Oscar Wilde

Summary

It's been a long chapter. Dynamic black-box testing covers a lot of ground. For new testers, this may be the single most important chapter in the book. It's likely that at your interviews or your first day on the job you'll be given software and asked to test it. Applying this chapter's techniques is a sure way to immediately find bugs.

Don't assume, though, that this is all there is to software testing. If it was, you could stop reading right now and ignore the remaining chapters. Dynamic black-box testing will just get you in the door. There's so much more to software testing, and you're just getting started.

The next two chapters introduce you to software testing when you have access to the code and can see how it works and what it does on the lowest levels. The same black-box techniques are still valid, but you'll be able to complement them with new techniques that will help you become an even more effective software tester.

Quiz

These quiz questions are provided for your further understanding. See Appendix A, "Answers to Quiz Questions," for the answers—but don't peek!

1. **True or False:** You can perform dynamic black-box testing without a product specification or requirements document.

2. If you're testing a program's ability to print to a printer, what generic test-to-fail test cases might be appropriate?

3. Start up Windows WordPad and select Print from the File menu. You'll get the dialog shown in Figure 5.12. What boundary conditions exist for the Print Range feature shown in the lower-left corner?

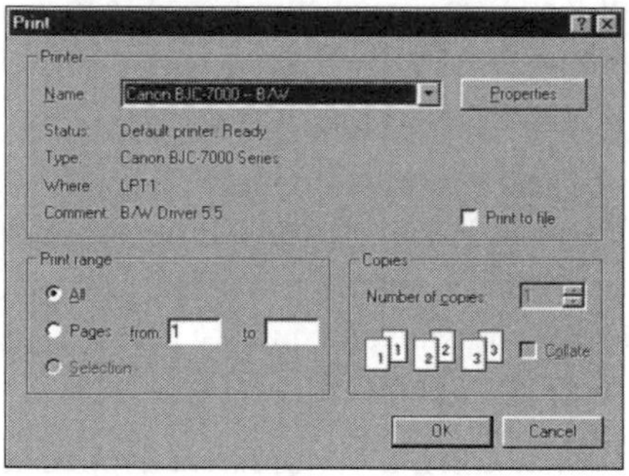

FIGURE 5.12
The Windows Print dialog box showing the Print Range feature.

4. Assume that you have a 10-character-wide ZIP code text box, such as the one shown in Figure 5.13. What equivalence partitions would you create for this text box?

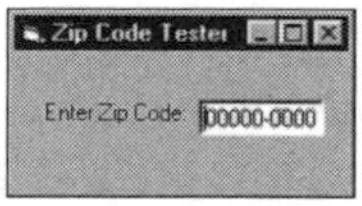

FIGURE 5.13
A sample ZIP code text box that holds up to 10 characters.

5. **True or False:** Visiting all the states that a program has assures that you've also traversed all the transitions among them.

6. There are many different ways to draw state transition diagrams, but there are three things that they all show. What are they?

7. What are some of the initial state variables for the Windows Calculator?

8. What actions do you perform on software when attempting to expose race condition bugs?

9. **True or False:** It's an unfair test to perform stress testing at the same time you perform load testing.

Examining the Code

IN THIS CHAPTER

Software testing isn't limited to treating the specification or the program like a black box as described in Chapters 4, "Examining the Specification," and 5, "Testing the Software with Blinders On." If you have some programming experience, even if it's just a little, you can also perform testing on the software design and code.

In some industries, such verification isn't as common as black-box testing. However, if you're testing military, financial, industrial, or medical software, or if you're lucky enough to be working in a highly disciplined development model, it may be routine to verify the product at this level.

This chapter introduces you to the basics of performing verification on the design and code. As a new software tester, it may not be your first task, but it's one that you can eventually move into if your interests lie in programming.

Highlights from this chapter include

- The benefits of static white-box testing
- The different types of static white-box reviews
- Coding guidelines and standards
- How to generically review code for errors

Static White-Box Testing: Examining the Design and Code

Remember the definitions of static testing and white-box testing from Chapter 4? *Static testing* refers to testing something that isn't running—examining and reviewing it. *White-box* (or clear-box) testing implies having access to the code, being able to see it and review it.

Static white-box testing is the process of carefully and methodically reviewing the software design, architecture, or code for bugs without executing it. It's sometimes referred to as *structural analysis*.

The obvious reason to perform static white-box testing is to find bugs early and to find bugs that would be difficult to uncover or isolate with dynamic black-box testing. The more independent people who review the software, the better, especially if it's at a low level and early in the development cycle.

A side benefit of performing static white-box testing is that it gives the team's black-box testers ideas for test cases to apply when they receive the software for testing. They may not necessarily understand the details of the code, but by listening to the review comments they can identify feature areas that sound troublesome or bug-prone.

> **NOTE**
>
> Development teams vary in who has the responsibility for static white-box testing. In some teams the programmers are the ones who organize and run the reviews, inviting the software testers as independent observers. In other teams the software testers are the ones who perform this task, asking the programmer who wrote the code and a couple of his peers to assist in the reviews. Ultimately, either approach can work. It's up to the development team to choose what works best for them.

The unfortunate thing about static white-box testing is that it's not always done. Many teams have the misconception that it's too time-consuming, too costly, or not productive. All of these are untrue—compared to the alternative of testing, finding, and still missing bugs at the back end of the project. The problem lies in the perception that a programmer's job is to write lines of code and that any task that takes away from his efficiency of churning out those lines is slowing down the process.

Fortunately, the tide is changing. Many companies are realizing the benefits of testing early and are hiring and training their programmers and testers to perform white-box testing. It's not rocket science (unless you're designing rockets), but getting started requires knowing a few basic techniques. If you're interested in taking it further, the opportunities are huge.

Formal Reviews

A *formal review* is the process under which static white-box testing is performed. A formal review can range from a simple meeting between two programmers to a detailed, rigorous inspection of the code.

There are four essential elements to a formal review:

- **Identify Problems.** The goal of the review is to find problems with the software—not just items that are wrong, but missing items as well. All criticism should be directed at the code, not the person who created it. Participants shouldn't take any criticism personally. Leave your egos, emotions, and sensitive feelings at the door.

- **Follow Rules.** A fixed set of rules should be followed. They may set the amount of code to be reviewed (usually a couple hundred lines), how much time will be spent (a couple hours), what can be commented on, and so on. This is important so that the participants know what their roles are and what they should expect. It helps the review run more smoothly.

- **Prepare.** Each participant is expected to prepare for and contribute to the review. Depending on the type of review, participants may have different roles. They need to know what their duties and responsibilities are and be ready to actively fulfill them at the review. Most of the problems found through the review process are found during preparation, not at the actual review.

- **Write a Report.** The review group must produce a written report summarizing the results of the review and make that report available to the rest of the product development team. It's imperative that others are told the results of the meeting—how many problems were found, where they were found, and so on.

What makes formal reviews work is following an established process. Haphazardly "getting together to go over some code" isn't sufficient and may actually be detrimental. If a process is run in an ad-hoc fashion, bugs will be missed and the participants will likely feel that the effort was a waste of time.

If the reviews are run properly, they can prove to be a great way to find bugs early. Think of them as one of the initial nets (see Figure 6.1) that catches the big bugs at the beginning of the process. Sure, smaller bugs will still get through, but they'll be caught in the next testing phases with the smaller nets with the tighter weave.

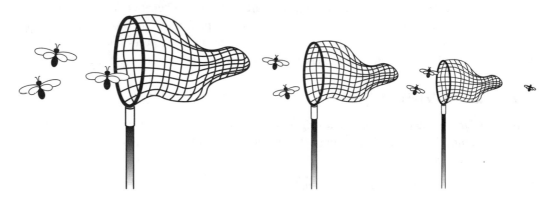

FIGURE 6.1
Formal reviews are the first nets used in catching bugs.

In addition to finding problems, holding formal reviews has a few indirect results:

- **Communications.** Information not contained in the formal report is communicated. For example, the black-box testers can get insight into where problems may lie. Inexperienced programmers may learn new techniques from more experienced programmers. Management may get a better feel for how the project is tracking its schedule.
- **Quality.** A programmer's code that is being gone over in detail, function by function, line by line, often results in the programmer being more careful. That's not to say that he would otherwise be sloppy—just that if he knows that his work is being carefully

reviewed by his peers, he might make an extra effort to triple-check it to make sure that it's right.

- **Team Camaraderie.** If a review is run properly, it can be a good place for testers and programmers to build respect for each other's skills and to better understand each other's jobs and job needs.

- **Solutions.** Solutions may be found for tough problems, although whether they are discussed depends on the rules for the review. It may be more effective to discuss solutions outside the review.

These indirect benefits shouldn't be relied on, but they do happen. On many teams, for whatever reasons, the members end up working in isolation. Formal reviews are a great way to get them in the same room, all discussing the same project problems.

Peer Reviews

The easiest way to get team members together and doing their first formal reviews of the software is through *peer reviews*, the least formal method. Sometimes called *buddy reviews*, this method is really more of an "I'll show you mine if you show me yours" type discussion.

Peer reviews are often held with just the programmer who wrote the code and one or two other programmers or testers acting as reviewers. That small group simply reviews the code together and looks for problems and oversights. To assure that the review is highly effective (and does not turn into a coffee break) all the participants need to make sure that the four key elements of a formal review are in place: Look for problems, follow rules, prepare for the review, and write a report. Because peer reviews are informal, these elements are often scaled back. Still, just getting together to discuss the code can find bugs.

Walkthroughs

Walkthroughs are the next step up in formality from peer reviews. In a walkthrough, the programmer who wrote the code formally presents (walks through) it to a small group of five or so other programmers and testers. The reviewers should receive copies of the software in advance of the review so they can examine it and write comments and questions that they want to ask at the review. Having at least one senior programmer as a reviewer is very important.

The presenter reads through the code line by line, or function by function, explaining what the code does and why. The reviewers listen and question anything that looks suspicious. Because of the larger number of participants involved in a walkthrough compared to a peer review, it's much more important for them to prepare for the review and to follow the rules. It's also very important that after the review the presenter write a report telling what was found and how he plans to address any bugs discovered.

Inspections

Inspections are the most formal type of reviews. They are highly structured and require training for each participant. Inspections are different from peer reviews and walkthroughs in that the person who presents the code, the *presenter* or *reader*, isn't the original programmer. This forces someone else to learn and understand the material being presented, potentially giving a different slant and interpretation at the inspection meeting.

The other participants are called *inspectors*. Each is tasked with reviewing the code from a different perspective, such as a user, a tester, or a product support person. This helps bring different views of the product under review and very often identifies different bugs. One inspector is even tasked with reviewing the code backward—that is, from the end to the beginning—to make sure that the material is covered evenly and completely.

Some inspectors are also assigned tasks such as *moderator* and *recorder* to assure that the rules are followed and that the review is run effectively.

After the inspection meeting is held, the inspectors might meet again to discuss the defects they found and to work with the moderator to prepare a written report that identifies the rework necessary to address the problems. The programmer then makes the changes and the moderator verifies that they were properly made. Depending on the scope and magnitude of the changes and on how critical the software is, a reinspection may be needed to locate any remaining bugs.

Inspections have proven to be very effective in finding bugs in any software deliverable, especially design documents and code, and are gaining popularity as companies and product development teams discover their benefits.

Coding Standards and Guidelines

In formal reviews, the inspectors are looking for problems and omissions in the code. There are the classic bugs where something just won't work as written. These are best found by careful analysis of the code—senior programmers and testers are great at this.

There are also problems where the code may operate properly but may not be written to meet a specific *standard* or *guideline*. It's equivalent to writing words that can be understood and get a point across but don't meet the grammatical and syntactical rules of the English language. Standards are the established, fixed, have-to-follow-them rules—the do's and don'ts. Guidelines are the suggested best practices, the recommendations, the preferred way of doing things. Standards have no exceptions, short of a structured waiver process. Guidelines can be a bit loose.

It may sound strange that some piece of software may work, may even be tested and shown to be very stable, but still be incorrect because it doesn't meet some criteria. It's important, though, and there are three reasons for adherence to a standard or guideline:

- **Reliability.** It's been shown that code written to a specific standard or guideline is more reliable and bug-free than code that isn't.
- **Readability/Maintainability.** Code that follows set standards and guidelines is easier to read, understand, and maintain.
- **Portability.** Code often has to run on different hardware or be compiled with different compilers. If it follows a set standard, it will likely be easier—or even completely painless—to move it to a different platform.

The requirements for your project may range from strict adherence to national or international standards to loose following of internal team guidelines. What's important is that your team has some standards or guidelines for programming and that these are verified in a formal review.

Examples of Programming Standards and Guidelines

Figure 6.2 shows an example of a programming standard that deals with the use of the C language goto, while, and if-else statements. Improper use of these statements often results in buggy code, and most programming standards explicitly set rules for using them.

TOPIC: 3.05   Control-Restriction on control structures

STANDARD
The **go to** statement (and hence labels as well) should not be used.

The **while** loop should be used instead of the **do-while**
loop, except where the logic of the problem explicit requires
doing the body at least once regardless of the loop condition.

If a single **if-else** can replace a continue, an **if-else**
should be used.

JUSTIFICATION
The **go to** statement is prohibited for the empirical reason that
its use is highly correlated with errors and hare-to-read code,
and for the abstract reason that algorithms should be
expressed in structures that facilitate checking the program
against the structure of the underlying process.

The **do-while** is discouraged because loops should be coded
in such a form as to "do nothing gracefully", i.e. they should
test their looping condition before executing the body.

FIGURE 6.2
A sample coding standard explains how several language control structures should be used. (Adapted from C++
Programming Guidelines *by Thomas Plum and Dan Saks. Copyright 1991, Plum Hall, Inc.)*

The standard has four main parts:

- *Title* describes what topic the standard covers.
- *Standard (or guideline)* describes the standard or guideline explaining exactly what's allowed and not allowed.
- *Justification* gives the reasoning behind the standard so that the programmer understands why it's good programming practice.
- *Example* shows simple programming samples of how to use the standard. This isn't always necessary.

Figure 6.3 is an example of a guideline dealing with C language features used in C++. Note how the language is a bit different. In this case, it starts out with "Try to avoid." Guidelines aren't as strict as standards, so there is some room for flexibility if the situation calls for it.

```
TOPIC: 7.02      C_ problems - Problem areas from C

GUIDELINE
Try to avoid C language features if a conflict with
programming in C++
    1.  Do not use setimp and longimp if there are any
        objects with destructors which could be created]
        between the execution of the setimp and the
        longimp.
    2.  Do not use the offsetof macro except when
        applied to members of just-a-struct.
    3.  Do not mix C-style FILE I/O (using stdio.h) with
        C++ style I/O (using iostream.h or stream.h) on
        the same file.
    4.  Avoid using C functions like memcpy or memcap for
        copying or comparing objects of a type other than
        array-of-char or just-a-struct.
    5.  Avoid the C macro NULL; use 0 instead.

JUSTIFICATION
Each of these features concerns an area of traditional C usage
which creates some problem in C++.
```

FIGURE 6.3

An example of a programming guideline shows how to use certain aspects of C in C++. (Adapted from C++ Programming Guidelines *by Thomas Plum and Dan Saks. Copyright 1991, Plum Hall, Inc.)*

It's a Matter of Style

There are standards, there are guidelines, and then there is style. From a software quality and testing perspective, style doesn't matter.

Every programmer, just like every book author and artist, has his or her own unique style. The rules may be followed, the language usage may be consistent, but it's still easy to tell who created what software.

That differentiating factor is style. In programming, it could be how verbose the commenting is or how the variables are named. It could be what indentation scheme is used in the loop constructs. It's the look and feel of the code.

Some teams, in their zeal to institute standards and guidelines, start critiquing the style of the code. As a software tester, be careful not to become caught up in this frenzy. When performing formal reviews on a piece of software, test and comment only on things that are wrong, missing, or don't adhere to written standards or guidelines. Ask yourself if what you're about to report is really a problem or just difference of opinion, a difference of style. The latter isn't a bug.

Obtaining Standards

If your project, because of its nature, must follow a set of programming standards, or if you're just interested in examining your software's code to see how well it meets a published standard or guideline, several sources are available for you to reference.

National and international standards for most computer languages and information technology can be obtained from:

- American National Standards Institute (ANSI), www.ansi.org
- International Engineering Consortium (IEC), www.iec.org
- International Organization for Standardization (ISO), www.iso.ch
- National Committee for Information Technology Standards (NCITS), www.ncits.org

There are also documents that demonstrate programming guidelines and best practices available from professional organizations such as

- Association for Computing Machinery (ACM), www.acm.org
- Institute of Electrical and Electronics Engineers, Inc (IEEE), www.ieee.org

You may also obtain information from the software vendor where you purchased your programming software. They often have published standards and guidelines available for free or for a small fee.

Generic Code Review Checklist

The rest of this chapter on static white-box testing covers some problems you should look for when verifying software for a formal code review. These checklists[1] are in addition to comparing the code against a standard or a guideline and to making sure that the code meets the project's design requirements.

To really understand and apply these checks, you should have some programming experience. If you haven't done much programming, you might find it useful to read an introductory book such as *Sams Teach Yourself Beginning Programming in 24 Hours* by Sams Publishing before you attempt to review program code in detail.

Data Reference Errors

Data reference errors are bugs caused by using a variable, constant, array, string, or record that hasn't been properly initialized for how it's being used and referenced.

- Is an uninitialized variable referenced? Looking for omissions is just as important as looking for errors.
- Are array and string subscripts integer values and are they always within the bounds of the array's or string's dimension?
- Are there any potential "off by one" errors in indexing operations or subscript references to arrays? Remember the code in Listing 5.1 from Chapter 5.
- Is a variable used where a constant would actually work better—for example, when checking the boundary of an array?
- Is a variable ever assigned a value that's of a different type than the variable? For example, does the code accidentally assign a floating-point number to an integer variable?
- Is memory allocated for referenced pointers?
- If a data structure is referenced in multiple functions or subroutines, is the structure defined identically in each one?

Data Declaration Errors

Data declaration bugs are caused by improperly declaring or using variables or constants.

- Are all the variables assigned the correct length, type, and storage class? For example, should a variable be declared as a string instead of an array of characters?

---

[1] *These checklist items were adapted from* Software Testing in the Real World: Improving the Process, *pp. 198-201. Copyright 1995 by Edward Kit. Used by permission of Pearson Education Limited, London. All rights reserved.*

- If a variable is initialized at the same time as it's declared, is it properly initialized and consistent with its type?
- Are there any variables with similar names? This isn't necessarily a bug, but it could be a sign that the names have been confused with those from somewhere else in the program.
- Are any variables declared that are never referenced or are referenced only once?
- Are all the variables explicitly declared within their specific module? If not, is it understood that the variable is shared with the next higher module?

Computation Errors

Computational or calculation errors are essentially bad math. The calculations don't result in the expected result.

- Do any calculations that use variables have different data types, such as adding an integer to a floating-point number?
- Do any calculations that use variables have the same data type but are different lengths—adding a byte to a word, for example?
- Are the compiler's conversion rules for variables of inconsistent type or length understood and taken into account in any calculations?
- Is the target variable of an assignment smaller than the right-hand expression?
- Is overflow or underflow in the middle of a numeric calculation possible?
- Is it ever possible for a divisor/modulus to be zero?
- For cases of integer arithmetic, does the code handle that some calculations, particularly division, will result in loss of precision?
- Can a variable's value go outside its meaningful range? For example, could the result of a probability be less than 0% or greater than 100%?
- For expressions containing multiple operators, is there any confusion about the order of evaluation and is operator precedence correct? Are parentheses needed for clarification?

Comparison Errors

Less than, greater than, equal, not equal, true, false. Comparison and decision errors are very susceptible to boundary condition problems.

- Are the comparisons correct? It may sound pretty simple, but there's always confusion over whether a comparison should be less than or less than or equal to.
- Are there comparisons between fractional or floating-point values? If so, will any precision problems affect their comparison? Is 1.00000001 close enough to 1.00000002 to be equal?

- Does each Boolean expression state what it should state? Does the Boolean calculation work as expected? Is there any doubt about the order of evaluation?
- Are the operands of a Boolean operator Boolean? For example, is an integer variable containing integer values being used in a Boolean calculation?

Control Flow Errors

Control flow errors are the result of loops and other control constructs in the language not behaving as expected. They are usually caused, directly or indirectly, by computational or comparison errors.

- If the language contains statement groups such as `begin...end` and `do...while`, are the ends explicit and do they match their appropriate groups?
- Will the program, module, subroutine, or loop eventually terminate? If it won't, is that acceptable?
- Is there a possibility of premature loop exit?
- Is it possible that a loop never executes? Is it acceptable if it doesn't?
- If the program contains a multiway branch such as a `switch...case` statement, can the index variable ever exceed the number of branch possibilities? If it does, is this case handled properly?
- Are there any "off by one" errors that would cause unexpected flow through the loop?

Subroutine Parameter Errors

Subroutine parameter errors are due to incorrect passing of data to and from software subroutines.

- Do the types and sizes of parameters received by a subroutine match those sent by the calling code? Is the order correct?
- If a subroutine has multiple entry points (yuck), is a parameter ever referenced that isn't associated with the current point of entry?
- If constants are ever passed as arguments, are they accidentally changed in the subroutine?
- Does a subroutine alter a parameter that's intended only as an input value?
- Do the units of each parameter match the units of each corresponding argument— English versus metric, for example?
- If global variables are present, do they have similar definitions and attributes in all referencing subroutines?

Input/Output Errors

These errors include anything related to reading from a file, accepting input from a keyboard or mouse, and writing to an output device such as a printer or screen. The items presented here are very simplified and generic. You should adapt and add to them to properly cover the software you're testing.

- Does the software strictly adhere to the specified format of the data being read or written by the external device?
- If the file or peripheral isn't present or ready, is that error condition handled?
- Does the software handle the situation of the external device being disconnected, not available, or full during a read or write?
- Are all conceivable errors handled by the software in an expected way?
- Have all error messages been checked for correctness, appropriateness, grammar, and spelling?

Other Checks

This best-of-the-rest list defines a few items that didn't fit well in the other categories. It's not by any means complete, but should give you ideas for specific items that should be added to a list tailored for your software project.

- Will the software work with languages other than English? Does it handle extended ASCII characters? Does it need to use Unicode instead of ASCII?
- If the software is intended to be portable to other compilers and CPUs, have allowances been made for this? Portability, if required, can be a huge issue if not planned and tested for.
- Has compatibility been considered so that the software will operate with different amounts of available memory, different internal hardware such as graphics and sound cards, and different peripherals such as printers and modems?
- Does compilation of the program produce any "warning" or "informational" messages? They usually indicate that something questionable is being done. Purists would argue that any warning message is unacceptable.

Summary

Examining the code—static white-box testing—has proven to be an effective means for finding bugs early. It's a task that requires a great deal of preparation to make it a productive exercise, but many studies have shown that the time spent is well worth the benefits gained. To make it even more attractive, commercial software is now available that automates a great deal of the work. Software is available that reads in a program's source files and checks it against published standards and your own customizable guidelines. Compilers have also improved to the point that if you enable all their levels of error checking, they will catch many of the problems listed previously in the generic code review checklist. These tools don't eliminate the tasks of code reviews or inspections—they just make it easier to accomplish and give testers more time to look even deeper for bugs.

If your team currently isn't doing testing at this level and you have some experience at programming, you might try suggesting it as a process to investigate. Programmers and managers may be apprehensive at first, not knowing if the benefits are that great—it's hard to claim, for example, that finding a bug during an inspection saved your project five days over finding it months later during black-box testing. But, static white-box testing is gaining momentum, and in some circles, projects can't ship reliable software without it.

Quiz

These quiz questions are provided for your further understanding. See Appendix A, "Answers to Quiz Questions," for the answers—but don't peek!

1. Name several advantages to performing static white-box testing.

2. **True or False:** Static white-box testing can find missing items as well as problems.

3. What key element makes formal reviews work?

4. Besides being more formal, what's the big difference between inspections and other types of reviews?

5. If a programmer was told that he could name his variables with only eight characters and the first character had to be capitalized, would that be a standard or a guideline?

6. Should you adopt the code review checklist from this chapter as your team's standard to verify its code?

Testing the Software with X-Ray Glasses

IN THIS CHAPTER

So far in Part II you've learned about three of the four fundamental testing techniques: static black box (testing the specification), dynamic black box (testing the software), and static white box (examining the code). In this chapter, you'll learn the fourth fundamental technique—dynamic white-box testing. You'll look into the software "box" with your X-ray glasses as you test the software.

In addition to your X-ray specs, you'll also need to wear your programmer's hat—if you have one. If you don't own one, don't be scared off. The examples used aren't that complex and if you take your time, you'll be able to follow them. Gaining even a small grasp of this type of testing will make you a much more effective black-box tester.

If you do have some programming experience, consider this chapter an introduction to a very wide-open testing field. Most software companies are hiring testers specifically to perform low-level testing of their software. They're looking for people with both programming and testing skills, which is often a rare mix and highly sought after.

Highlights from this chapter include

- What dynamic white-box testing is
- The difference between debugging and dynamic white-box testing
- What unit and integration testing are
- How to test low-level functions
- The data areas that need to be tested at a low level
- How to force a program to operate a certain way
- What different methods you can use to measure the thoroughness of your testing

Dynamic White-Box Testing

By now you should be very familiar with the terms *static*, *dynamic*, *white box*, and *black box*. Knowing that this chapter is about dynamic white-box testing should tell you exactly what material it covers. Since it's dynamic, it must be about testing a running program and since it's white-box, it must be about looking inside the box, examining the code, and watching it as it runs. It's like testing the software with X-ray glasses.

Dynamic white-box testing, in a nutshell, is using information you gain from seeing what the code does and how it works to determine what to test, what not to test, and how to approach the testing. Another name commonly used for dynamic white-box testing is *structural testing* because you can see and use the underlying structure of the code to design and run your tests.

Why would it be beneficial for you to know what's happening inside the box, to understand how the software works? Consider Figure 7.1. This figure shows two boxes that perform the basic calculator operations of addition, subtraction, multiplication, and division.

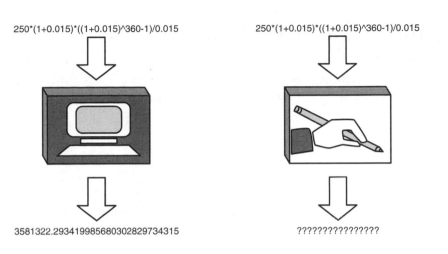

250*(1+0.015)*((1+0.015)^360-1)/0.015   250*(1+0.015)*((1+0.015)^360-1)/0.015

3581322.293419985680302829734315   ???????????????????

FIGURE 7.1

You would choose different test cases if you knew that one box contained a computer and the other a person with a pencil and paper.

If you didn't know how the boxes worked, you would apply the dynamic black-box testing techniques you learned in Chapter 5, "Testing the Software with Blinders On." But, if you could look in the boxes and see that one contained a computer and the other contained a person with a pencil and paper, you would probably choose a completely different test approach for each one. Of course, this example is very simplistic, but it makes the point that knowing how the software operates will influence how you test.

Dynamic white-box testing isn't limited just to seeing what the code does. It also can involve directly testing and controlling the software. The four areas that dynamic white-box testing encompasses are

- Directly testing low-level functions, procedures, subroutines, or libraries. In Microsoft Windows, these are called Application Programming Interfaces (APIs).

- Testing the software at the top level, as a completed program, but adjusting your test cases based on what you know about the software's operation.

- Gaining access to read variables and state information from the software to help you determine whether your tests are doing what you thought. And, being able to force the software to do things that would be difficult if you tested it normally.

- Measuring how much of the code and specifically what code you "hit" when you run your tests and then adjusting your tests to remove redundant test cases and add missing ones.

Each area is discussed in the remainder of this chapter. Think about them as you read on and consider how they might be used to test software that you're familiar with.

Dynamic White-Box Testing versus Debugging

It's important not to confuse dynamic white-box testing with *debugging*. If you've done some programming, you've probably spent many hours debugging code that you've written. The two techniques may appear similar because they both involve dealing with software bugs and looking at the code, but they're very different in their goals (see Figure 7.2).

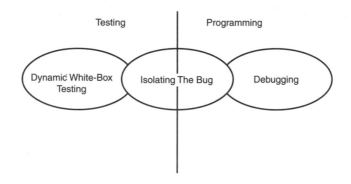

FIGURE 7.2
Dynamic white-box testing and debugging have different goals but they do overlap in the middle.

The goal of dynamic white-box testing is to find bugs. The goal of debugging is to fix them. They do overlap, however, in the area of isolating where and why the bug occurs. You'll learn more about this in Chapter 18, "Reporting What You Find," but for now, think of the overlap this way. As a software tester, you should narrow down the problem to the simplest test case that demonstrates the bug. If it's white-box testing, that could even include information about what lines of code look suspicious. The programmer who does the debugging picks the process up from there, determines exactly what is causing the bug, and attempts to fix it.

NOTE

It's important to have a clear separation between your work and the programmer's work. Programmers write the code, testers find the bugs and may need to write some code to drive their tests, and programmers fix the bugs. Without this separation, issues can arise where tasks are overlooked or work is duplicated.

If you're performing this low-level testing, you will use many of the same tools that programmers use. If the program is compiled, you will use the same compiler but possibly with different settings to enable better error detection. You will likely use a code-level debugger to single-step through the program, watch variables, set break conditions, and so on. You may also write your own programs to test separate code modules given to you to validate.

Testing the Pieces

Recall from Chapter 2, "The Software Development Process," the various models for software development. The big-bang model was the easiest but the most chaotic. Everything was put together at once and, with fingers crossed, the team hoped that it all worked and that a product would be born. By now you've probably deduced that testing in such a model would be very difficult. At most, you could perform dynamic black-box testing, taking the product in one entire blob and exploring it to see what you could find.

You've learned that this approach is very costly because the bugs are found late in the game. From a testing perspective, there are two reasons for the high cost:

- It's difficult and sometimes impossible to figure out exactly what caused the problem. The software is a huge Rube Goldberg machine that doesn't work—the ball drops in one side, but buttered toast and hot coffee doesn't come out the other. There's no way to know which little piece is broken and causing the entire contraption to fail.

- Some bugs hide others. A test might fail. The programmer confidently debugs the problem and makes a fix, but when the test is rerun, the software still fails. So many problems were piled one on top the other that it's impossible to get to the core fault.

Unit and Integration Testing

The way around this mess is, of course, to never have it happen in the first place. If the code is built and tested in pieces and gradually put together into larger and larger portions, there won't be any surprises when the entire product is linked together (see Figure 7.3).

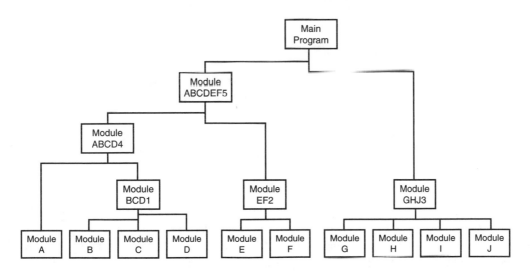

FIGURE 7.3
Individual pieces of code are built up and tested separately, and then integrated and tested again.

Testing that occurs at the lowest level is called *unit testing* or *module testing*. As the units are tested and the low-level bugs are found and fixed, they are integrated and *integration testing* is performed against groups of modules. This process of incremental testing continues, putting together more and more pieces of the software until the entire product—or at least a major portion of it—is tested at once in a process called *system testing*.

With this testing strategy, it's much easier to isolate bugs. When a problem is found at the unit level, the problem must be in that unit. If a bug is found when multiple units are integrated, it must be related to how the modules interact. Of course, there are exceptions to this, but by and large, testing and debugging is much more efficient than testing everything at once.

There are two approaches to this incremental testing: *bottom-up* and *top-down*. In bottom-up testing (see Figure 7.4), you write your own modules, called *test drivers*, that exercise the modules you're testing. They hook in exactly the same way that the future real modules will. These drivers send test-case data to the modules under test, read back the results, and verify that they're correct. You can very thoroughly test the software this way, feeding it all types and quantities of data, even ones that might be difficult to send if done at a higher level.

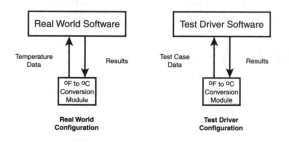

FIGURE 7.4

A test driver can replace the real software and more efficiently test a low-level module.

Top-down testing may sound like big-bang testing on a smaller scale. After all, if the higher-level software is complete, it must be too late to test the lower modules, right? Actually, that's not quite true. Look at Figure 7.5. In this case, a low-level interface module is used to collect temperature data from an electronic thermometer. A display module sits right above the interface, reads the data from the interface, and displays it to the user. To test the top-level display module, you'd need blow torches, water, ice, and a deep freeze to change the temperature of the sensor and have that data passed up the line.

Rather than test the temperature display module by attempting to control the temperature of the thermometer, you could write a small piece of code called a *stub* that acts just like the interface module by feeding temperature values from a file directly to the display module. The display module would read the data and show the temperature just as though it was reading directly from a real thermometer interface module. It wouldn't know the difference. With this test stub configuration, you could quickly run through numerous test values and validate the operation of the display module.

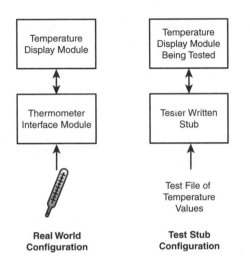

FIGURE 7.5
A test stub sends test data up to the module being tested.

An Example of Unit Testing

A common function available in many compilers is one that converts a string of ASCII characters into an integer value.

What this function does is take a string of numbers, – or + signs, and possible extraneous characters such as spaces and letters, and converts them to a numeric value—for example, the string "12345" gets converted to the number 12,345. It's a fairly common function that's often used to process values that a user might type into a dialog box—for example, someone's age or an inventory count.

The C language function that performs this operation is atoi(), which stands for "ASCII to Integer." Figure 7.6 shows the specification for this function. If you're not a C programmer, don't fret. Except for the first line, which shows how to make the function call, the spec is in English and could be used for defining the same function for any computer language.

If you're the software tester assigned to perform dynamic white-box testing on this module, what would you do?

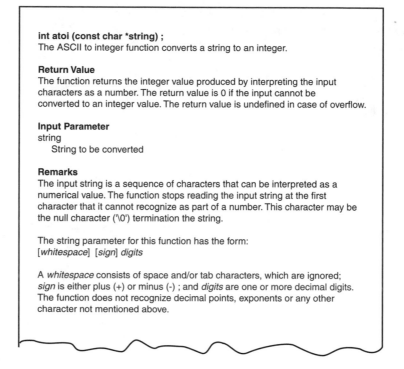

```
int atoi (const char *string) ;
The ASCII to integer function converts a string to an integer.

Return Value
The function returns the integer value produced by interpreting the input
characters as a number. The return value is 0 if the input cannot be
converted to an integer value. The return value is undefined in case of overflow.

Input Parameter
string
    String to be converted

Remarks
The input string is a sequence of characters that can be interpreted as a
numerical value. The function stops reading the input string at the first
character that it cannot recognize as part of a number. This character may be
the null character ('\0') termination the string.

The string parameter for this function has the form:
[whitespace] [sign] digits

A whitespace consists of space and/or tab characters, which are ignored;
sign is either plus (+) or minus (-) ; and digits are one or more decimal digits.
The function does not recognize decimal points, exponents or any other
character not mentioned above.
```

FIGURE 7.6

The specification sheet for the C language atoi() *function.*

First, you would probably decide that this module looks like a bottom module in the program, one that's called by higher up modules but doesn't call anything itself. You could confirm this by looking at the internal code. If this is true, the logical approach is to write a test driver to exercise the module independently from the rest of the program.

This test driver would send test strings that you create to the atoi() function, read back the return values for those strings, and compare them with your expected results. The test driver would most likely be written in the same language as the function—in this case, C—but it's also possible to write the driver in other languages as long as they interface to the module you're testing.

This test driver can take on several forms. It could be a simple dialog box, as shown in Figure 7.7, that you use to enter test strings and view the results. Or it could be a standalone program that reads test strings and expected results from a file. The dialog box, being user driven, is very interactive and flexible—it could be given to a black-box tester to use. But the standalone driver can be very fast reading and writing test cases directly from a file.

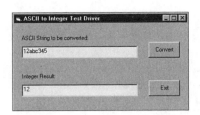

FIGURE 7.7
A dialog box test driver can be used to send test cases to a module being tested.

Next, you would analyze the specification to decide what black-box test cases you should try and then apply some equivalence partitioning techniques to reduce the total set (remember Chapter 5?). Table 7.1 shows examples of a few test cases with their input strings and expected output values. This table isn't intended to be a comprehensive list.

TABLE 7.1   Sample ASCII to Integer Conversion Test Cases

Input String	Output Integer Value
"1"	1
"-1"	−1
"+1"	1
"0"	0
"-0"	0
"+0"	0
"1.2"	1
"2-3"	2
"abc"	0
"a123"	0
and so on	

Lastly, you would look at the code to see how the function was implemented and use your white-box knowledge of the module to add or remove test cases.

> **NOTE**
>
> Creating your black-box testing cases based on the specification, before your white-box cases, is important. That way, you are truly testing what the module is intended

to do. If you first create your test cases based on a white-box view of the module, by examining the code, you will be biased into creating test cases based on how the module works. The programmer could have misinterpreted the specification and your test cases would then be wrong. They would be precise, perfectly testing the module, but they wouldn't be accurate because they wouldn't be testing the intended operation.

Adding and removing test cases based on your white-box knowledge is really just a further refinement of the equivalence partitions done with inside information. Your original black-box test cases might have assumed an internal ASCII table that would make cases such as "a123" and "z123" different and important. After examining the software, you could find that instead of an ASCII table, the programmer simply checked for numbers, – and + signs, and blanks. With that information, you might decide to remove one of these cases because both of them are in the same equivalence partition.

With close inspection of the code, you could discover that the handling of the + and – signs looks a little suspicious. You might not even understand how it works. In that situation, you could add a few more test cases with embedded + and – signs, just to be sure.

Data Coverage

The previous example of white-box testing the atoi() function was greatly simplified and glossed over some of the details of looking at the code to decide what adjustments to make to the test cases. In reality, there's quite a bit more to the process than just perusing the software for good ideas.

The logical approach is to divide the code just as you did in black-box testing—into its data and its states (or program flow). By looking at the software from the same perspective, you can more easily map the white-box information you gain to the black-box cases you've already written.

Consider the data first. Data includes all the variables, constants, arrays, data structures, keyboard and mouse input, files and screen input and output, and I/O to other devices such as modems, networks, and so on.

Data Flow

Data flow coverage involves tracking a piece of data completely through the software. At the unit test level this would just be through an individual module or function. The same tracking could be done through several integrated modules or even through the entire software product—although it would be more time-consuming to do so.

If you test a function at this low level, you would use a debugger and watch variables to view the data as the program runs (see Figure 7.8). With black-box testing, you only know what the value of the variable is at the beginning and at the end. With dynamic white-box testing you could also check intermediate values during program execution. Based on what you see you might decide to change some of your test cases to make sure the variable takes on interesting or even risky interim values.

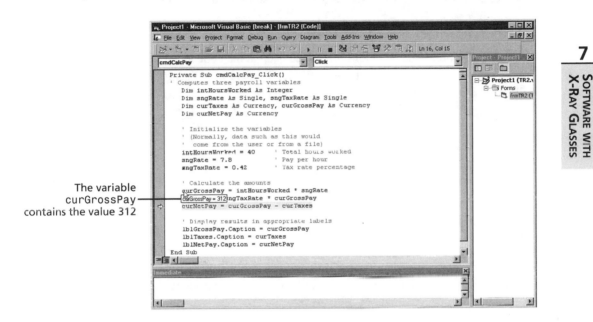

The variable
curGrossPay
contains the value 312

FIGURE 7.8
A debugger and watch variables can help you trace a variable's values through a program.

Sub-Boundaries

Sub-boundaries were discussed in Chapter 5 in regard to embedded ASCII tables and powers-of-two. These are probably the most common examples of sub-boundaries that can cause bugs, but every piece of software will have its own unique sub-boundaries, too. Here are a few more examples:

- A module that computes taxes might switch from using a data table to using a formula at a certain financial cut-off point.

- An operating system running low on RAM may start moving data to temporary storage on the hard drive. This sub-boundary may not even be fixed. It may change depending on how much space remains on the disk.

- To gain better precision, a complex numerical analysis program may switch to a different equation for solving the problem depending on the size of the number.

If you perform white-box testing, you need to examine the code carefully to look for sub-boundary conditions and create test cases that will exercise them. Ask the programmer who wrote the code if she knows about any of these situations and pay special attention to internal tables of data because they're especially prone to sub-boundary conditions.

Formulas and Equations

Very often, formulas and equations are buried deep in the code and their presence or effect isn't always obvious from the outside. A financial program that computes compound interest will definitely have this formula somewhere in the software:

$$A=P(1+r/n)^{nt}$$

where

P = principal amount

r = annual interest rate

n = number of times the interest is compounded per year

t = number of years

A = amount after time t

A good black-box tester would hopefully choose a test case of $n=0$, but a white-box tester, after seeing the formula in the code, would know to try $n=0$ because that would cause the formula to blow up with a divide-by-zero error.

But, what if n was the result of another computation? Maybe the software sets the value of n based on other user input or algorithmically tries different n values in an attempt to find the lowest payment. You need to ask yourself if there's any way that n can ever become zero and figure out what inputs to feed the program to make that happen.

TIP

Scour your code for formulas and equations, look at the variables they use, and create test cases and equivalence partitions for them in addition to the normal inputs and outputs of the program.

Error Forcing

The last type of data testing covered in this chapter is *error forcing*. If you're running the software that you're testing in a debugger, you don't just have the ability to watch variables and see what values they hold—you can also force them to specific values.

In the preceding compound interest calculation, if you couldn't find a direct way to set the number of compoundings (n) to zero, you could use your debugger to force it to zero. The software would then have to handle it…or not.

> **NOTE**
>
> Be careful if you use error forcing and make sure you aren't creating a situation that can never happen in the real world. If the programmer checked that n was greater than zero at the top of the function and n was never used until the formula, setting it to zero and causing the software to fail would be an invalid test case.

If you take care in selecting your error forcing scenarios and double-check with the programmer to assure that they're valid, error forcing can be an effective tool. You can execute test cases that would otherwise be difficult to perform.

Forcing Error Messages

A great way to use error forcing is to cause all the error messages in your software to appear. Most software uses internal error codes to represent each error message. When an internal error condition flag is set, the error handler takes the variable that holds the error code, looks up the code in a table, and displays the appropriate message.

Many errors are difficult to create—like hooking up 2,049 printers. But if all you want to do is test that the error messages are correct (spelling, language, formatting, and so on), using error forcing can be a very efficient way to see all of them. Keep in mind, though, that you aren't testing the code that detects the error, just the code that displays it.

Code Coverage

As with black-box testing, testing the data is only half the battle. For comprehensive coverage you must also test the program's states and the program's flow among them. You must attempt to enter and exit every module, execute every line of code, and follow every logic and decision path through the software. Examining the software at this level of detail is called *code-coverage analysis.*

Code-coverage analysis is a dynamic white-box testing technique because it requires you to have full access to the code to view what parts of the software you pass through when you run your test cases.

The simplest form of code-coverage analysis is using your compiler's debugger to view the lines of code you visit as you single-step through the program. Figure 7.9 shows an example of the Visual Basic debugger in operation.

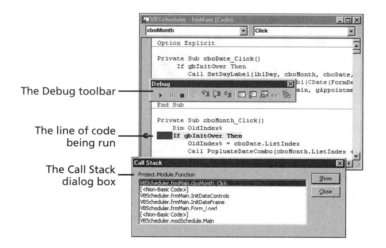

FIGURE 7.9

The debugger allows you to single-step through the software to see what lines of code and modules you execute while running your test cases.

For very small programs or individual modules, using a debugger is often sufficient. However, performing code coverage on most software requires a specialized tool known as a *code-coverage analyzer*. Figure 7.10 shows an example of such a tool.

Code-coverage analyzers hook into the software you're testing and run transparently in the background while you run your test cases. Each time a function, a line of code, or a logic decision is executed, the analyzer records the information. You can then obtain statistics that identify which portions of the software were executed and which portions weren't. With this data you'll know

- What parts of the software your test cases don't cover. If the code in a specific module is never executed, you know that you need to write additional test cases for testing that module's function.

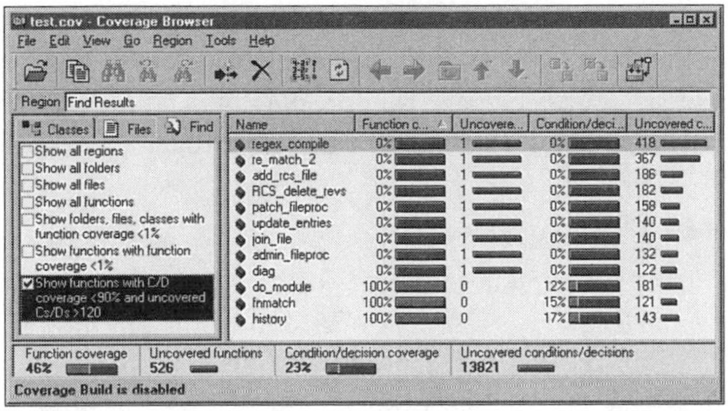

FIGURE 7.10

A code-coverage analyzer provides detailed information about how effective your test cases are. (This figure is copyright and courtesy of Bullseye Testing Technology.)

- Which test cases are redundant. If you run a series of test cases and they don't increase the percentage of code covered, they are likely in the same equivalence partition.

- What new test cases need to be created for better coverage. You can look at the code that has low coverage, see how it works and what it does, and create new test cases that will exercise it.

You will also have a general feel for the quality of the software. If your test cases cover 90 percent of the software and don't find any bugs, the software is in pretty good shape. If, on the other hand, your tests cover only 50 percent of the software and you're still finding bugs, you know you still have work to do.

Program Statement and Line Coverage

The most straightforward form of code coverage is called *statement coverage* or *line coverage*. If you're monitoring statement coverage while you test your software, your goal is to make sure that you execute every statement in the program at least once. In the case of the short program shown in Listing 7.1, 100 percent statement coverage would be the execution of lines 1 through 4.

LISTING 7.1   It's Very Easy to Test Every Line of This Simple Program

```
PRINT "Hello World"
PRINT "The date is: "; Date$
PRINT "The time is: "; Time$
END
```

You might think this would be the perfect way to make sure that you tested your program completely. You could run your tests and add test cases until every statement in the program is touched. Unfortunately, statement coverage is misleading. It can tell you if every statement is executed, but it can't tell you if you've taken all the paths through the software.

Branch Coverage

Attempting to cover all the paths in the software is called *path testing*. The simplest form of path testing is called *branch coverage* testing. Consider the program shown in Listing 7.2.

LISTING 7.2   The IF Statement Creates Another Branch Through the Code

```
PRINT "Hello World"
IF Date$ = "01-01-2000" THEN
    PRINT "Happy New Year"
    END IF
PRING "The date is: "; Date$
PRINT "The time is: "; Time$
END
```

If you test this program with the goal of 100 percent statement coverage, you would need to run only a single test case with the Date$ variable set to January 1, 2000. The program would then execute the following path:

> Lines 1, 2, 3, 4, 5, 6, 7

Your code coverage analyzer would state that you tested every statement and achieved 100 percent coverage. You could quit testing, right? Wrong! You may have tested every *statement*, but you didn't test every *branch*.

Your gut may be telling you that you still need to try a test case for a date that's not January 1, 2000. If you did, the program would execute the other path through the program:

> Lines 1, 2, 5, 6, 7

Most code coverage analyzers will account for code branches and report both statement coverage and branch coverage results separately, giving you a much better idea of your test's effectiveness.

Condition Coverage

Just when you thought you had it all figured out, there's yet another complication to path testing. Listing 7.3 shows a slight variation to Listing 7.2. An extra condition is added to the IF statement in line 2 that checks the time as well as the date. *Condition coverage* testing takes the extra conditions on the branch statements into account.

LISTING 7.3   The Multiple Conditions in the IF Statement Create More Paths Through the Code

```
PRINT "Hello World"
IF Date$ = "01-01-2000" AND Time$ = "00:00:00" THEN
    PRINT "Happy New Year"
    END IF
PRINT "The date is: "; Date$
PRINT "The time is: "; Time$
END
```

In this sample program, to have full condition coverage testing, you need to have the four sets of test cases shown in Table 7.2. These cases assure that each possibility in the IF statement are covered.

TABLE 7.2   Test Cases to Achieve Full Coverage of the Multiple IF Statement Condition

Date$	Time$	Line # Execution
01-01-0000	11:11:11	1,2,5,6,7
01-01-0000	00:00:00	1,2,5,6,7
01-01-2000	11:11:11	1,2,5,6,7
01-01-2000	00:00:00	1,2,3,4,5,6,7

If you were concerned only with branch coverage, the first three conditions would be redundant and could be equivalence partitioned into a single test case. But, with condition coverage testing, all four cases are important because they exercise different conditions of the IF statement in line 4.

As with branch coverage, code coverage analyzers can be configured to consider conditions when reporting their results. If you test for all the possible conditions, you will achieve branch coverage and therefore achieve statement coverage.

> **NOTE**
>
> If you manage to test every statement, branch, and condition (and that's impossible except for the smallest of programs), you still haven't tested the program completely. Remember, all the data errors discussed in the first part of this chapter are still possible. The program flow and the data together make up the operation of the software.

Summary

This chapter showed you how having access to the software's source code while the program is running can open up a whole new area of software testing. Dynamic white-box testing is a very powerful approach that can greatly reduce your test work by giving you "inside" information about what to test. By knowing the details of the code, you can eliminate redundant test cases and add test cases for areas you didn't initially consider. Either way, you can greatly improve your testing effectiveness.

Chapters 4 through 7 covered the fundamentals of software testing:

- *Static black-box* testing involves examining the specification and looking for problems before they get written into the software.
- *Dynamic black-box* testing involves testing the software without knowing how it works.
- *Static white-box* testing involves examining the details of the written code through formal reviews and inspections.
- *Dynamic white-box* testing involves testing the software when you can see how it works and basing your tests on that information.

In a sense, this is all there is to software testing. Of course, reading about it in four chapters and putting it into practice are very different things. Being a good software tester requires lots of dedication and hard work. It takes practice and experience to know when and how to best apply these fundamental techniques.

In Part III, "Applying Your Testing Skills," you'll learn about different types of software testing and how you can apply the skills from your "black and white testing box" to real-world scenarios.

Quiz

These quiz questions are provided for your further understanding. See Appendix A, "Answers to Quiz Questions," for the answers—but don't peek!

1. Why does knowing how the software works influence how and what you should test?
2. What's the difference between dynamic white-box testing and debugging?
3. What are two reasons that testing in a big-bang software development model is nearly impossible? How can these be addressed?
4. **True or False:** If your product development is in a hurry, you can skip module testing and proceed directly to integration testing.
5. What's the difference between a test stub and a test driver?
6. **True or False:** Always design your black-box test cases first.
7. Of the three code coverage measures described, which one is the best? Why?
8. What's the biggest problem of white-box testing, either static or dynamic?

Applying Your Testing Skills

PART III

For my birthday I got a humidifier and a dehumidifier...I put them in the same room and let them fight it out.

—Steven Wright, comedian

Discovery consists of looking at the same thing as everyone else does and thinking something different.

—Albert Szent-Gyorgyi, 1937 Nobel Prize winner in physiology and medicine

IN THIS PART

Configuration Testing

IN THIS CHAPTER

Life could be so simple. All computer hardware could be identical. All software could be written by the same company. There wouldn't be confusing option buttons to click or check boxes to check. Everything would interface perfectly the first time, every time. How boring.

In the real world, 50,000-square-foot computer superstores are offering PCs, printers, monitors, network cards, modems, scanners, digital cameras, peripherals, net-cams, and hundreds of other computer doodads from thousands of companies—all able to connect to your PC!

If you're just getting started at software testing, one of your first tasks may be configuration testing. You'll be making sure that your software works with as many different hardware combinations as possible. If you're not testing software for a PC or a Mac—that is, if you're testing some proprietary system—you will still need to consider some configuration issues. You can easily tailor what you learn in this chapter to your situation.

The first part of this chapter deals with the generalities of PC configuration testing and then moves into the specifics of testing printers, display adapters (video cards), and sound cards for a PC. Although the examples are based on desktop computers, you can extrapolate the methods to just about any type of configuration test problem. New and different devices are released every day, and it will be your job to figure out how to test them.

Highlights of this chapter include

- Why configuration testing is necessary
- Why configuration testing can be a huge job
- A basic approach to configuration testing
- How to find the hardware you need to test with
- What to do if you're not testing software for a desktop computer

An Overview of Configuration Testing

The next time you're in one of those computer superstores, look at a few software boxes and read over the system requirements. You'll see things such as PC with 486/66 MHz processor, Super VGA, 256-color monitor, 16-bit audio card, MIDI game port, and so on. *Configuration testing* is the process of checking the operation of the software you're testing with all these various types of hardware. Consider the different configuration possibilities for a standard Windows-based PC used in homes and businesses:

- **The PC.** There are dozens of well-known computer manufacturers, such as Compaq, Dell, Gateway, Hewlett Packard, IBM, and others. Each one designs and builds PCs using their own designed components or parts from other manufacturers. Many lesser-known manufacturers and many hobbyists even build their own PCs.

- **Components.** Most PCs are modular and built up from various *system boards, component cards,* and other internal devices such as disk drives, CD-ROM drives, video, sound, modem, and network cards (see Figure 8.1). There are TV cards and specialized cards for video capture and home automation. There are even input/output cards that can give a PC the ability to control a small factory! These internal devices are built by hundreds of different manufacturers.

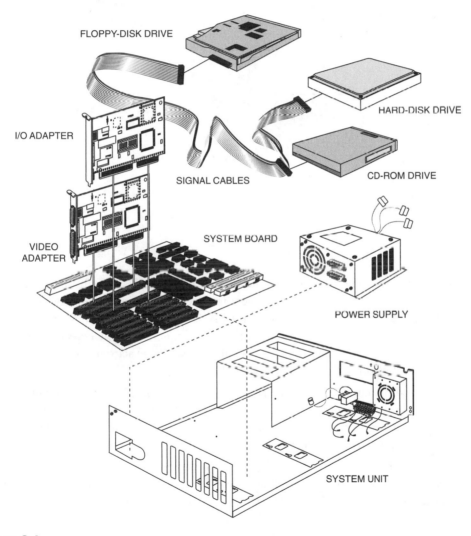

8

CONFIGURATION
TESTING

FIGURE 8.1

Numerous internal components make up a PC's configuration.

- **Peripherals.** Peripherals, shown in Figure 8.2, are the printers, scanners, mice, keyboards, monitors, cameras, joysticks, and other devices that plug into your system and operate externally to the PC.

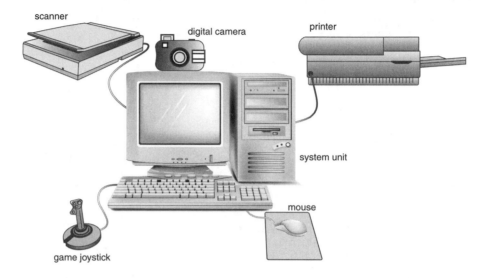

scanner

digital camera

printer

system unit

mouse

game joystick

FIGURE 8.2

A PC can connect to a wide assortment of peripherals.

- **Interfaces.** The components and peripherals plug into your PC through various types of interface connectors (see Figure 8.3). These interfaces can be internal or external to the PC. Typical names for them are ISA, PCI, USB, PS/2, RS/232, and Firewire. There are so many different possibilities that hardware manufacturers will often create the same peripheral with different interfaces. It's possible to buy the exact same mouse in three different configurations!

- **Options and memory.** Many components and peripherals can be purchased with different hardware options and memory sizes. Printers can be upgraded to support extra fonts or accept more memory to speed up printing. Graphics cards with more memory can support additional colors and higher resolutions.

- **Device Drivers.** All components and peripherals communicate with the operating system and the software applications through low-level software called *device drivers*. These drivers are often provided by the hardware device manufacturer and are installed when you set up the hardware. Although technically they are software, for testing purposes they are considered part of the hardware configuration.

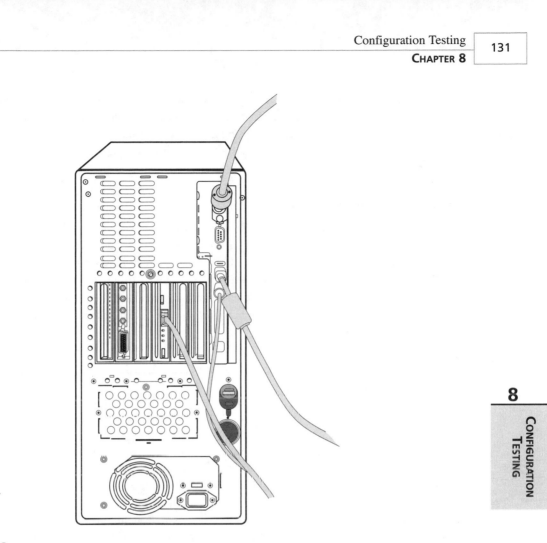

FIGURE 8.3

The back of a PC shows numerous interface connectors for attaching peripherals.

If you're a tester gearing up to start configuration testing on a piece of software, you need to consider which of these configuration areas would be most closely tied to the program. A highly graphical computer game will require lots of attention to the video and sound areas. A greeting card program will be especially vulnerable to printer issues. A fax or communications program will need to be tested with numerous modems and network configurations.

You may be wondering why this is all necessary. After all, there are standards to meet for building hardware, whether it's for an off-the-shelf PC or a specialized computer in a hospital. You would expect that if everyone designed their hardware to a set of standards, software would just work with it without any problems. In an ideal world, that would happen, but unfortunately, standards aren't always followed. Sometimes, the standards are fairly loose—call them guidelines. Card and peripheral manufacturers are always in tight competition with one another and frequently bend the rules to squeeze in an extra feature or to get in a last little bit of performance gain. Often the device drivers are rushed and packed into the box as the hardware goes out the door. The result is software that doesn't work correctly with certain hardware configurations.

Isolating Configuration Bugs

Those configuration bugs can bite hard. Remember the Disney Lion King bug described in Chapter 1? That was a configuration problem. The software's sound didn't work only on a few, but very popular, hardware configurations. If you've ever been playing a game or using a graphics program and the colors suddenly go crazy or pieces of windows get left behind as you drag them, you've probably discovered a display adapter configuration bug. If you've ever spent hours (or days!) trying to get an old program to work with your new printer, it's probably a configuration bug.

> **NOTE**
>
> The sure way to tell if a bug is a configuration problem and not just an ordinary bug is to perform the exact same operation that caused the problem, step by step, on another computer with a completely different configuration. If the bug doesn't occur, it's very likely a configuration problem. If the bug happens on more than one configuration, it's probably just a regular bug.

Assume that you test your software on a unique configuration and discover a problem. Who should fix the bug—your team or the hardware manufacturer? That could turn out to be a million-dollar question.

First you need to figure out where the problem lies. This is usually a dynamic white-box testing and programmer-debugging effort. A configuration problem can occur for several reasons, all requiring someone to carefully examine the code while running the software under different configurations to find the bug:

- Your software may have a bug that appears under a broad class of configurations. An example is if your greeting card program works fine with laser printers but not with inkjet printers.

- Your software may have a bug specific only to one particular configuration—it doesn't work on the OkeeDoKee Model BR549 InkJet Deluxe printer.

- The hardware device or its device drivers may have a bug that only your software reveals. Maybe your software is the only one that uses a unique display card setting. When your software is run with a specific video card, the PC crashes.

- The hardware device or its device drivers may have a bug that can be seen with lots of other software—although it may be particularly obvious with yours. An example would be if a specific printer driver always defaulted to draft mode and your photo printing software had to set it to high-quality every time it printed.

In the first two cases, it seems fairly straightforward that your project team is responsible for fixing the bug. It's your problem. You should fix it.

In the last two cases, things get blurry. Say the bug is in a printer and that printer is the most popular in the world, with tens of millions in use. Your software obviously needs to work with that printer. It's a good bet that your team will have to make changes to your software, even though the software is doing everything right, to work around the bug in the printer.

In the end, it's your team's responsibility to address the problem, no matter where it lies. Your customers don't care why or how the bug is happening, they just want the new software they purchased to work on their system's configuration.

Of Purple Fuzz and Sound Cards

In 1997 Microsoft released its ActiMates Barney character and supporting CD-ROM learning software for kids. These animatronic dolls interacted with the software through a two-way radio in the doll and another radio connected to a PC.

The PC's radio connected to a seldom-used interface on most sound cards called a MIDI connector. This interface is used for music keyboards and other musical instruments. Microsoft assumed the connector would be a good choice because most people don't own musical devices. It would likely not have anything plugged into it and would be available for use with the ActiMates radio.

During configuration testing, a typical amount of bugs showed up. Some were due to sound card problems, some were in the ActiMates software. There was one bug, however, that could never quite be pinned down. It seemed that occasionally, randomly, the PC running the software would just lock up and would require rebooting. This problem occurred only with the most popular sound card on the market—of course.

With just weeks left in the schedule, a concerted effort was put together to resolve the problem. After a great deal of configuration testing and debugging, the bug was isolated to the sound card's hardware. It seems that the MIDI connector always had

> this bug, but, being so seldom used, no one had ever seen it. The ActiMates software exposed it for the first time.
>
> There was a mad scramble, lots of denials and finger pointing, and lots of late nights. In the end, the sound card manufacturer conceded that there was a problem and promised to work around the bug in updated versions of its device driver. Microsoft included a fixed driver on the ActiMates CD-ROM and made changes to the software that attempted to make the bug occur less frequently. Despite all those efforts, sound card compatibility problems were the top reason that people called in for assistance with the product.

Sizing Up the Job

The job of configuration testing can be a huge undertaking. Suppose that you're testing a new software game that runs under Microsoft Windows. The game is very graphical, has lots of sound effects, allows multiple players to compete against each other over the phone lines, and can print out game details for strategy planning.

At the least, you'll need to consider configuration testing with different graphics cards, sound cards, modems, and printers. The Windows Add New Hardware Wizard (see Figure 8.4) allows you to select hardware in each of these categories—and 25 others.

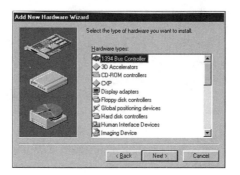

FIGURE 8.4

The Microsoft Windows Add New Hardware Wizard dialog box allows you add new hardware to your PC's current configuration.

Under each hardware category are the different manufacturers and models (see Figure 8.5). Keep in mind, these are only the models with support built into Windows. Many other models provide their own setup disks with their hardware.

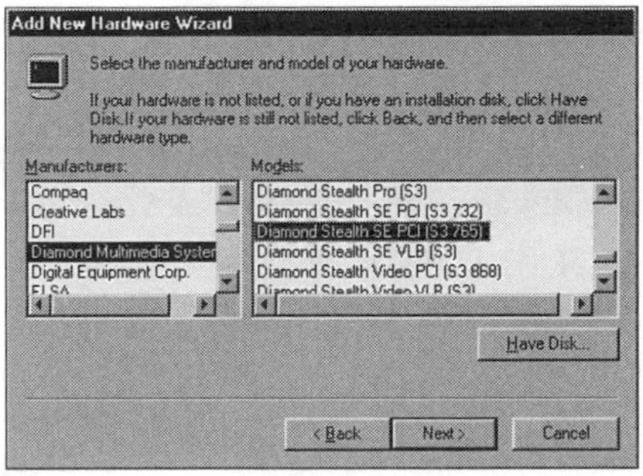

FIGURE 8.5
Each type of hardware has numerous manufacturers and models.

If you decided to perform a full, comprehensive configuration test, checking every possible make and model combination, you'd have a huge job ahead of you.

There are approximately 336 possible display cards, 210 sound cards, 1500 modems, and 1200 printers. The number of test combinations is $336 \times 210 \times 1500 \times 1200$, for a total in the billions—way too many to consider!

If you limited your testing to exclude combinations, just testing each card individually at about 30 minutes per configuration, you'd be at it for about a year. Keep in mind that's just one pass through the configurations. It's not uncommon with bug fixes to run two or three configuration test passes before a product is released.

The answer to this mess, as you've hopefully deduced, is *equivalence partitioning*. You need to figure out a way to reduce the huge set of possible configurations to the ones that matter the most. You'll assume some risk by not testing everything, but that's what software testing is all about.

Approaching the Task

The decision-making process that goes into deciding what devices to test with and how they should be tested is a fairly straightforward equivalence partition project. What's important, and what makes the effort a success or not, is the information you use to make the decisions. If you're not experienced with the hardware that your software runs on, you should learn as much as you can and bring in other experienced testers or programmers to help you. Ask a lot of questions and make sure you get your plan approved.

The following sections show the general process that you should use when planning your configuration testing.

Decide the Types of Hardware You'll Need

Does your application print? If so, you'll need to test printers. If it has sound, you'll need to test sound cards. If it's a photo or graphics program, you'll likely need scanners and digital cameras. Look closely at your software feature set to make sure that you cover everything. Put your software disk on a table and ask yourself what hardware pieces you need to put together to make it work.

Online Registration

An example of a feature that you can easily overlook when selecting what hardware to test with is online registration. Many programs today allow users to register their software during installation via modem. Users type in their name, address, and other personal data, click a button, and the modem dials out to a computer at the software company where it downloads the information and completes the registration. The software may not do anything else with online communications. But, if it has online registration, you will need to consider modems as part of your configuration testing.

Decide What Hardware Brands, Models, and Device Drivers Are Available

If you're putting out a cutting-edge graphics program, you probably don't need to test that it prints well on a 1987 black-and-white dot-matrix printer. (Remember those?) Work with your sales and marketing people to create a list of hardware to test with. If they can't or won't help, grab some recent editions and back issues of *PC Magazine* or *Mac World* to get an idea of what hardware is available and what is (and was) popular. Both magazines, as well as others, have annual reviews of printers, sound cards, and display adapters.

Do some research to see if some of the devices are clones of each other and therefore equivalent—falling under the same equivalence partition. For example, a printer manufacturer may sell his printer to another company that then puts a different cover and label on it. From your standpoint, it's the same printer.

Decide what device drivers you're going to test with. Your options are usually the drivers included with the operating system, the drivers included with the device, or the latest drivers available on the hardware or operating system company's Web site. Usually, all three are different. Ask yourself what customers have or what they can get.

Decide Which Hardware Features, Modes, and Options Are Possible

Color printers can print in black and white or color, they can print in different quality modes, and can have settings for printing photos or text. Display cards, as shown in Figure 8.6, can have different color settings and screen resolutions.

FIGURE 8.6

The display properties of number of colors and screen area are possible configurations for a display card.

Every device has options, and your software may not need to support all of them. A good example of this is computer games. Many require a minimum number of display colors and resolution. If the configuration has less than that, they simply won't run.

Pare Down the Identified Hardware Configurations to a Manageable Set

Given that you don't have the time or budget to test everything, you need to reduce the thousands of potential configurations into the ones that matter—the ones you're going to test.

One way to do this is to put all the configuration information into a spreadsheet with columns for the manufacturer, model, driver versions, and options. Figure 8.7 shows an example of a table that identifies various printer configurations. You and your team can review the chart and decide which configuration you want to test.

8

CONFIGURATION
TESTING

Popularity (1=most, 10=least)	Type (Laser / InkJet)	Age (years)	Manufacturer	Model	Device Driver Version	Options	Options
1	Laser	3	HAL Printers	LDIY2000	1.0	B/W	Draft Quality
5	InkJet	1	HAL Printers	IJDIY2000	1.0a	Color B/W	Draft Quality Draft Quality
5	InkJet	1	HAL Printers	IJDIY2000	2.0	Color B/W	Art Photo Draft Quality
10	Laser	5	OkeeDohKee	LJ100	1.5	B/W	100dpi 200dpi 300dpi
2	InkJet	2	OkeeDohKee	EasyPrint	1.0	Auto	600dpi

FIGURE 8.7

Organize your configuration information into a spreadsheet.

Notice that Figure 8.7 also has columns for information about the device's popularity, its type, and its age. When creating your equivalence partitions, you might decide that you want to test only the most popular printers, or ones that are less than five years old. With the type information—in this case, laser or inkjet—you could decide to test 75 percent lasers and 25 percent inkjets.

NOTE

Ultimately, the decision-making process that you use to equivalence partition the configurations into smaller sets is up to you and your team. There is no right formula. Every software project is different and will have different selection criteria. Just make sure that everyone on the project team, especially your project manager, is aware of what configurations are being tested and what variables went into selecting them.

Identify Your Software's Unique Features That Work with the Hardware Configurations

The key word here is *unique*. You don't want to, nor do you need to, completely test your software on each configuration. You need to test only those features that are different from each other (different equivalence partitions) that interact with the hardware.

For example, if you're testing a word processor such as WordPad (see Figure 8.8), you don't need to test the file save and load feature in each configuration. File saving and loading has nothing to do with printing. A good test would be to create a document that contains different (selected by equivalence partitioning, of course) fonts, point sizes, colors, embedded pictures, and so on. You would then attempt to print this document on each chosen printer configuration.

FIGURE 8.8
You can use a sample document made up of different fonts and styles to configuration test a printer.

Selecting the unique features to try isn't as easy as it sounds. You should first make a black-box pass by looking at your product and pulling out the obvious ones. Then talk with others on your team, especially the programmers, to get a white-box view. You may be surprised at what features are remotely tied to the configuration.

Design the Test Cases to Run on Each Configuration

You'll learn the details of writing test cases in Chapter 17, "Writing and Tracking Test Cases," but, for now, consider that you'll need to write down the steps required to test each configuration. This can be as simple as

1. Select and set up the next test configuration from the list.

2. Start the software.

3. Load in the file `configtest.doc`.

4. Confirm that the displayed file is correct.

5. Print the document.

6. Confirm that there are no error messages and that the printed document matches the standard.

7. Log any discrepancies as a bug.

In reality, the steps would be much more involved, including more detail and specifics on exactly what to do. The goal is to create steps that anyone can run. After all, you don't want to personally be doing these tests forever.

Execute the Tests on Each Configuration

You need to run the test cases and carefully log and report your results (see Chapter 18, "Reporting What You Find") to your team, and to the hardware manufacturers if necessary. As described earlier in this chapter, it's often difficult and time-consuming to identify the specific source of configuration problems. You'll need to work closely with the programmers and white-box testers to isolate the cause and decide if the bugs you find are due to your software or to the hardware.

If the bug is specific to the hardware, consult the manufacturer's Web site for information on reporting problems to them. Be sure to identify yourself as a software tester and what company you work for. Many companies have separate staff set up to assist software companies writing software to work with their hardware. They may ask you to send copies of your test software, your test cases, and supporting details to help them isolate the problem.

Rerun the Tests Until the Results Satisfy Your Team

It's not uncommon for configuration testing to run the entire course of a project. Initially a few configurations might be tried, then a full test pass, then smaller and smaller sets to confirm bug fixes. Eventually you will get to a point where there are no known bugs or to where the bugs that still exist are in uncommon or unlikely test configurations. At that point, you can call your configuration testing complete.

Obtaining the Hardware

One thing that hasn't been mentioned so far is where you obtain all this hardware. Even if you take great pains, and risk, to equivalence partition your configurations to the barest minimum, you still could require dozens of different hardware setups. It would be an expensive proposition to go out and buy everything at retail, especially if you will use the hardware only once for the one test pass. Here are a few ideas for overcoming this problem:

- Buy only the configurations that you can or will use most often. A great plan is for every tester on the team to have different hardware. This may drive your purchasing department and the group that maintains your company's PCs crazy (they like everyone to have exactly the same configuration) but it's a very efficient means of always having different configurations available to test on. Even if your test team is very small, three or four people having just a few configurations would be a great help.

- Contact the hardware manufacturers and ask if they will lend or even give you the hardware. If you explain that you're testing new software and you want to assure that it works on their hardware, many will do this for you. They have an interest in the outcome, too, so tell them that you'll furnish them with the results of the tests and, if you can, a copy of the finished software. It's good to build up these relationships, especially if you find a bug and need a contact person at the hardware company to report it to.

- Send a memo or email to everyone in your company asking what hardware they have in their office or even at home—and if they would allow you to run a few tests on it. To perform the configuration testing, you may need to drive around town, but it's a whole lot cheaper than attempting to buy all the hardware.

Configuration Testing VCRs

The Microsoft ActiMates product line of animatronic dolls not only interfaced with a PC, but also a VCR. Specially coded commands, invisible to a viewer, were mixed in with the video on the tape. A special box connected to the VCR decoded the commands and sent them by radio to the doll. The test team obviously needed to perform configuration testing on VCRs. They had many PC configurations but no VCRs.

They found two ways to get the job done:

- They asked about 300 employees to bring in their VCRs for a day of testing. The program manager awarded gift certificates as a means of persuading people to bring them in.

- They paid the manager of a local electronics superstore to stay at the store after hours (actually, all night) while they pulled each VCR off the shelf, connected their equipment, and ran the tests. They dusted and cleaned the VCRs and bought the manager dinner to show their thanks.

When it was all over, they had tested about 150 VCRs, which they determined was a very good equivalence partition of the VCRs in people's homes.

- If you have the budget, work with your project manager to contract out your test work to a professional configuration and compatibility test lab. These companies do nothing but configuration testing and have every piece of PC hardware known to man. OK, maybe not that much, but they do have a lot.

  These labs can help you, based on their experience, select the correct hardware to test. Then, they will allow you to come in and use their equipment, or they will provide a complete turn-key service. You provide the software, the step-by-step test process, and the expected results. They'll take it from there, running the tests and reporting what passed and what failed. Of course this can be costly, but much less so than buying the hardware yourself or worse, not testing and having customers find the problems.

Identifying Hardware Standards

If you're interested in performing a little static black-box analysis—that is, reviewing the specifications that the hardware companies use to create their products—you can look in a couple of places. Knowing some details of the hardware specifications can help you make more informed equivalence partition decisions.

For Apple hardware, visit the Apple Hardware Web site at `http://developer.apple.com/hardware/`. There you'll find information and links about developing and testing hardware and device drivers for Apple computers. Another Apple link, `http://developer.apple.com/testing/`, points you to specific testing information, including links to test labs that perform configuration testing.

For PCs, the best link is `http://www.pcdesignguide.org/`. This site, sponsored jointly between Intel and Microsoft, provides information and links to the standards used to develop hardware and peripherals for PCs. The standards are revised annually and are named PC99, PC2000, and so on.

Microsoft publishes a set of standards for software and hardware to receive the Windows logo. That information is at `http://msdn.microsoft.com/certification/` and `http://www.microsoft.com/hwtest`.

Configuration Testing Other Hardware

So, what if you're not testing software that runs on a PC or a Mac? Was this chapter a waste of your time? No way! Everything you learned can be applied to testing generic or proprietary systems, too. It doesn't matter what the hardware and software is and what it connects to; if it connects to anything else, configuration issues need to be tested.

If you're testing software for an industrial controller, a network, medical devices, or a phone system, ask yourself the same questions that you would if you were testing software for a desktop computer:

- What external hardware will operate with this software?
- What models and versions of that hardware are available?
- What features or options does that hardware support?

Create equivalence partitions of the hardware based on input from the people who work with the equipment, your project manager, or your sales people. Develop test cases, collect the selected hardware, and run the tests. Configuration testing follows the same testing techniques that you've already learned.

Summary

This chapter got you thinking about how to approach configuration testing. It's a job that new software testers are frequently assigned because it is easily defined, is a good introduction to basic organization skills and equivalence partitioning, is a task that will get you working with lots of other project team members, and is one for which your manager can readily verify the results. The downside is that it can become overwhelming.

If you're assigned to perform configuration testing for your project, take a deep breath, reread this chapter, carefully plan your work, and take your time. When you're done, your boss will have another job for you: compatibility testing, the subject of the next chapter.

Quiz

These quiz questions are provided for your further understanding. See Appendix A, "Answers to Quiz Questions," for the answers—but don't peek!

1. What's the difference between a component and a peripheral?
2. How can you tell if a bug you find is a general problem or a specific configuration problem?
3. How could you guarantee that your software would never have a configuration problem?
4. **True or False:** A cloned sound card doesn't need to be considered as one of the configurations to test.
5. In addition to age and popularity, what other criteria might you use to equivalence partition hardware for configuration testing?
6. Is it acceptable to release a software product that has configuration bugs?

8

CONFIGURATION
TESTING

Compatibility Testing

IN THIS CHAPTER

In Chapter 8 you learned about hardware configuration testing and how to assure that software works properly with the hardware it was designed to run on and connect with. This chapter deals with a similar area of interaction testing—checking that your software operates correctly with other software.

Testing whether one program plays well with others has become increasingly important as consumers demand the ability to share data among programs of different types and from different vendors and take advantage of the ability to run multiple programs at once.

It used to be that a program could be developed as a standalone application. It would be run in a known, understood, benign environment, isolated from anything that could corrupt it. Today, that program likely needs to import and export data to other programs, run with different operating systems and Web browsers, and interoperate with other software being run simultaneously on the same hardware. The job of software compatibility testing is to make sure that this interaction works as users would expect.

The highlights of this chapter include

- What it means for software to be compatible
- How standards define compatibility
- What platforms are and what they mean for compatibility
- Why being able to transfer data among software applications is the key to compatibility

Compatibility Testing Overview

Software compatibility testing means checking that your software interacts with and shares information correctly with other software. This interaction could occur between two programs simultaneously running on the same computer or even on different computers connected through the Internet thousands of miles apart. The interaction could also be as simple as saving data to a floppy disk and hand-carrying it to another computer across the room.

Examples of compatible software are

- Cutting text from a Web page and pasting it into a document opened in your word processor
- Saving accounting data from one spreadsheet program and then loading it into a completely different spreadsheet program
- Having photograph touchup software work correctly on different versions of the same operating system
- Having your word processor load in the names and addresses from your contact management program and print out personalized invitations and envelopes

- Upgrading to a new database program and having all your existing databases load in and work just as they did with the old program

What compatibility means for your software depends on what your team decides to specify and what levels of compatibility are required by the system that your software will run on. Software for a standalone medical device that runs its own operating system, stores its data on its own memory cartridges, and doesn't connect to any other device would have no compatibility considerations. However, the fifth version of a word processor (see Figure 9.1) that reads and writes different files from other word processors, allows multiuser editing over the Internet, and supports inclusion of embedded pictures and spreadsheets from various applications has a multitude of compatibility issues.

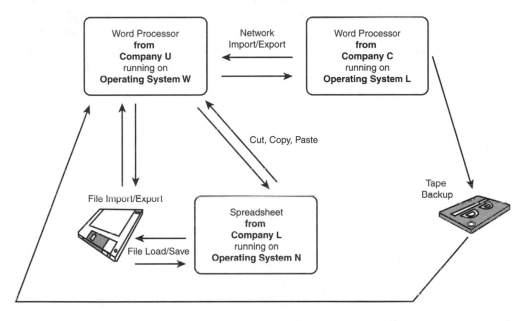

FIGURE 9.1
Compatibility across different software applications can quickly become very complicated.

If you're assigned the task of performing software compatibility testing on a new piece of software, you'll need to get the answers to a few questions:

- What other *platforms* (operating system, Web browser, or other operating environment) and other application software is your software designed to be compatible with? If the software you're testing is a platform, what applications are designed to run under it?

- What compatibility standards or guidelines should be followed that define how your software should interact with other software?

- What types of data will your software use to interact and share information with other platforms and software?

Gaining the answers to these questions is basic static testing—both black-box and white-box. It involves thoroughly analyzing the specification for the product and any supporting specifications. It could also entail discussions with the programmers and possibly close review of the code to assure that all links to and from your software are identified. The rest of this chapter discusses these questions in more detail.

Platform and Application Versions

Selecting the target platforms or the compatible applications is really a program management or a marketing task. Someone who's very familiar with the customer base will decide whether your software is to be designed for a specific operating system, Web browser, or some other platform. They'll also identify the version or versions that the software needs to be compatible with. For example, you've probably seen notices such as these on software packages or startup screens:

> Works best with Netscape 4.0
>
> Requires Windows 95 or greater
>
> For use with Linux kernel 2.2.16

This information is part of the specification and tells the development and test teams what they're aiming for. Each platform has its own development criteria and it's important, from a project management standpoint, to make this platform list as small as possible but still fill the customer's needs.

Backward and Forward Compatibility

Two terms you'll hear regarding compatibility testing are *backward compatible* and *forward compatible*. If something is backward compatible, it will work with previous versions of the software. If something is forward compatible, it will work with future versions of the software.

The simplest demonstration of backward and forward compatibility is with a `.txt` or text file. As shown in Figure 9.2, a text file created using Notepad 98 running under Windows 98 is backward compatible all the way back to MS-DOS 1.0. It's also forward compatible to Windows 2000 and likely will be beyond that.

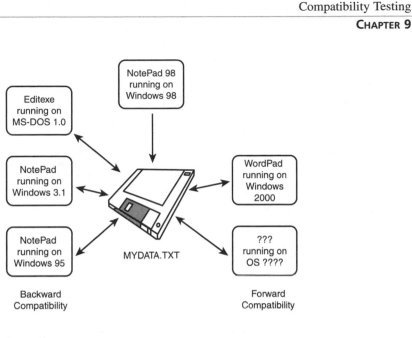

FIGURE 9.2
Backward and forward compatibility define what versions will work with your software or data files.

NOTE

It's not a requirement that all software or files be backward or forward compatible. That's a product feature decision your software designers need to make. You should, though, provide input on how much testing will be required to check forward and backward compatibility for the software.

The Impact of Testing Multiple Versions

Testing that multiple versions of platforms and software applications work properly with each other can be a huge task. Consider the situation of having to compatibility test a new version of a popular operating system. The programmers have made numerous bug fixes and performance improvements and have added many new features to the code. There could be tens or hundreds of thousands of existing programs for the current versions of the OS. The project's goal is to be 100 percent compatible with them. See Figure 9.3.

This is a big job, but it's just another example of how equivalence partitioning can be applied to reduce the amount of work.

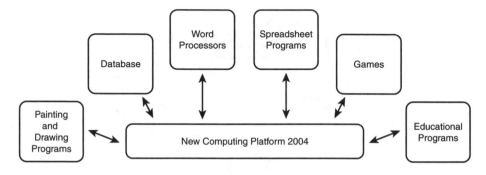

Figure 9.3

If you compatibility test a new platform, you must check that existing software applications work correctly with it.

> **Note**
>
> To begin the task of compatibility testing, you need to equivalence partition all the possible software combinations into the smallest, effective set that verifies that your software interacts properly with other software.

In short, you can't test all the thousands of software programs on your operating system, so you need to decide which ones are the most important to test. The key word is *important*. The criteria that might go into deciding what programs to choose could be

- **Popularity.** Use sales data to select the top 100 or 1,000 most popular programs.
- **Age.** You might want to select programs and versions that are less than three years old.
- **Type.** Break the software world into types such as painting, writing, accounting, databases, communications, and so on. Select software from each category for testing.
- **Manufacturer.** Another criteria would be to pick software based on the company that created it.

Just as in hardware configuration testing, there is no right "textbook" answer. You and your team will need to decide what matters most and then use that criteria to create equivalence partitions of the software you need to test with.

The previous example dealt with compatibility testing a new operating system platform. The same issues apply to testing a new application (see Figure 9.4). You need to decide what platform versions you should test your software on and what other software applications you should test your software with.

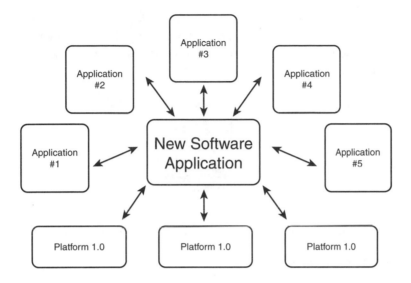

FIGURE 9.4
Compatibility testing a new application may require you to test it on multiple platforms and with multiple applications.

Standards and Guidelines

So far in this chapter you've learned about selecting the software that you'll compatibility test with your program. Now, it's time to look at how you'll approach the actual testing. Your first stop should be researching the existing standards and guidelines that might apply to your software or the platform.

There are really two levels of these requirements: high-level and low-level. High-level standards are the ones that guide your product's general compliance, its look and feel, its supported features, and so on. Low-level standards are the nitty-gritty details, such as the file formats and the network communications protocols. Both are important and both need to be tested to assure compatibility.

High-Level Standards and Guidelines

Will your software run under Windows, Mac, or Linux operating systems? Is it an Internet application? If so, what browsers will it run on? Each of these is considered a platform and most have their own set of standards and guidelines that must be followed if an application is to claim that it's compatible with the platform.

An example of this is the Certified for Microsoft Windows logo (see Figure 9.5). To be awarded this logo, your software must undergo and pass compatibility testing by an independent testing laboratory. The goal is to assure that the software runs stably and reliably on the operating system.

FIGURE 9.5

The Certified for Microsoft Windows logo signifies that the software meets all the criteria defined by the guidelines.

A few examples of the logo requirements are that the software

- Supports mice with more than three buttons
- Supports installation on disk drives other than C: and D:
- Supports long filenames
- Doesn't read, write, or otherwise use the old system files `win.ini`, `system.ini`, `autoexec.bat`, or `config.sys`

These may sound like simple, matter-of-fact requirements, but they're only four items out of a 77-page document. It's a great deal of work to assure that your software complies with all the logo requirements, but it makes for much more compatible software.

NOTE

The details of the Windows logo can be obtained at `http://msdn.microsoft.com/certification/`. Details for using the Apple Mac logo are at `http://developer.apple.com/mkt/maclogo.html`.

Low-Level Standards and Guidelines

Low-level standards are, in a sense, more important than the high-level standards. You could create a program that would run on Windows that didn't have the look and feel of other Windows software. It wouldn't be granted the Certified for Microsoft Windows logo. Users might not be thrilled with the differences from other applications, but they could use the product.

If, however, your software is a graphics program that saves its files to disk as .pict files (a standard Macintosh file format for graphics) but the program doesn't follow the standard for .pict files, your users won't be able to view the files in any other program. Your software wouldn't be compatible with the standard and would likely be a short-lived product.

Similarly, communications protocols, programming language syntax, and any means that programs use to share information must adhere to published standards and guidelines.

These low-level standards are often taken for granted, but from a tester's perspective must be tested. You should treat low-level compatibility standards as an extension of the software's specification. If the software spec states, "The software will save and load its graphics files as .bmp, .jpg, and .gif formats," you need to find the standards for these formats and design tests to confirm that the software does indeed adhere to them.

Data Sharing Compatibility

The sharing of data among applications is what really gives software its power. A well-written program that supports and adheres to published standards and allows users to easily transfer data to and from other software is a great compatible product.

The most familiar means of transferring data from one program to another is saving and loading disk files. As discussed in the previous section, adhering to the low-level standards for the disk and file formats is what makes this sharing possible. Other means, though, are sometimes taken for granted but still need to be tested for compatibility. Here are a few examples:

- *File save* and *file load* are the data-sharing methods that everyone is aware of. You save your data to a floppy disk (or some other means of network, magnetic, or optical storage) and then transfer it over to another computer running different software. The data format of the files needs to meet standards for it to be compatible on both computers.

- *File export* and *file import* are the means that many programs use to be compatible with older versions of themselves and with other programs. Figure 9.6 shows the Microsoft Word File Open dialog box and some of the 23 different file formats that can be imported into the word processor.

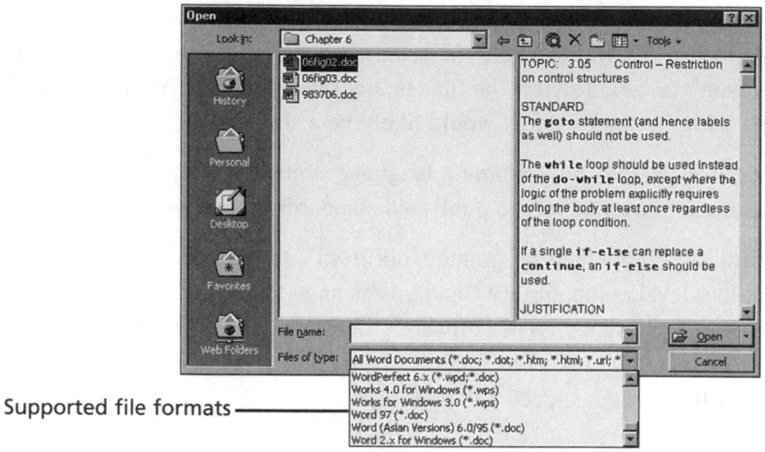

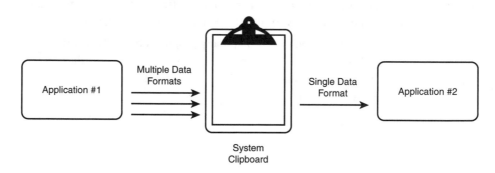

Supported file formats ———

FIGURE 9.6

Microsoft Word can import 23 different file formats.

To test the file import feature, you would need to create test documents in each compatible file format—probably using the original software that wrote that format. Those documents would need to have equivalence partitioned samples of the possible text and formatting to check that the importing code properly converts it to the new format.

- *Cut*, *copy*, and *paste* are the most familiar methods for sharing data among programs without transferring the data to a disk. In this case, the transfer happens in memory through an intermediate program called the *Clipboard*. Figure 9.7 shows how this transfer occurs.

FIGURE 9.7

The System Clipboard is a temporary hold place for different types of data that's being copied from one application to another.

The Clipboard is designed to hold several different data types. Common ones in Windows are text, pictures, and sounds. These data types can also be different formats—for example, the text can be plain old text, HTML, or rich text. Pictures can be bitmaps, metafiles, or `.tifs`.

Whenever a user performs a cut or copy, the data that's chosen is placed in the Clipboard. When he does a paste, it's copied from the Clipboard to the destination software.

If you're compatibility testing a program, you need to make sure that its data can be properly copied in and out of the Clipboard to other programs. This feature is so frequently used, people forget that there's a lot of code behind making sure that it works and is compatible across lots of different software.

- *DDE* (pronounced D-D-E) and *OLE* (pronounced oh-lay) are the methods in Windows of transferring data between two applications. DDE stands for Dynamic Data Exchange and OLE stands for Object Linking and Embedding. Other platforms support similar methods.

There's no need to get into the gory details of these technologies in this book, but the primary difference between these two methods and the Clipboard is that with DDE and OLE data can flow from one application to the other in real time. Cutting and copying is a manual operation. With DDE and OLE, the transfer can happen automatically.

An example of how these might be used could be a written report done in a word processor that has a pie-chart created by a spreadsheet program. If the report's author copied and pasted the chart into the report, it would be a snapshot in time of the data. If, however, the author linked the pie chart into the report as an object, when the underlying numbers for the chart change, the new graphics will automatically appear in the report.

This is all pretty fancy, yes, but it's also a testing challenge to make sure that the all the object linking embedding and data exchanging happens correctly.

Summary

This chapter introduced you to the basics of compatibility testing. In reality, an entire book could be written on the subject, and a single chapter doesn't do the topic justice. Every platform and every application is unique, and the compatibility issues on one system can be totally different than on another.

As a new software tester, you may be assigned a task of compatibility testing your software. That may seem strange, given that it's potentially such a large and complex task, but you'll likely be assigned just a piece of the entire job. If your project is a new operating system, you may be asked to compatibility test just word processors or graphics programs. If your project is an applications program, you may be asked to compatibility test it on several different platforms.

Each is a manageable task that you can easily handle if you approach your testing with these three things in mind:

- Equivalence partition all the possible choices of compatible software into a manageable set. Of course, your project manager should agree with your list and understand the risk involved in not testing everything.

- Research the high-level and low-level standards and guidelines that might apply to your software. Use these as extensions of your product's specification.

- Test the different ways that data can flow between the software programs you're testing. This data exchange is what makes one program compatible with another.

Quiz

These quiz questions are provided for your further understanding. See Appendix A, "Answers to Quiz Questions," for the answers—but don't peek!

1. **True or False:** All software must undergo some level of compatibility testing.

2. **True or False:** Compatibility is a product feature and can have different levels of compliance.

3. If you're assigned to test compatibility of your product's data file formats, how would you approach the task?

4. How can you test forward compatibility?

Foreign-Language Testing

IN THIS CHAPTER

Si tu eres fluente en mas de un idioma y competente en provando programas de computadora, tu tienes una habilidad muy deceada en el mercado.

Wenn Sie eine zuverläßig Software Prüferin sind, und fließend eine fremd sprache, ausser English, sprechen können, dann können Sie gut verdienen.

Translated roughly from Spanish and German, the preceding two sentences read: *If you are a competent software tester and are fluent in a language other than English, you have a very marketable skill set.*

Most software today is released to the entire world, not just to a certain country or in a specific language. Microsoft shipped Windows 98 with support for 73 different languages, from Afrikaans to Hungarian to Vietnamese. Most other software companies do the same, realizing that the U.S. English market is less than half of their potential customers. It makes business sense to design and test your software for worldwide distribution.

This chapter covers what's involved in testing software written for other countries and languages. It might seem like a straightforward process, but it's not, and you'll learn why.

Highlights of this chapter include

- Why just translating is not enough
- How words and text are affected
- Why footballs and telephones are important
- The configuration and compatibility issues
- How large of a job testing another language is

Making the Words and Pictures Make Sense

Have you ever read a user's manual for an appliance or a toy that was poorly converted word for word from another language? "Put in a bolt number five past through green bar and tighten no loose to nut." Got it?

That's a poor *translation*, and it's what software can look like to a non-English speaker if little effort is put into building the software for foreign languages. It's easy to individually convert all the words, but to make the overall instructions meaningful and useful requires much more work and attention.

Good translators can do that. If they're fluent in both languages, they can make the foreign text read as well as the original. Unfortunately, what you'll find in the software industry is that even a good translation isn't sufficient.

Take Spanish, for example. It should be a simple matter to convert English text to Spanish, right? Well, which Spanish are you referring to? Spanish from Spain? What about Spanish from Costa Rica, Peru, or the Dominican Republic? They're all Spanish, but they're different enough that software written for one might not be received well by the others. Even English has this problem. There's not just U.S. English, there's also Canadian, Australian, and British English. It would probably seem strange to you to see the words *colour*, *neighbour*, and *rumour* in your word processor.

What needs to be accounted for, besides the language, is the *region* or *locale*—the user's country or geographic area. The process of adapting software to a specific locale, taking into account its language, dialect, local conventions, and culture, is called *localization*. Testing the software is called *localization testing*.

Translation Issues

Although translation is just a part of the overall localization effort, it's an important one from a test standpoint. The most obvious problem is how to test something that's in another language. Well, you or someone on your test team will need to be at least semi-fluent in the language you're testing, being able to navigate the software, read any text it displays, and type the necessary commands to run your tests. It might be time to sign up for the community college course in Slovenian you always wanted to take.

> **NOTE**
>
> It's important that you or someone on your test team be at least a little familiar with the language you're testing. Of course, if you're shipping your program in 32 different languages, they may be difficult. The solution is to contract out this work to a localization testing company. Numerous such companies worldwide can perform testing in nearly any language. For more information, search the Internet for "localization testing."

It's not a requirement that everyone on the test team speak the language that the software is being localized into; you probably need just one person. Many things can be checked without knowing what the words say. It would be helpful, sure, to know a bit of the language, but you'll see that you might be able to do a fair amount of the testing without being completely fluent.

Text Expansion

The most straightforward example of a translation problem that can occur is due to something called *text expansion*. Although English may appear at times to be wordy, it turns out that when English is translated into other languages, more characters are usually necessary to say the same thing. Figure 10.1 shows how the size of a button needs to expand to hold the translated text of two common computer words. A good rule of thumb is to expect up to 100 percent increase in size for individual words—on a button, for example. Expect a 50 percent increase in size for sentences and short paragraphs—typical phrases you would see in dialog boxes and error messages.

FIGURE 10.1

When translated into other languages, the words Minimize and Maximize can vary greatly in size, often forcing the UI to be redesigned to accommodate them.

Because of this expansion, you need to carefully test areas of the software that could be affected by longer text. Look for text that doesn't wrap correctly, is truncated, or is hyphenated incorrectly. This could occur anywhere—onscreen, in windows, boxes, buttons, and so on. Also look for cases where the text had enough room to expand, but did so by pushing something else out of the way.

Another possibility is that this longer text can cause a major program failure or even a system crash. A programmer could have allocated enough internal memory for the English text messages, but not enough for the translated strings. The English version of the software will work fine but the German version will crash when the message is displayed. A white-box tester could catch this problem without knowing a single word of the language.

ASCII, DBCS, and Unicode

Chapter 5, "Testing the Software with Blinders On," briefly discussed the ASCII character set. ASCII can represent only 256 different characters—not nearly enough to represent all the possible characters in all languages. When software started being developed for different languages, solutions needed to be found to overcome this limitation. An approach common in the days of MS-DOS, but still in use today, is to use a technique called *code pages*. Essentially, a code page is a replacement ASCII table, with a different code page for each language. If your software runs in Quebec on a French PC, it could load and use a code page that supports French characters. Russian uses a different code page for its Cyrillic characters, and so on.

This solution is fine, although a bit clunky, for languages with less than 256 characters, but Japanese, Chinese, and other languages with thousands of symbols cause problems. A system called *DBCS* (for *Double-Byte Character Set*) is used by some software to provide more than 256 characters. Using 2 bytes instead of 1 byte allows for up to 65,536 different characters.

Code pages and DBCS are sufficient in many situations but suffer from a few problems. Most important is the issue of compatibility. If a Hebrew document is loaded onto a German computer running a British word processor, the result can be gibberish. Without the proper code pages or the proper conversion from one to the other, the characters can't be interpreted correctly, or even at all.

The solution to this mess is the Unicode standard.

> Unicode provides a unique number for every character,
> no matter what the platform,
> no matter what the program,
> no matter what the language.

> *"What is Unicode?"*
> *from the Unicode Consortium Web site,*
> www.unicode.org

Because Unicode is a worldwide standard supported by the major software companies, hardware manufacturers, and other standards groups, it's becoming more commonplace. Most major software applications support it. Figure 10.2 shows many of the different characters supported. If it's at all possible that your software will ever be localized, you and the programmers on your project should cut your ties to "ol' ASCII" and switch to Unicode to save yourself time, aggravation, and bugs.

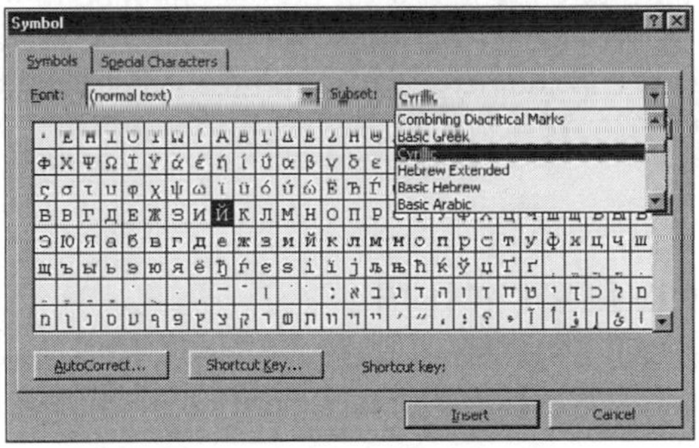

FIGURE 10.2
This Microsoft Word 2000 dialog shows support for the Unicode standard.

Hot Keys and Shortcuts

In English, it's Search. In French, it's *Réchercher*. If the hotkey for selecting Search in the English version of your software is Alt+S, that will need to change in the French version.

In localized versions of your software, you'll need to test that all the hotkeys and shortcuts work properly and aren't too difficult to use—for example, requiring a third keypress. And, don't forget to check that the English hotkeys and shortcuts are disabled.

Extended Characters

A common problem with localized software, and even non-localized software, is in its handling of *extended characters*. Referring back to that ancient ASCII table, extended characters are the ones that are outside the normal English alphabet of A–Z and a–z. Examples of these would be the accented characters such as the *é* in *José* or the *ñ* in *El Niño*. If your software is properly written to use Unicode or even if it correctly manages code pages or DBCS, this shouldn't be an issue, but a tester should never assume anything, so it's worthwhile to check.

The way to test this is to look for all the places that your software can accept character input or send output. In each place, try to use extended characters to see if they work just as regular characters would. Dialog boxes, logins, and any text field are fair game. Can you send and receive extended characters through a modem? Can you name your files with them or even have the characters in the files? Will they print out properly? What happens if you cut, copy, and paste them between your program and another one?

> **TIP**
>
> The simplest way to ensure that you test for proper handling of extended characters is to add them to your equivalence partition of the standard characters that you test. Along with those bug-prone characters sitting on the ASCII table boundaries, throw in an *Æ*, an *Ø*, and a *ß*.

Computations on Characters

Related to extended characters are problems with how they're interpreted by software that performs calculations on them. Two examples of this are word sorting and upper- and lowercase conversion.

Does your software sort or alphabetize word lists? Maybe in a list box of selectable items such as filenames or Web site addresses? If so, how would you sort the following words?

Kopiëren	*Reiste*
Ärmlich	*Arg*
Reiskorn	*résumé*
Reißaus	*kopieën*
reiten	*Reisschnaps*
reißen	*resume*

If you're testing software to be sold to one of the many Asian cultures, are you aware that the sort order is based on the order of the brush strokes used to paint the character? The preceding list would likely have a completely different sort order if written in Mandarin Chinese. Find out what the sorting rules are for the language you're testing and develop tests to specifically check that the proper sort order occurs.

The other area where calculation on extended characters breaks down is with upper- and lower-case conversion. It's a problem because the "trick" solution that many programmers learn in school is to simply add or subtract 32 to the ASCII value of the letter to convert it between cases. Add 32 to the ASCII value of *A* and you get the ASCII value of *a*. Unfortunately, that doesn't work for extended characters. If you tried this technique using the Apple Mac extended character set, you'd convert *Ñ* (ASCII 132) to § (ASCII 164) instead of *ñ* (ASCII 150)—not exactly what you'd expect.

Sorting and alphabetizing are just two examples. Carefully look at your software to determine if there are other situations where calculations are performed on letters or words. Spell-checking perhaps?

Reading Left to Right and Right to Left

A huge issue for translation is that some languages, such as Hebrew and Arabic, read from right to left, not left to right. Imagine flipping your entire user interface into a mirror image of itself.

Thankfully, most major operating systems provide built-in support for handling these languages. Without this, it would be a nearly impossible task. Even so, it's still not a simple matter of translating the text. It requires a great deal of programming to make use of the OS's features to do the job. From a testing standpoint, it's probably safe to consider it a completely new product, not just a localization.

Text in Graphics

Another translation problem occurs when text is used in graphics. See Figure 10.3 for several examples.

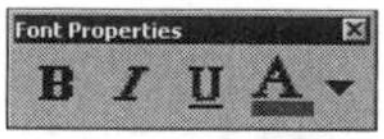

FIGURE 10.3

Word 2000 has examples of text in bitmaps that would be difficult to translate.

The icons in Figure 10.3 are the standard ones for selecting Bold, Italic, Underline, and Font Color. Since they use the English letters B, I, U, and A, they'll mean nothing to someone from Japan who doesn't read English. They might pick up on the meaning based on their look—the **B** is a bit dark, the *I* is leaning, and the U has a line under it—but software isn't supposed to be a puzzle.

The impact of this is that when the software is localized, each icon will have to be changed to reflect the new languages. If there were many of these icons, it could get prohibitively expensive to localize the program. Look for text-in-graphic bugs early in the development cycle so they don't make it through to the end.

Keep the Text out of the Code

The final translation problem to cover is a white-box testing issue—keep the text out of the code. What this means is that all text strings, error messages, and really anything that could possibly be translated should be stored in a separate file independent of the source code. You should never see a line of code such as:

```
Print "Hello World"
```

Most localizers are not programmers, nor do they need to be. It's risky and inefficient to have them modifying the source code to translate it from one language to another. What they should modify is a simple text file, called a *resource file*, that contains all the messages the software can display. When the software runs, it references the messages by looking them up, not knowing or caring what they say. If the message is in English or Dutch, it gets displayed just the same.

That said, it's important for a white-box testers to search the code to make sure there are no embedded strings that weren't placed in the external file. It would be pretty embarrassing to have an important error message in an Spanish program appear in English.

Another variation of this problem is when the code dynamically generates a text message. For example, it might piece together snippets of text to create a larger message. The code could take three strings:

1. "You pressed the"
2. a variable string containing the name of the key just pressed
3. "key just in time!"

and put them together to create a message. If the variable string had the value "stop nuclear reaction," the total message would read:

> You pressed the stop nuclear reaction key just in time!

The problem is that the word order is not the same in all languages. Although it pieces together nicely in English, with each phrase translated separately, it could be gibberish when stuck together in Mandarin Chinese or even German. Don't let strings crop into the code and don't let them be built up into larger strings by the code.

Localization Issues

As mentioned previously, translation issues are only half the problem. Text can easily be translated and allowances made for different characters and lengths of strings. The difficulty occurs in changing the software so that it's appropriate for the foreign market.

REMINDER

> Remember those terms from Chapter 3: *precision, accuracy,* and *reliability and quality*?

Well-translated and well-tested software is precise and reliable, but probably not accurate or of high quality. It might look and feel great, read perfectly, and never crash, but to someone from another locale, it might just seem plain-old wrong. Assuring that the product is correctly localized gets you to this next step.

Content

What would you think of a new software encyclopedia for the U.S. English market if it had the content shown in Figure 10.4?

Football

Our Queen

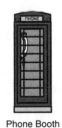
Phone Booth

Always drive on the left

FIGURE 10.4
These content samples would seem strange in a U.S. English encyclopedia.

In the United States, a soccer ball isn't the same thing as a football! You don't drive on the left! These may not seem right to you, but in other countries they would be perfectly accurate. If you're testing a product that will be localized, you need to carefully examine the content to make sure it's appropriate to the area where it will be used.

Content is all the other "stuff" besides the code that goes into the product (see Chapter 2, "The Software Development Process"). The following list shows various types of content that you should carefully review for localization issues. Don't consider it a complete list; there can be many more examples depending on the product. Think about what other items in your software might be problematic if it was sent to another country.

Sample documents	Icons
Pictures	Sounds
Video	Help files
Maps with disputed boundaries	Marketing material
Packaging	Web links

A Nose Too Long

In 1993, Microsoft released two products for kids called Creative Writer and Fine Artist. These products used a helper character named McZee to guide the kids through the software. A great deal of research went into the design of McZee to select his look, color, mannerisms, personality, and so on. He turned out to be a rather strange looking fellow with buck teeth, dark purple skin, and a big nose.

Unfortunately, after a great deal of work was done drawing the animations that would appear on the screen, a call came in from one of Microsoft's foreign offices. They had received a preliminary version of the software and after reviewing it said that it was unacceptable. The reason: McZee's nose was too long. In their culture, people with large noses weren't common and, right or wrong, they associated having a large nose with lots of negative stereotypes. They said that the product wouldn't sell if it was localized for their locale.

It would have been way too costly to create two different McZees, one for each market, so the artwork completed up to that point was thrown out, and McZee had his first nose job.

The bottom line is that the content that goes with the software, whether it's text, graphics, sounds, or whatever, is especially prone to having localization issues. Test the content with an eye for these types of problems and, if you're not experienced with the culture of the locale that the software is destined for, be sure to call in someone who is.

Data Formats

Different locales use different formats for data units such as currency, time, and measurement. Just as with content, these are localization, not translation, issues. A U.S. English publishing program that works with inches couldn't simply undergo a text translation to use centimeters. It would require code changes to alter the underlying formulas, gridlines, and so on.

Table 10.1 shows many of the different categories of units that you'll need to become familiar with if you're testing localized software.

TABLE 10.1 Data Format Considerations for Localized Software

Unit	Considerations
Measurements	Metric or English
Numbers	Comma, decimal, or space separators; how negatives are shown; # symbol for number
Currency	Different symbols and where they're placed
Dates	Order of month, day, year; separators; leading zeros; long and short formats
Times	12-hour or 24-hour, separators
Calendars	Different calendars and starting days
Addresses	Order of lines; postal code used
Telephone numbers	Parenthesis or dash separators
Paper sizes	Different paper and envelope sizes

Fortunately, most operating systems designed for use in multiple locales support these different units and their formats. Figure 10.5 shows an example from Windows 98. Having this built-in support makes it easier, but by no means foolproof, for programmers to write localized software.

NOTE

How a unit is displayed isn't necessarily how it's treated internally by the software. For example, the Date tab on the Regional Settings program shows a short date style of m/d/yy. That doesn't imply that the operating system handles only a 2-digit year (and hence is a Y2K bug). In this case, the setting means only a 2-digit year is displayed. The operating system still supports a 4-digit year for computations, which is one more thing to consider when testing.

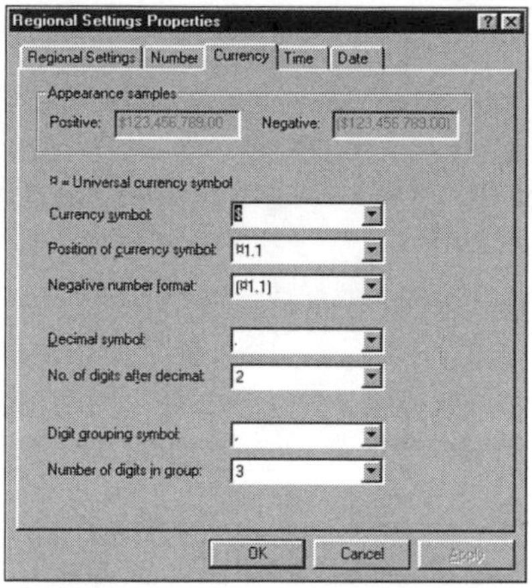

FIGURE 10.5

The Windows 98 Regional Settings options allow a user to select how numbers, currency, times, and dates will be displayed.

If you're testing localized software, you'll need to become very familiar with the units of measure used by the target locale. To properly test the software, you'll need to create different equivalence partitions of test data from the ones you create for testing the original version of the software.

Configuration and Compatibility Issues

The information covered in Chapters 8 and 9 on configuration and compatibility testing is very important when testing localized versions of software. The problems that can crop up when software interacts with different hardware and software are amplified by all the new and different combinations. Performing this testing isn't necessarily more difficult, just a bit larger of a task. It can also tax your logistical skills to locate and acquire the foreign version of hardware and software to test with.

Foreign Platform Configurations

Windows 98 supports 73 different languages and 66 different keyboards. It does this, as shown in Figure 10.6, through the Keyboard Properties dialog via Control Panel. The drop-down list for languages runs from Afrikaans to Ukrainian and includes eight different versions of English other than U.S. English (Australian, British, Canadian, Caribbean, Irish, Jamaican, New Zealand, and South African), five different German dialects, and 20 different Spanish dialects.

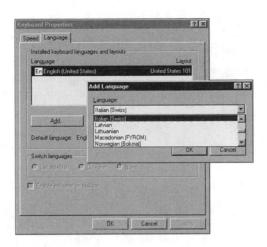

FIGURE 10.6
Windows 98 supports the use of different keyboards and languages through the Keyboard Properties dialog.

Figure 10.7 shows examples of three different keyboard layouts designed for different countries. You'll notice that each has keys specific to its own language, but also has English characters. This is fairly common, since English is often spoken as a second language in many countries, and allows the keyboard to be used with both native and English language software.

Keyboards are probably the piece of hardware with the largest language dependencies, but depending on what you're testing, there can be many others. Printers, for example, would need to print all the characters your software sends to them and properly format the output on the various paper sizes used in different countries. If your software uses a modem, there might be issues related to the phone lines or communication protocol differences. Basically, any peripheral that your software could potentially work with needs to be considered for a place in your equivalence partitions for platform configuration and compatibility testing.

NOTE

When designing your equivalence partitions, don't forget that you should consider all the hardware and software that can make up the platform. This includes the hardware, device drivers for the hardware, and the operating system. Running a French printer on a Mac, with a British operating system, and a German version of your software might be a perfectly legitimate configuration for your users.

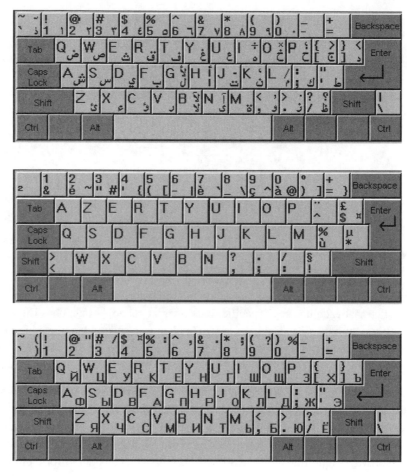

FIGURE 10.7

The Arabic, French, and Russian keyboards support characters specific to those languages. Courtesy of Fingertip Software, Inc. (www.fingertipsoft.com).

Data Compatibility

Just as with platform configuration testing, compatibility testing of data takes on a whole new meaning when you add localization to the equation. Figure 10.8 shows how complex it can get moving data from one application to another. In this example, a German application that uses metric units and extended characters can move data to a different French program by saving and loading to disk or using cut and paste. That French application can then export the data for import to yet another English application. That English program, which uses English units and non-extended characters, can then move it all back to original German program.

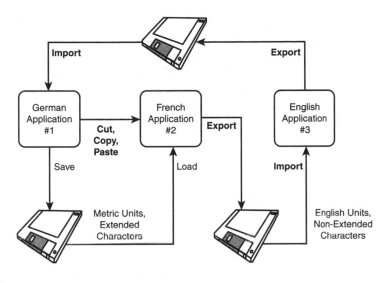

FIGURE 10.8

Data compatibility testing of localized software can get fairly complex.

During this round and round of data transfers, with all the conversions and handling of measurement units and extended characters, there are numerous places for bugs. Some of these bugs might be due to design decisions. For example, what should happen to data moved from one application to another if it needs to change formats? Should it be automatically converted, or should the user be prompted for a decision? Should it show an error or should the data just move and the units change?

These important questions need to be answered before you can start testing the compatibility of your localized software. As soon as you have those specifications, your compatibility testing should proceed as it normally would—just with more test cases in your equivalence partitions.

How Much Should You Test?

The big uncertainty that looms over localization testing is in determining how much of the software you should test. If you spent six months testing the U.S. English version, should you spend six months testing a version localized into French? Should you spend even more because of additional configuration and compatibility issues?

This complex issue comes down to two questions:

- Was the project intended to be localized from the very beginning?
- Was programming code changed to make the localized version?

If the software was designed from the very beginning to account for all the things discussed in this chapter, the risk is much smaller that a localized version will be very buggy and require lots of testing. If, on the other hand, the software was written specifically for the U.S. English market and then it was decided to localize it into another language, it would probably be wise to treat the software as a completely new release requiring full testing.

The other question deals with what needs to change in the overall software product. If the localization effort involves changing only content such as graphics and text—not code—the test effort can sometimes be just a validation of the changes. If, however, because of poor design or other problems, the underlying code must change, the testing needs take that into account and check functionality as well as content.

> **NOTE**
>
> The amount of localization testing required is a risk-based decision, just as all testing is. As you gain experience in testing, you'll learn what variables go into the decision-making process.

> **NOTE**
>
> One method used by teams who know they are going to localize their product is to test for *localizability*. That is, they test the first version of the product, assuming that it will eventually be localized. The white-box testers examine the code for text strings, proper handling of units of measure, extended characters, and other code-level issues. They may even create their own "fake" localized version. The black-box testers carefully review the spec and the product itself for localizing problems such as text in graphics and configuration issues. They can use the "fake" version to test for compatibility.
>
> Eventually, when the product is localized, many of the problems that would have shown up later have already been found and fixed, making the localization effort much less painful and costly.

Summary

Ha Ön egy rátermett és képzett softver ismerő, és folyékonyan beszél egy nyelvet az Angolon kívül, Ön egy nagyon piacképes szakképzett személy.

That's the same first sentence of this chapter—only written in Hungarian this time. Don't worry if you can't read it. You've learned in this chapter that knowing the language is only part of the overall testing required for a localized product. Much work can be done by checking the product for localizability and for testing language-independent areas.

If you are fluent in a language other than English, keep reading this book, and learn all you can about software testing. With the global economy and the worldwide adoption of technology and computers you will, as the Hungarian phrase roughly says, "have a very marketable skill set."

For more information on localization programming and testing for Windows, visit `www.microsoft.com/globaldev`. For the Mac, consult the book *Guide to Macintosh Software Localization*, published by Addison-Wesley.

Quiz

These quiz questions are provided for your further understanding. See Appendix A, "Answers to Quiz Questions," for the answers—but don't peek!

1. What's the difference between translation and localization?
2. Do you need to know the language to be able to test a localized product?
3. What is text expansion and what common bugs can occur because of it?
4. Identify several areas where extended characters can cause problems.
5. Why is it important to keep text strings out of the code?
6. Name a few types of data formats that could vary from one localized program to another.

Usability Testing

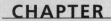
IN THIS CHAPTER

Software is written to be used. That sounds pretty obvious, but it's sometimes forgotten in the rush to design, develop, and test a complex product. So much time and effort is spent on the technology aspects of writing the code that the development team ignores the most important aspect of software—that someone will eventually use the stuff. It really doesn't matter whether the software is embedded in a microwave oven, a telephone switching station, or an Internet stock trading Web site. Eventually the bits and bytes bubble up to where a live person will interact with it. *Usability* is how appropriate, functional, and effective that interaction is.

You may have heard the term *ergonomics*, the science of designing everyday things so that they're easy and functional to use. An ergonomist's main concern is in achieving usability.

Now, you're not going to get the knowledge of a four-year ergonomics degree in the 15 or so pages of this chapter, nor do you need to. Remember from Chapter 1 the fifth rule of what constitutes a bug: The software is difficult to understand, hard to use, slow, or—in the software tester's eyes—will be viewed by the end user as just plain not right. That's your blank check for usability testing.

You're likely the first person to use the software—hopefully, while it's still in development and can be fixed. You've become familiar with the specification and investigated who the customers will be. If you have problems using the software while you're testing it, odds are the customers will, too.

Because there are so many different types of software, it's impossible to go into detail about usability issues for all of them. Usability of a nuclear reactor shutdown sequence is pretty different from usability of a voicemail menu system. What you'll learn in this chapter are the basics of what to look for—with a bias toward software that you use on your PC every day. You can then take those ideas and apply them to whatever software you have to test.

Highlights of this chapter include

- What usability testing involves
- What to look for when testing a user interface
- What special usability features are needed by the disabled

User Interface Testing

The means that you use to interact with a software program is called its *user interface*, or UI. All software has some sort of UI. Purists might argue that this isn't true, that software such as what's in your car to control the fuel/air ratio in the engine doesn't have a user interface. In truth, it doesn't have a conventional UI, but the extra pressure you need to apply to the gas pedal and the audible sputtering you hear from the tailpipe is indeed a user interface.

The computer UI we're all familiar with has changed over time. The original computers had toggle switches and light bulbs. Paper tape, punch cards, and teletypes were popular user interfaces in the '60s and '70s. Video monitors and simple line editors such as MS-DOS came next. Now we're using personal computers with sophisticated graphical user interfaces (GUIs).

Although these UIs were very different, technically they all provided the same interaction with the computer—the means to give it input and receive output.

What Makes a Good UI?

Many software companies spend large amounts of time and money researching the best way to design the user interfaces for their software. They use special usability labs run by ergonomic specialists. The labs are equipped with one-way mirrors and video cameras to record exactly how people use their software. Everything the users (subjects) do from what keys they press, how they use the mouse, what mistakes they make, and what confuses them is analyzed to make improvements to the UI.

You may be wondering what a software tester could possibly contribute with such a detailed and scientific process. By the time the software is specified and written, it should have the perfect UI. But, if that's the case, why are there so many VCRs blinking 12:00?

First, not every software development team designs their interface so scientifically. Many UIs are just thrown together by the programmers—who may be good at writing code, but aren't necessarily ergonomics experts. Other reasons might be that technological limitations or time constraints caused the UI to be sacrificed. As you learned in Chapter 10, "Foreign Language Testing," the reason might be that the software wasn't properly localized. In the end, the software tester needs to assume the responsibility of testing the product's usability, and that includes its user interface.

You might not feel that you're properly trained to test a UI, but you are. Remember, you don't have to design it. You just have to pretend you're the user and find problems with it.

NOTE

Because of the subjectivity of usability bugs, disagreements commonly arise between testers and UI designers. A UI is often considered art by the person who created it, and a tester saying that something is wrong can come across as insulting to the "artist." Usability is a sensitive area for reporting bugs. See Chapter 18, "Reporting What You Find," for techniques you can use to make your point known without getting someone upset.

Here's a list of seven important traits common to a good UI. It doesn't matter if the UI is on a digital watch or is the Mac OS interface, they all still apply.

- Follows standards and guidelines
- Intuitive
- Consistent
- Flexible
- Comfortable
- Correct
- Useful

If you read a UI design book, you may also see other traits being listed as important. Most of them are inherent or follow from these seven. For example, "easy to learn" isn't listed above, but if something is intuitive and consistent, it's probably easy to learn. As a tester, if you concentrate on making sure your software's UI meets these criteria, you'll have a darn good interface. Each trait is discussed in detail in the following sections.

Follows Standards or Guidelines

The single most important user interface trait is that your software follows existing standards and guidelines—or has a really good reason not to. If your software is running on an existing platform such as Mac or Windows, the standards are set. Apple's are defined in the book *Macintosh Human Interface Guidelines*, published by Addison-Wesley, and Microsoft's in the book *Microsoft Windows User Experience*, published by Microsoft Press.

Each book goes into meticulous detail about how software that runs on each platform should *look* and *feel* to the user. Everything is defined from when to use check boxes instead of an option button (when both states of the choice are clearly opposite and unambiguous) to when it's proper to use the information, warning, and critical messages as shown in Figure 11.1.

FIGURE 11.1
Did you ever notice that there are three different levels of messages in Windows? When and how to use each one is defined in the user interface standards for Windows.

> **NOTE**
>
> If you're testing software that runs on a specific platform, you need to treat the standards and guidelines for that platform as an addendum to your product's specification. Create test cases based on it just as you would from the product's spec.

These standards and guidelines were developed (hopefully) by experts in software usability. They have accounted for a great deal of formal testing, experience, and trial and error to devise rules that work well for their users. If your software strictly follows the rules, most of the other traits of a good UI will happen automatically. Not all of them will because your team may want to improvise on them a bit, or the rules may not perfectly fit with your software. In those cases, you need to really pay attention to usability issues.

It's also possible that your platform doesn't have a standard, or maybe your software *is* the platform. In those situations, your design team will be the ones creating the usability standards for your software. You won't be able to take for granted the rules that someone else has already figured out, and the remaining traits of a good user interface will be even more important for you to follow.

Intuitive

In 1975 the MITS (Micro Instrumentation Telemetry Systems) Altair 8800 was released as one of the first personal computers. Its user interface (see Figure 11.2) was nothing but switches and lights—not exactly intuitive to use.

FIGURE 11.2

The MITS Altair 8800 and its less-than-intuitive user interface. (Photo courtesy of the Computer Museum of America, www.computer-museum.org.*)*

The Altair was designed for computer hobbyists, people who are a lot more forgiving of user interface issues. Today, users want much more out of their software than what the Altair 8800 provided. Everyone from grandmothers to little kids to Ph.D.s are using computers in their daily lives. The computers with the most intuitive UIs are the ones that people don't even realize they're using.

When you're testing a user interface, consider the following things and how they might apply to gauging how intuitive your software is:

- Is the user interface clean, unobtrusive, not busy? The UI shouldn't get in the way of what you want to do. The functions you need or the response you're looking for should be obvious and be there when you expect them.

- Is the UI organized and laid out well? Does it allow you to easily get from one function to another? Is what to do next obvious? At any point can you decide to do nothing or even back up or back out? Are your inputs acknowledged? Do the menus or windows go too deep?

- Is there excessive functionality? Does the software attempt to do too much, either as a whole or in part? Do too many features complicate your work? Do you feel like you're getting information overload?

- If all else fails, does the help system really help you?

Consistent

Consistency within your software and with other software is a key attribute. Users develop habits and expect that if they do something a certain way in one program, another will do the same operation the same way. Figure 11.3 shows an example of how two Windows applications, which should be following a standard, aren't consistent. In Notepad, Find is accessed through the Search menu or by pressing F3. In WordPad, a very similar program, it's accessed through the Edit menu or by pressing Ctrl+F.

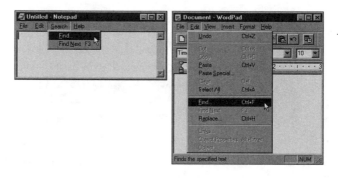

FIGURE 11.3
Windows Notepad and WordPad are inconsistent in how the Find feature is accessed.

Inconsistencies such as this frustrate users as they move from one program to another. It's even worse if the inconsistency is within the same program. If there's a standard for your software or your platform, follow it. If not, pay particular attention to your software's features to make sure that similar operations are performed similarly. Think about a few basic items as you review your product:

- **Shortcut keys and menu selections.** In a voicemail system, pressing 0, not other numbers, is almost always the "get-out" button that connects you to a real person. In Windows, pressing F1 always gets you help.

- **Terminology and naming.** Are the same terms used throughout the software? Are features named consistently? For example, is Find always called Find, or is it sometimes called Search?

- **Audience.** Does the software consistently talk to the same audience level? A fun greeting card program with a colorful user interface shouldn't display error messages of arcane technobabble.

- **Placement and keyboard equivalents for buttons.** Did you ever notice that when the OK and Cancel buttons are in a dialog box, OK is always on the top or left and Cancel is on the right or bottom? For the same reason, the keyboard equivalents are usually Esc for Cancel and Enter for the dialog's selected button. Consistency matters.

Flexible

Users like choices—not too many, but enough to allow them to select what they want to do and how they want to do it. The Windows Calculator (see Figure 11.4) has two views: Standard and Scientific. Users can decide which one they need for their task or the one they're most comfortable using.

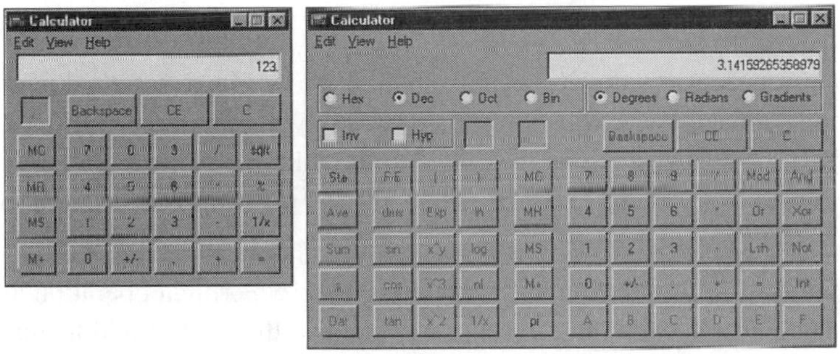

FIGURE 11.4
The Windows Calculator shows its flexibility by having two different views.

Of course, with flexibility comes complexity. In the Calculator example you'll have a much larger test effort than if there's just one view. The test impact of flexibility is felt most in the areas covered in Chapter 5, "Testing Software with Blinders On," with states and with data:

- **State jumping.** Flexible software provides more options and more ways to accomplish the same task. The result is additional paths among the different states of the software. Your state transition diagrams can become much more complex and you'll need to spend more time deciding which interconnecting paths should be tested.

- **State termination and skipping.** This is most evident when software has power-user modes where a user who's very familiar with the software can skip numerous prompts or windows and go directly to where they want to go. A voicemail system that allows you to directly punch in your party's extension is an example. If you're testing software that allows this, you'll need to make sure that all the state variables are correctly set if all the intermediate states are skipped or terminated early.

- **Data input and output.** Users want different ways to enter their data and see their results. To put text into a WordPad document, you can type it, paste it, load it from six different file formats, insert it as an object, or drag it with the mouse from another program. The Microsoft Excel spreadsheet program allows you to view your data in 14 different standard and 20 different custom graphs. Who even knew there were that many possibilities? Testing all the different ways to get data in and out of your software can very quickly increase the effort necessary and make for tough choices when creating your equivalence partitions.

Comfortable

Software should be comfortable to use. It shouldn't get in the way or make it difficult for a user to do his work. Software comfort is a pretty touchy-feely concept. Researchers have spent their careers trying to find the right formula to make software comfortable. It can be a difficult concept to quantify, but you can look for a few things that will give you a better idea of how to identify good and bad software comfort:

- **Appropriateness.** Software should look and feel proper for what it's doing and who it's for. A financial business application should probably not go crazy with loud colors and sound effects. A space game, on the other hand, will have much more leeway with the rules. Software should neither be too garish nor too plain for the task it's intended to perform.

- **Error handling.** A program should warn users before a critical operation and allow users to restore data lost because of a mistake. People take the Undo/Redo feature for granted today, but it wasn't long ago that these features didn't exist.

- **Performance.** Being fast isn't always a good thing. More than one program has flashed error messages too quickly to read. If an operation is slow, it should at least give the user feedback on how much longer it will take and show that it's still working and hasn't frozen. Status bars, as shown in Figure 11.5, are a popular way to accomplish this.

FIGURE 11.5

Status bars show how much of the work has been completed and how much is left to go.

Correct

The comfort trait is admittedly a bit fuzzy and often can be left to interpretation. Correctness, though, isn't. When you're testing for correctness, you're testing whether the UI does what it's supposed to do. Figure 11.6 is an example of a UI that isn't correct.

FIGURE 11.6
This software has a completely useless Abort button.

This figure shows a message box from a popular page-scanning program for Windows. The box appears when a scan is started and is supposed to provide a way for the user to stop the scan mid-process. Unfortunately, it doesn't work. Note that the cursor is an hourglass. An hourglass means (according to the Windows standard) that the software is busy and can't accept any input. Then why is the Abort button there? You can repeatedly click the Abort button during the entire scan, which can take a minute or more, and nothing happens. The scan continues uninterrupted until it completes.

Correctness problems such as this are usually obvious and will be found in your normal course of testing against the product specification. You should pay attention to some areas in particular, however:

- **Marketing differences.** Are there extra or missing functions, or functions that perform operations different from what the marketing material says? Notice that you're not comparing the software to the specification—you're comparing it to the sales information. They're usually different.

- **Language and spelling.** Programmers know how to spell only computer language keywords and often create some very interesting user messages. The following is an order confirmation message from a popular e-commerce Web site—hopefully fixed by the time you read this:

  If there are any discreptency with the information below, please contact us immediately to ensure timely delivery of the products that you ordered.

- **Bad media.** Media is any supporting icons, images, sounds, or videos that go with your software's UI. Icons should be the same size and have the same palette. Sounds should all be of the same format and sampling rate. The correct ones should be displayed when chosen from the UI.

- **WYSIWYG (what you see is what you get).** Make sure that whatever the UI tells you that you have is really what you do have. When you click the Save button, is the document onscreen exactly what's saved to disk? When you load it back, does it perfectly compare with the original?

Useful

The final trait of a good user interface is whether it's useful. Remember, you're not concerned with whether the software itself is useful, just whether the particular feature is. A popular term used in the software industry to describe unnecessary or gratuitous features is *dancing bologna*. It doesn't matter whether the dancing bologna is in a solitaire program or a heart monitor machine, it's bad for the user and means extra testing for you.

When you're reviewing the product specification, preparing to test, or actually performing your testing, ask yourself if the features you see actually contribute to the software's value. Do they help users do what the software is intended to do? If you don't think they're necessary, do some research to find out why they're in the software. It's possible that there are reasons you're not aware of, or it could just be dancing bologna.

Testing for the Disabled: Accessibility Testing

A serious topic that falls under the area of usability testing is that of *accessibility testing*, or testing for the disabled. A 1994–1995 government Survey of Income and Program Participation (SIPP) used by the U.S. Census Bureau found that in 1994, about 54 million people in the country had some sort of disability. Table 11.1 shows the complete breakdown.

TABLE 11.1 People with Disabilities

Age	Percentage of People with Disabilities
0–21	10%
22–44	14.9%
45–54	24.5%
55–64	36.3%
65–79	47.3%
80+	71.5%

With our aging population and the penetration of technology into nearly every aspect of our lives, the usability of software becomes more important every day.

Although there are many types of disabilities, the following ones make using computers and software especially difficult:

- **Visual impairments.** Color blindness, extreme near and far sightedness, tunnel vision, dim vision, blurry vision, and cataracts are examples of visual limitations. People with one or more of these would have their own unique difficulty in using software. Think about trying to see where the mouse pointer is located or where text or small graphics appear onscreen. What if you couldn't see the screen at all?

- **Hearing impairments.** Someone may be partially or completely deaf, have problems hearing certain frequencies, or picking a specific sound out of background noise. Such a person may not be able to hear the sounds or voices that accompany an onscreen video, audible help, or system alerts.

- **Motion impairments.** Disease or injury can cause a person to lose fine, gross, or total motor control of his hands or arms. It may be difficult or impossible for some people to properly use a keyboard or a mouse. For example, they may not be able to press more than one key at a time or may find it impossible to press a key only once. Accurately moving a mouse may not be possible.

- **Cognitive and language.** Dyslexia and memory problems may make it difficult for someone to use complex user interfaces. Think of the issues outlined previously in this chapter and how they might impact a person with cognitive and language difficulties.

It's the Law

Fortunately, developing software with a user interface that can be used by the disabled isn't just a good idea, a guideline, or a standard—it's the law. In the United States, three laws apply to this area:

- The Americans with Disability Act states that businesses with 15 or mores employees must make reasonable accommodations for employees, or potential employees, with disabilities. The ADA has recently been applied to commercial Internet Web sites, mandating that they be made accessible.

- Section 508 of the Rehabilitation Act is very similar to the ADA and applies to any organization that receives federal funding.

- Section 255 of the Telecommunications Act requires that all hardware and software that transfers information over the Internet, a network, or the phone lines be made so that it can be used by people with disabilities. If it's not directly usable, it must be compatible (see Chapter 8, "Configuration Testing," and Chapter 9, "Compatibility Testing") with existing hardware and software accessibility aids.

Accessibility Features in Software

Software can be made accessible in one of two ways. The easiest is to take advantage of support built into its platform or operating system. Windows, Mac OS, Sun Java, and IBM OS/2 all support accessibility to some degree. Your software only needs to adhere to the platform's standards for communicating with the keyboard, mouse, sound card, and monitor to be accessibility enabled. Figure 11.7 shows an example of Windows 98's accessibility settings control panel.

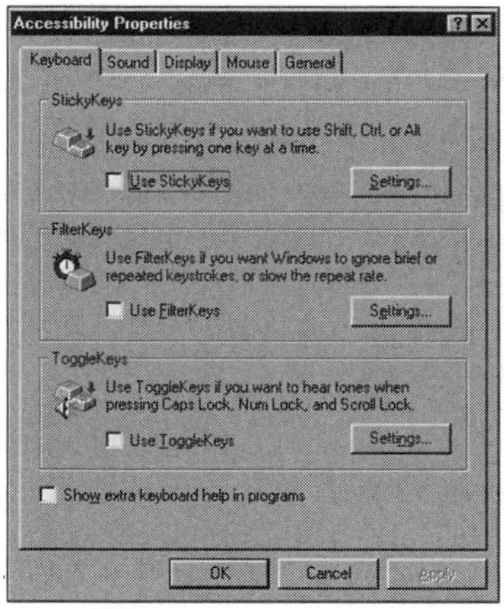

FIGURE 11.7

The Windows accessibility features are set from this control panel.

If the software you're testing doesn't run on these platforms or is its own platform, it will need to have its own accessibility features specified, programmed, and tested.

The latter case is obviously a much larger test effort than the first, but don't take built-in support for granted, either. You'll need to test accessibility features in both situations to make sure that they comply.

> **NOTE**
>
> If you're testing usability for your product, be sure to create test cases specifically for accessibility. You'll feel good knowing that this area is thoroughly tested.

Each platform is slightly different in the features that it offers, but they all strive to make it easier for applications to be accessibility enabled. Windows provides the following capabilities:

- *StickyKeys* allows the Shift, Ctrl, or Alt keys to stay in effect until the next key is pressed.

- *FilterKeys* prevents brief, repeated (accidental) keystrokes from being recognized.

- *ToggleKeys* plays tones when the Caps Lock, Scroll Lock, or NumLock keyboard modes are enabled.

- *SoundSentry* creates a visual warning whenever the system generates a sound.

- *ShowSounds* tells programs to display captions for any sounds or speech they make. These captions need to be programmed into your software.

- *High Contrast* sets up the screen with colors and fonts designed to be read by the visually impaired. Figure 11.8 shows an example of this.

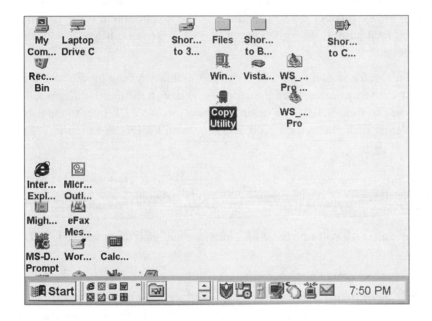

FIGURE 11.8
The Windows desktop can be switched to this high contrast mode for easier viewing by the visually impaired.

- *MouseKeys* allows use of keyboard keys instead of the mouse to navigate.

- *SerialKey* sets up a communications port to read in keystrokes from an external non-keyboard device. Although the OS should make these devices look like a standard keyboard, it would be a good idea to add them to your configuration testing equivalence partitions.

For more information about the accessibility features built into the popular OS platforms, consult the following Web sites:

- `http://www.microsoft.com/enable`
- `http://www.apple.com/education/k12/disability`
- `http://www-3.ibm.com/able`
- `http://www.sun.com/tech/access`

Summary

The software is difficult to understand, hard to use, slow, or—in the software tester's eyes—will be viewed by the end user as just plain not right.

As a software tester checking the usability of a software product, that's your mantra. You're the first person to use the product in a meaningful way, the first person to see it all come together in its proposed final form. If it's hard to use or doesn't make sense to you, customers will have the same issues.

Above all, don't let the vagueness or subjectivity of usability testing hinder your test effort. It's vague and subjective by nature. Even the experts who design the user interfaces will admit to that—well, some of them will. If you're testing a new product's UI, refer to the lists in this chapter that define what makes for a good one. If it doesn't meet these criteria, it's a bug.

Quiz

These quiz questions are provided for your further understanding. See Appendix A, "Answers to Quiz Questions," for the answers—but don't peek!

1. **True or False:** All software has a user interface and therefore must be tested for usability.
2. Is user interface design a science or an art?
3. If there's no definitive right or wrong user interface, how can it be tested?
4. List some examples of poorly designed or inconsistent UIs in products you're familiar with.
5. What four types of disabilities could affect software usability?
6. If you're testing software that will be accessibility enabled, what areas do you need to pay close attention to?

Testing the Documentation

IN THIS CHAPTER

In Chapter 2, "The Software Development Process," you learned that there's a great deal of work and a great number of non-software pieces that make up a software product. Much of that non-software is its documentation.

In simpler days, software documentation was at most a readme file copied onto the software's floppy disk or a short 1-page insert put into the box. Now it's much, much more, sometimes requiring more time and effort to produce than the software itself.

As a software tester, you typically aren't constrained to just testing the software. Your responsibility will likely cover all the parts that make up the entire software product. Assuring that the documentation is correct is your job, too.

In this chapter you'll learn about testing software documentation and how to include it in your overall software test effort. Highlights of this chapter include

- The different types of software documentation
- Why documentation testing is important
- What to look for when testing documentation

Types of Software Documentation

If your software's documentation consists of nothing but a simple readme file, testing it would not be a big deal. You'd make sure that it included all the material that it was supposed to, that everything was technically accurate, and (for good measure) you might run a spell check and a virus scan on the disk. That would be it. But, the days of documentation consisting of just a readme file are gone.

Today, software documentation can make up a huge portion of the overall product. Sometimes, it can seem as if the product is nothing but documentation with a little bit of software thrown in.

Here's a list of software components that can be classified as documentation. Obviously, not all software will have all the components, but it's possible:

- **Packaging text and graphics.** This includes the box, carton, wrapping, and so on. The documentation might contain screen shots from the software, lists of features, system requirements, and copyright information.
- **Marketing material, ads, and other inserts.** These are all the pieces of paper you usually throw away, but they are important tools used to promote the sale of related software, add-on content, service contracts, and so on. The information for them must be correct for a customer to take them seriously.
- **Warranty/registration.** This is the card that the customer fills out and sends in to register the software. It can also be part of the software and display onscreen for the user to read, acknowledge, and even complete online.

- **EULA.** Pronounced "you-la," it stands for *End User License Agreement*. This is the legal document that the customer agrees to that says, among other things, that he won't copy the software nor sue the manufacturer if he's harmed by a bug. The EULA is sometimes printed on the envelope containing the media—the floppy or CD. It also may pop up onscreen during the software's installation. An example is shown in Figure 12.1.

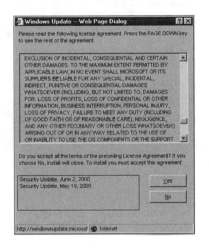

FIGURE 12.1
The EULA is part of the software's documentation and explains the legal terms of use for the software.

- **Labels and stickers.** These may appear on the media, on the box, or on the printed material. There may also be serial number stickers and labels that seal the EULA envelope. Figure 12.2 shows an example of a disk label and all the information that needs to be checked.

- **Installation and setup instructions.** Sometimes this information is printed on the media, but it also can be included as a separate sheet of paper or, if it's complex software, as an entire manual.

- **User's manual.** The usefulness and flexibility of online manuals has made printed manuals much less common than they once were. Most software now comes with a small, concise "getting started"–type manual with the detailed information moved to online format. The online manuals can be distributed on the software's media, on a Web site, or a combination of both.

- **Online help.** Online help often gets intertwined with the user's manual, sometimes even replacing it. Online help is indexed and searchable, making it much easier for users to find the information they're looking for. Many online help systems allow natural language queries so users can type **Tell me how to copy text from one program to another** and receive an appropriate response.

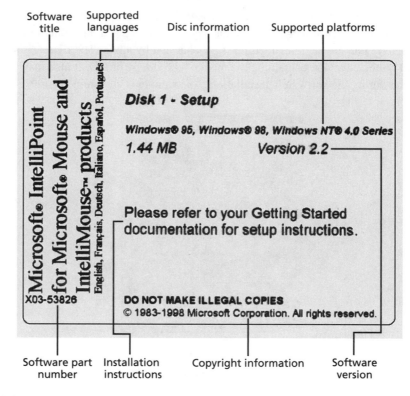

FIGURE 12.2
There's lots of documentation on a disk label for the software tester to check.

- **Tutorials, wizards, and CBT (Computer Based Training).** These tools blend programming code and written documentation. They're often a mixture of both content and high-level, macro-like programming and are often tied in with the online help system. A user can ask a question and the software then guides him through the steps to complete the task. Microsoft's Office Assistant, sometimes referred to as the "paper clip guy" (see Figure 12.3), is an example of such a system.

- **Samples, examples, and templates.** An example of these would be a word processor with forms or samples that a user can simply fill in to quickly create professional-looking results. A compiler could have snippets of code that demonstrate how to use certain aspects of the language.

- **Error messages.** These have already been discussed a couple times in this book as an often neglected area, but they ultimately fall under the category of documentation.

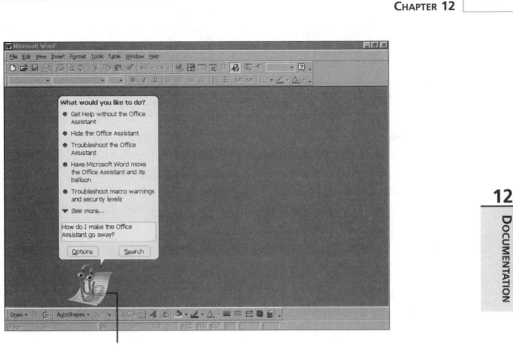

Office Assistant

FIGURE 12.3
The Microsoft Office Assistant is an example of a very elaborate help and tutorial system.

The Importance of Documentation Testing

Software users consider all these individual non-software components parts of the overall software product. They don't care whether the pieces were created by a programmer, a writer, or a graphic artist. What they care about is the quality of the entire package.

> **NOTE**
>
> If the installation instructions are wrong or if an incorrect error message leads them astray, users will view those as bugs with the software—ones that should have been found by a software tester.

Good software documentation contributes to the product's overall quality in three ways:

- **It improves usability.** Remember from Chapter 11, "Usability Testing," all the issues related to a product's usability? Much of that usability is related to the software documentation.

12

TESTING THE
DOCUMENTATION

- **It improves reliability.** Reliability is how stable and consistent the software is. Does it do what the user expects and when he expects it? If the user reads the documentation, uses the software, and gets unexpected results, that's poor reliability. As you'll see in the rest of this chapter, testing the software and the documentation against each other is a good way to find bugs in both of them.

- **It lowers support costs.** In Chapter 2 you learned that problems found by a customer can cost 10 to 100 times as much as if they were found and fixed early in the product's development. The reason is that users who are confused or run into unexpected problems will call the company for help, which is expensive. Good documentation can prevent these calls by adequately explaining and leading users through difficult areas.

NOTE

As a software tester, you should treat the software's documentation with the same level of attention and give it the same level of effort that you do the code. They are one and the same to the user.

What to Look for When Reviewing Documentation

Testing the documentation can occur on two different levels. If it's non-code, such as a printed user's manual or the packaging, testing is a static process much like what's described in Chapters 4 and 6. Think of it as technical editing or technical proofreading. If the documentation and code are more closely tied, such as with a hyperlinked online manual or with a helpful paper clip guy, it becomes a dynamic test effort that should be checked with the techniques you learned in Chapters 5 and 7. In this situation, you really are testing software.

NOTE

Whether or not the documentation is code, a very effective approach to testing it is to treat it just like a user would. Read it carefully, follow every step, examine every figure, and try every example. With this simple real-world approach, you'll find bugs both in the software and the documentation.

Table 12.1 is a simple checklist to use as a basis for building your documentation test cases.

TABLE 12.1   A Documentation Testing Checklist

What to Check	What to Consider
General Areas	
Audience	Does the documentation speak to the correct level of audience, not too novice, not too advanced?
Terminology	Is the terminology proper for the audience? Are the terms used consistently? If acronyms or abbreviations are used, are they standard ones or do they need to be defined? Make sure that your company's acronyms don't accidentally make it through. Are all the terms indexed and cross-referenced correctly?
Content and subject matter	Are the appropriate topics covered? Are any topics missing? How about topics that shouldn't be included, such as a feature that was cut from the product and no one told the manual writer. Is the material covered in the proper depth?
Correctness	
Just the facts	Is all the information factually and technically correct? Look for mistakes caused by the writers working from outdated specs or sales people inflating the truth. Check the table of contents, the index, and chapter references. Try the Web site URLs. Is the product support phone number correct? Try it.
Step by step	Read all the text carefully and slowly. Follow the instructions exactly. Assume nothing! Resist the temptation to fill in missing steps; your customers won't know what's missing. Compare your results to the ones shown in the documentation.
Figures and screen captures	Check figures for accuracy and precision. Are they of the correct image and is the image correct? Make sure that any screen captures aren't from prerelease software that has since changed. Are the figure captions correct?
Samples and examples	Load and use every sample just as a customer would. If it's code, type or copy it in and run it. There's nothing more embarrassing than samples that don't work—and it happens all the time!
Spelling and grammar	In an ideal world, these types of bugs wouldn't make it through to you. Spelling and grammar checkers are too commonplace not to be used. It's possible, though, that someone forgot to perform the check or that a specialized or technical term slipped through. It's also possible that the checking had to be done manually, such as in a screen capture or a drawn figure. Don't take it for granted.

12

**TESTING THE
DOCUMENTATION**

Finally, if the documentation is software driven, test it as you would the rest of the software. Check that the index list is complete, that searching finds the correct results, and that the hyperlinks and hotspots jump to the correct pages. Use equivalence partition techniques to decide what test cases to try.

The Realities of Documentation Testing

To close this chapter, it's important for you to learn a few things that make documentation development and testing a bit different from software development. Chapter 3 was titled "The Realities of Software Testing." You might call these issues the realities of documentation testing:

- Documentation often gets the least attention, budget, and resources. There seems to be the mentality that it's a software project first and foremost and all the other stuff is less important. In reality, it's a software product that people are buying and all that other stuff is at least as important as the bits and bytes. If you're responsible for testing an area of the software, make sure that you budget time to test the documentation that goes along with that code. Give it the same attention that you do the software and if it has bugs, report them.

- It's possible that the people writing the documentation aren't experts in what the software does. Just as you don't have to be an accounting expert to test a spreadsheet program, the writer doesn't have to be an expert in the software's features to write its documentation. As a result, you can't rely on the person creating the content to make sense out of poorly written specs or complex or unclear product features. Work closely with writers to make sure they have the information they need and that they're up-to-date with the product's design. Most importantly, tell them about difficult-to-use or difficult-to-understand areas of the code that you discover so they can better explain those areas in the documentation.

- Printed documentation takes time to produce, sometimes weeks or even months. Software, however, can now be published almost instantly to the Internet or CD. Because of this time difference, a software product's documentation may need to be finalized—locked down—before the software is completed. If the software functionality changes or bugs are discovered during this critical period, the documentation can't be changed to reflect them. That's why the readme file was invented. It's how those last-minute changes are communicated to users. The solution to this problem is to have a good development model, follow it, hold your documentation release to the last possible minute, and release as much documentation as possible, online, with the software.

Summary

Hopefully this chapter opened your eyes to how much more there can be to a software product than the code the programmers write. The software's documentation, in all its forms, created by writers, illustrators, indexers, and so on, can easily take more effort to develop and test than the actual software.

From the user's standpoint, it's all the same product. An online help index that's missing an important term, an incorrect step in the installation instructions, or a blatant misspelling are bugs just like any other software failure. If you properly test the documentation, you'll find the bugs before your users do.

In the next chapter you'll learn about testing something that's almost all documentation— almost all text, graphics, and hyperlinks with a software platform underneath it. You'll be able to apply the techniques you've learned so far in this book to testing Internet Web sites.

Quiz

These quiz questions are provided for your further understanding. See Appendix A, "Answers to Quiz Questions," for the answers—but don't peek!

1. Start up Windows Paint (see Figure 12.4) and look for several examples of documentation that should be tested. What did you find?

FIGURE 12.4

What examples of documentation can you find in Windows Paint?

2. The Windows Paint Help Index contains more than 200 terms from *adding custom colors* to *zooming*. Would you test that each of these takes you to the correct help topics? What if there were 10,000 indexed terms?

3. **True or False:** Testing error messages falls under documentation testing.

4. In what three ways does good documentation contribute to the product's overall quality?

Web Site Testing

IN THIS CHAPTER

The testing techniques that you've learned in previous chapters have been fairly generic. They've been presented by using small programs such as Windows WordPad, Calculator, and Paint to demonstrate testing fundamentals and how to apply them. This final chapter of Part III is geared toward testing a specific type of software—Internet Web pages. It's a fairly timely topic, something that you're likely familiar with, and a good real-world example to apply the techniques that you've learned so far.

What you'll find in this chapter is that Web site testing encompasses many areas, including configuration testing, compatibility testing, usability testing, documentation testing, and, if the site is a worldwide site, localization testing. Of course, black-box, white-box, static, and dynamic testing are always a given.

This chapter isn't meant to be a complete how-to guide for testing Internet Web sites (that's another book) but it will give you a straightforward practical example of testing something real and give you a good head start if your first job happens to be looking for bugs in someone's Web site.

Highlights of this chapter include

- What fundamental parts of a Web page need testing
- What basic white-box and black-box techniques apply to Web page testing
- How configuration and compatibility testing apply
- Why usability testing is the primary concern of Web pages
- How to use tools to help test your Web site

Web Page Fundamentals

In the most simple terms, Internet Web pages are just documents of text, pictures, sounds, video, and hyperlinks—much like the CD-ROM multimedia titles that were popular in the mid 1990s. As in those programs, Web users can navigate from page to page by clicking hyperlinked text or pictures, searching for words or phrases, and viewing the information they find.

The Internet, though, has introduced two twists to the multimedia document concept that revolutionizes the technology:

- Unlike data that is stored solely on a CD-ROM, Web pages aren't constrained to a single PC. Users can link to and search worldwide across the entire Internet for information on any Web site.
- Web page authoring isn't limited to programmers using expensive and technical tools. The average person can create a simple Web page almost as easily as writing a letter in a word processor.

But, just as giving someone a paint brush doesn't make him an artist, giving someone the ability to create Web pages doesn't make him an expert in multimedia publishing. Couple that with the technology explosion that continually adds new Web site features, and you have the perfect opportunity for a software tester.

Figure 13.1 shows a popular news Web site that demonstrates many of the possible Web page features. A partial list of them includes

- Text of different sizes, fonts, and colors (okay, you can't see the colors in this book)
- Graphics and photos
- Hyperlinked text and graphics
- Varying advertisements
- Drop-down selection boxes
- Fields in which the users can enter data

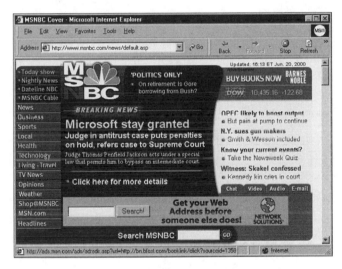

FIGURE 13.1

A typical Web page has many testable features.

A great deal of functionality also isn't as obvious, features that make the Web site much more complex:

- Customizable layout that allows users to change where information is positioned onscreen
- Customizable content that allows users to select what news and information they want to see

- Dynamic drop-down selection boxes

- Dynamically changing text

- Dynamic layout and optional information based on screen resolution

- Compatibility with different Web browsers, browser versions, and hardware and software platforms

- Lots of hidden formatting, tagging, and embedded information that enhances the Web page's usability

Granted, short of a secure e-commerce Web site, this is probably one of the more complex and feature-rich Web pages on the Internet. If you have the tester mentality (and hopefully you've gained it by reading this far in the book), looking at such a Web page should whet your appetite to jump in and start finding bugs. The remainder of this chapter will give you clues on where to look.

Black-Box Testing

Remember all the way back to Chapters 4 through 7, the ones that covered the fundamentals of testing? In those vitally important chapters, you learned about black-box, white-box, static, and dynamic testing—the raw skills of a software tester. Web pages are the perfect means to practice what you've learned. You don't have to go out and buy different programs—you can simply jump to a Web page, one of your favorites or a completely new one, and begin testing.

The easiest place to start is by treating the Web page or the entire Web site as a black box. You don't know anything about how it works, you don't have a specification, you just have the Web site in front of you to test. What do you look for?

Figure 13.2 shows a screen image of Apple's Web site, www.apple.com, a fairly straightforward and typical Web site. It has all the basic elements—text, graphics, hyperlinks to other pages on the site, and hyperlinks to other Web sites. A few of the pages have form fields in which users can enter information and a few pages play videos. One interesting thing about this site that's not so common is that it's localized for 27 different locales, from Asia to the UK.

If you have access to the Internet, take some time now and explore Apple's Web site. Think about how you would approach testing it. What would you test? What would your equivalence partitions be? What would you choose not to test?

FIGURE 13.2

What would you test in a straightforward Web site such as this?

After exploring a bit, what did you decide? Hopefully you realized that it's a pretty big job. If you looked at the site map (www.apple.com/find/sitemap.html), you found links to more than 60 different sub-sites, each one with several pages.

> **NOTE**
>
> When testing a Web site, you first should create a state table (see Chapter 5, "Testing the Software with Blinders On"), treating each page as a different state with the hyperlinks as the lines connecting them. A completed state map will give you a better view of the overall task.

Thankfully, most of the pages are fairly simple, made up of just text, graphics, links, and the occasional form. Testing them isn't difficult. The following sections give some ideas of what to look for.

Text

Web page text should be treated just like documentation and tested as described in Chapter 12, "Testing the Documentation". Check the audience level, the terminology, the content and subject matter, the accuracy—especially of information that can become outdated—and always, always check spelling.

> **NOTE**
>
> Don't rely on spell checkers to be perfect, especially when they're used on Web page content. They might only check the regular text but not what's contained in the graphics, scrolling marquees, forms, and so on. You could perform what you think is a complete spell check and still have misspellings on the page.

If there is contact information such as email addresses, phone numbers, or postal addresses, check them to make sure that they're correct. Make sure that the copyright notices are correct and dated appropriately.

Test that each page has a correct title. This text appears in the browser's title bar (upper-left corner of Figure 13.2) and what is listed when you add the page to your favorites or bookmarks.

An often overlooked type of text is called *ALT text*, for *ALTernate text*. Figure 13.3 shows an example of ALT text. When a user puts the mouse cursor over a graphic on the page he gets a pop-up description of what the graphic represents. Web browsers that don't display graphics use ALT text. Also, with ALT text blind users can use graphically rich Web sites—an audible reader interprets the ALT text and reads it out through the computer's speakers.

Check for text layout issues by resizing your browser window to be very small or very large. This will reveal bugs where the designer or programmer assumed a fixed page width or height. It will also reveal hard-coded formatting such as line breaks that might look great with certain layouts but not with others.

Hyperlinks

Links can be tied to text or graphics. Each link should be checked to make sure that it jumps to the correct destination and opens in the correct window. If you don't have a specification for the Web site, you'll need to test whether the jump worked correctly.

Make sure that hyperlinks are obvious. Text links are usually underlined, and the mouse pointer should change to a hand pointer when it's over any kind of hyperlink—text or graphic.

If the link opens up an email message, fill out the message, send it, and make sure you get a response.

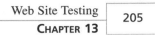

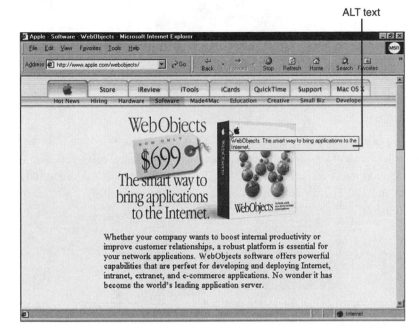

FIGURE 13.3
ALT text provides textual descriptions of graphics images on Web pages.

Look for *orphan pages*, which are part of the Web site but can't be accessed through a hyperlink because someone forgot to hook them up. You'll likely need to get a list from the Web site's designer and compare that with your own state table. Even better, get a list of the actual pages on the Web server and perform simple code-coverage analysis to determine if you indeed are testing all the pages, that none are missing, and that there are no extra pages.

Graphics

Many possible bugs with graphics are covered later under usability testing, but you can check a few obvious things with a simple black-box approach. For example, do all graphics load and display properly? If a graphic is missing or is incorrectly named, it won't load and the Web page will display an error where the graphic was to be placed (see Figure 13.4).

If text and graphics are intermixed on the page, make sure that the text wraps properly around the graphics. Try resizing the browser's window to see if strange wrapping occurs around the graphic.

How's the performance of loading the page? Are there so many graphics on the page, resulting in a large amount of data to be transferred and displayed, that the Web site's performance is too slow? What if it's displayed over a slow dial-up modem connection on a poor-quality phone line?

13

WEB SITE TESTING

FIGURE 13.4

If a graphic can't load onto a Web page, an error box is put in its location.

Forms

Forms are the text boxes, list boxes, and other fields for entering or selecting information on a Web page. Figure 13.5 shows a simple example from Apple's Web site. It's a signup form for potential Mac developers. There are fields for entering your first name, middle initial, last name, and email address. There's an obvious bug on this page—hopefully it's fixed by the time you read this.

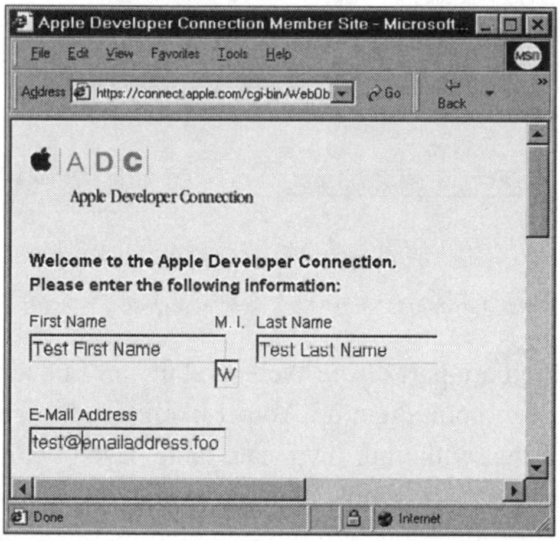

FIGURE 13.5

Make sure your Web site's form fields are positioned properly. Notice in this Apple Developer signup form that the middle initial (M.I.) field is misplaced.

Test forms just as you would if they were fields in a regular software program—remember Chapter 5? Are the fields the correct size? Do they accept the correct data and reject the wrong data? Is there proper confirmation when you finally press Enter? Are optional fields truly optional and the required ones truly required? What happens if you enter **9999999999999999999999999999**?

Objects and Other Simple Miscellaneous Functionality

Your Web site may contain features such as a hit counter, scrolling marquee text, changing advertisements, or internal site searches (not to be confused with search engines that search the entire Web). When planning your tests for a Web site, take care to identify all the features present on each page. Treat each unique feature as you would a feature in a regular program and test it individually with the standard testing techniques that you've learned. Does it have its own states? Does it handle data? Could it have ranges or boundaries? What test cases apply and how should they be equivalence classed? A Web page is just like any other software.

Gray-Box Testing

You're already familiar with black-box and white-box testing, but another type of testing, *gray-box testing*, is a mixture of the two—hence the name. With gray-box testing, you straddle the line between black-box and white-box testing. You still test the software as a black-box, but you supplement the work by taking a peek (not a full look, as in white-box testing) at what makes the software work.

Web pages lend themselves nicely to gray-box testing. Most Web pages are built with HTML (Hypertext Markup Language). Listing 13.1 shows a few lines of the HTML used to create the Web page shown in Figure 13.6.

LISTING 13.1 Sample HTML Showing Some of What's Behind a Web Page

```
<html>
<head>
<meta http-equiv="Content-Type" content="text/html; charset=iso-8859-1">
<meta name="GENERATOR" content="Microsoft FrontPage 4.0">
<title>Superior Packing Systems</title>
<meta name="Microsoft Theme" content="sandston 111, default">
<meta name="Microsoft Border" content="t, default">
</head>
<body background="_themes/sandston/stonbk.jpg" bgcolor="#FFFFCC"
  text="#333333" link="#993300" vlink="#666633" alink="#CC6633">
  <!--msnavigation--><table border="0" cellpadding="0" cellspacing="0"
  width="100%"><tr><td><!--mstheme--><font face="Arial, Helvetica">
<h1 align="center"><!--mstheme--><font color="#660000">
  <img src="_derived/index.htm_cmp_sandston110_bnr.gif" width="600"
  height="60" border="0" alt="Superior Packing Systems"><br>
  <br>
<a href="./"><img src="_derived/home_cmp_sandston110_gbtn.gif" width="95"
  height="20" border="0" alt="Home" align="middle"></a> <a href="services.htm">
  <img src="_derived/services.htm_cmp_sandston110_gbtn.gif" width="95"
  height="20" border="0" alt="Services" align="middle"></a>
  <a href="contact.htm"><img
src="_derived/contact.htm_cmp_sandston110_gbtn.gif"
  width="95" height="20" border="0" alt="Contact Us" align="middle">
  </a><!--mstheme--></font></h1>
```

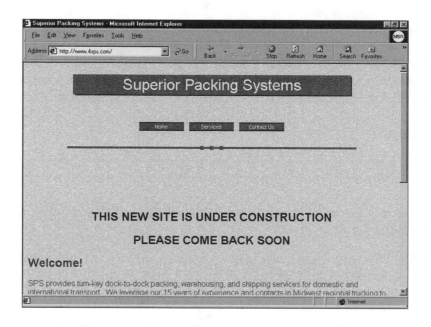

FIGURE 13.6
Part of this Web page is created by the HTML in Listing 13.1.

NOTE

If you're not familiar with creating your own Web site, you might want to read a little on the subject. An introductory book such as *Sams Teach Yourself to Create Web Pages in 24 Hours, Second Edition,* would be a great way to learn the basics and help you discover a few ways to apply gray-box testing techniques.

HTML and Web pages can be tested as a gray box because HTML isn't a programming language—it's a *markup language*. In the early days of word processors, you couldn't just select text and make it **bold** or *italic*. You had to embed markups, sometimes called *field tags*, in the text. For example, to create the bolded phrase

This is bold text.

you would enter something such as this into your word processor:

[begin bold]This is bold text.[end bold]

HTML works the same way. To create the line in HTML you would enter

<b>This is bold text.</b>

HTML has evolved to where it now has hundreds of different field tags and options, as evidenced by the HTML in Listing 13.1. But, in the end, HTML is nothing but a fancy old-word-processor-like markup language. The difference between HTML and a program is that HTML doesn't execute or run, it just determines how text and graphics appear onscreen.

TIP

To see the HTML for a Web page using Internet Explorer, right-click a blank area of the page (not on a graphic) and select View Source from the menu. Other Web browsers vary slightly from this, but most offer some means to view the HTML that creates the page.

Since HTML is so easy for you, as the tester, to view, you might as well take advantage of it and supplement your testing. If you're a black-box tester, it's the perfect opportunity to start moving toward white-box testing.

Start by learning to create your own simple Web pages. Learn the basic and common HTML tags. Look at the HTML for many different pages on the Web, see what techniques are used and how those techniques make things work on the page. Once you become familiar with HTML, you'll be able to look at the Web pages you're testing in a whole new way and be a more effective tester.

White-Box Testing

In Figure 13.1, you saw an example of a Web page with much static content in the form of text and images. This static content was most likely created with straight HTML. That same Web page also has customizable and dynamic changing content. Remember, HTML isn't a programming language—it's merely a tagging system for text and graphics. To create these extra dynamic features requires the HTML to be supplemented with programming code that can execute and follow decision paths.

You've likely heard of the popular Web programming languages that can create these types of features: DHTML, Java, JavaScript, ActiveX, VBScript, Perl, CGI, ASP, and XML. As explained in Chapters 6, "Examining the Code," and 7, "Testing the Software with X-Ray Glasses," to apply white-box testing, you don't necessarily need to become an expert in these languages, just familiar enough to be able to read and understand them and to devise test cases based on what you see in the code.

This chapter can't possibly go into all the details of white-box testing a Web site, but several features could be more effectively tested with a white-box approach. Of course, they could also be tested as a black-box, but the potential complexity is such that to really make sure you find the important bugs that you have some knowledge of the Web site's system structure and programming:

- **Dynamic Content.** Dynamic content is graphics and text that changes based on certain conditions—for example, the time of day, the user's preferences, or specific user actions. It's possible that the programming for the content is done in a simple scripting language such as JavaScript and is embedded within the HTML. This is known as *client-side* programming. You can apply gray-box testing techniques when you examine the script and view the HTML. For efficiency, most dynamic content programming is located on the Web site's server; it's called *server-side* programming and would require you to have access to the Web server to view the code.

- **Database-Driven Web Pages.** Many e-commerce Web pages that show catalogs or inventories are database driven. The HTML provides a simple layout for the Web content and then pictures, text descriptions, pricing information, and so on are pulled from a database on the Web site's server and plugged into the pages.

- **Programmatically Created Web Pages.** Many Web pages, especially ones with dynamic content, are programmatically generated—that is, the HTML and possibly even the programming is created by software. A Web page designer may type entries in a database and drag and drop elements in a layout program, press a button, and out comes the HTML that displays a Web page. If this sounds scary, it's really no different than a computer language compiler creating machine code. If you're testing such a system, you have to check that the HTML it creates is what the designer expects.

- **Server Performance and Loading.** Popular Web sites might receive millions of individual hits a day. Each one requires a download of data from the Web site's server to the browser's computer. If you wanted to test a system for performance and loading, you'd have to find a way to simulate the millions of connections and downloads.

- **Security.** Web site security issues are always in the news as hackers try new and different ways to gain access to a Web site's internal data. Financial, medical, and other Web sites that contain personal data are especially at risk and require intimate knowledge of server technology to test them for proper security.

The Security Testing Myth

There are often highly publicized stories about computer hackers breaking into super-secure Web sites and obtaining secret or sensitive information. The press will play up that the hackers did it with a simple three-line computer program or through a blatant open back-door. It often seems as though the average person could have found the hole. Don't be misled—those hackers worked long and hard to discover their way in. Sure, the end result might have been a three-line program, but e=mc^2 is only five characters and Einstein worked a long time to figure out that equation. As a software tester, if you're looking for security holes in a Web site, be prepared for a difficult challenge. It's not as easy as it seems.

Configuration and Compatibility Testing

It's time to get back to what you can do, today, to test a Web page. Recall from Chapter 8, "Configuration Testing," and Chapter 9, "Compatibility Testing," what configuration and compatibility testing are. Configuration testing is the process of checking the operation of your software with various types of hardware and software platforms and their different settings. Compatibility testing is checking your software's operation with other software. Web pages are perfect examples of where you can apply this type of testing.

Assume that you have a Web site to test. You need to think about what the possible hardware and software configurations might be that could affect the operation or appearance of the site. Here's a list to consider:

- **Hardware Platform.** Is it a Mac, PC, a TV browsing device, a hand-held, or a wristwatch? Each hardware device has its own operating system, screen layout, communications software, and so on. Each can affect how the Web site appears onscreen.

- **Browser Software and Version.** There are many different Web browsers and browser versions. Some run on only one type of hardware platform, others run on multiple platforms. Some examples are Netscape Navigator 3.04 and 4.05, Internet Explorer 3.02, 4.01, and 5.0, Mosaic 3.0, Opera, and Emacs.

  Each browser and version supports a slightly different set of features. A Web site might look great under one browser but not display at all under another. Web designers can choose to design a site using the least common denominator of features so that it looks the same on all of them, or write specialized code to make the site work best on each one. How would this impact your testing?

13

WEB SITE TESTING

- **Browser Plug-Ins.** Many browsers can accept plug-ins or extensions to gain additional functionality. An example of this would be to play specific types of audio or video files.

- **Browser Options.** Most Web browsers allow for a great deal of customization. Figure 13.7 shows an example of this. You can select security options, choose how ALT text is handled, decide what plug-ins to enable, and so on. Each option has potential impact on how your Web site operates—and, hence, is a test scenario to consider.

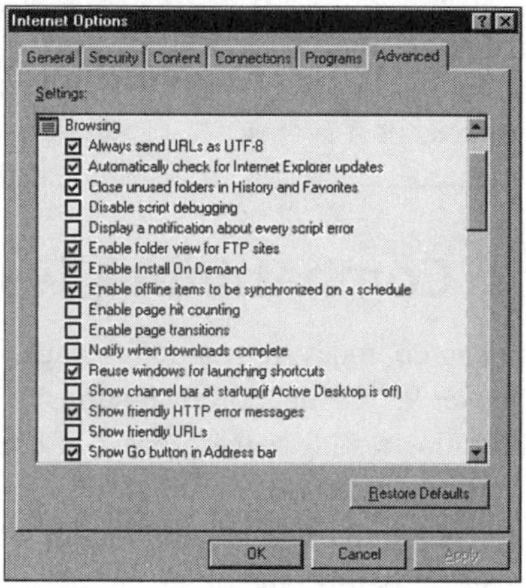

FIGURE 13.7
This example shows how configurable the Internet Explorer Web browser is.

- **Video Resolution and Color Depth.** Many platforms can display in various screen resolutions and colors. A PC running Windows, for example, can have screen dimensions of 640×480, 800×600, 1,024×768, 1280×1024, and up. Your Web site may look different, or even wrong, in one resolution, but not in another. Text and graphics can wrap differently, be cut off, or not appear at all.

  The number of colors that the platform supports can also impact the look of your site. There can be as few as 16 colors and as many as 2^{24}. Could your Web site be used on a system with only 16 colors?

- **Text Size.** Did you know that a user can change the size of the text used in the browser? Could your site be used with very small or very large text? What if it was being run on a small screen, in a low resolution, with large text?

- **Modem Speeds.** Enough can't be said about performance. Someday everyone will have high-speed connections with Web site data delivered as fast as you can view it. Until then, you need to test that your Web site works well at a wide range of modem speeds.

If you consider all the possibilities outlined here, testing even the simplest Web site can become a huge task. It's not enough that the Web site looks good on your PC—if you want to ensure that it works well for its intended audience, you need to research the possible configurations they might have. With that information, you can create equivalence partitions of the configurations you feel are most important to test.

A good place to start your search is Georgia Tech's Graphic, Visualization, & Usability Center's (GVU) annual WWW User Survey. It's located at `www.gvu.gatech.edu/user_surveys`. The technology demographics information lists platforms, connection speeds, types of connections, browsers, email programs, video size and resolution, and many other attributes. It's a great first step in deciding what configurations to test.

Usability Testing

Usability and Web sites are sometimes mutually exclusive terms. You've no doubt seen pages that are difficult to navigate, outdated, slow, or just plain ugly. Not surprisingly, these sites were probably never seen by a software tester. A programmer or someone with little or no design experience (or maybe too much design experience) created the pages and uploaded them for the world to see without considering how usable they were.

As described in Chapter 11, "Usability Testing," usability testing is a difficult process to define. What looks bad to you might look great to someone else—some people think that Elvis on velvet is art. Fortunately, following and testing a few basic rules can help make Web sites more usable.

Jakob Nielsen, `www.useit.com`, a respected expert on Web site design and usability, has performed extensive research on Web site usability. The following list is adapted from his *Top Ten Mistakes in Web Design*:

- **Gratuitous Use of Bleeding-Edge Technology.** Your Web site shouldn't try to attract users by bragging about its use of the latest Web technology. It may attract a few nerds, but mainstream users will care more about useful content and the site's ability to offer good customer service. Using the latest and greatest technology before it's even released is a sure way to discourage users; if their system crashes while visiting your site, you can bet that many of them won't be back. Unless you're in the business of selling Internet products or services, it's better to wait until some experience has been gained with the technology. When desktop publishing was young, people put 20 different fonts in their documents; try to avoid similar design bloat on the Web.

- **Scrolling Text, Marquees, and Constantly Running Animations.** Never allow page elements that move incessantly. Moving images have an overpowering effect on human peripheral vision. A Web page shouldn't emulate Times Square in New York City in its constant attack on the human senses—give your user some peace and quiet to actually read the text!

- **Long Scrolling Pages.** Users typically don't like to scroll beyond the information visible onscreen when a page comes up. All critical content and navigation options should be on the top part of the page. Recent studies have shown that users are becoming more willing to scroll now than they were in the early years of the Web, but it's still a good idea to minimize scrolling on navigation pages.

- **Non-Standard Link Colors.** Hyperlinks to pages that users haven't seen should be blue; links to previously seen pages should be purple or red. Don't mess with these colors because the ability to understand which links have been followed is one of the few navigational aids that's standard in most Web browsers. Consistency is key to teaching users what the link colors mean.

- **Outdated Information.** Your development team should have a Web "gardener"—someone to root out the weeds and replant the flowers as the Web site changes. Unfortunately, most teams would rather spend their time creating new content than doing maintenance. In practice, maintenance is a cheap way of enhancing the content on your Web site since many old pages keep their relevance and should be linked into the new pages. Of course, some pages are better off being removed completely from the server after their expiration date.

- **Overly Long Download Times.** Traditional human-factor guidelines indicate that 0.1 second is about the limit for users to feel that the system is reacting instantaneously. One second is about the limit for a user's flow of thought to stay uninterrupted. Ten seconds is the maximum response time before a user loses interest.

  On the Web, users have been trained to endure so much suffering that it may be acceptable to increase this limit to 15 seconds for a few pages. But don't aim for this—aim for less.

- **Lack of Navigation Support.** Don't assume that users know as much about your site as you do. They will always have difficulty finding information, so they need support in the form of a strong sense of structure and place. Your site's design should start with a good understanding of the structure of the information space and communicate that structure explicitly to users. Provide a site map to let users know where they are and where they can go. The site should also have a good search feature because even the best navigation support will never be enough.

- **Orphan Pages.** Make sure that all pages include a clear indication of what Web site they belong to since users may access pages directly without coming in through your home page. For the same reason, every page should have a link to your home page as well as some indication of where they fit within the structure of your information space.

- **Complex Web Site Addresses (URLs).** Even though machine-level addressing like the URL should never have been exposed in the user interface, it's there and research has found that users actually try to decode the URLs of pages to infer the structure of Web sites. Users do this because of the lack of support for navigation (see above) and sense of location in current Web browsers. Thus, a URL should contain human-readable names that reflect the nature of the Web site's contents.

Also, users often type in a URL, so the Web site should try to minimize the risk of typos by using short names with all lowercase characters and no special characters (many people don't know how to type a ~).

- **Using Frames.** Frames are an HTML technology that allows a Web site to display another Web site within itself, hence the name *frame*—like a picture frame. Splitting a page into frames can confuse users since frames break the fundamental user model of the Web page. All of a sudden they can't bookmark the current page and return to it (the bookmark points to another version of the frameset), URLs stop working, and printouts become difficult. Even worse, the predictability of user actions goes out the door—who knows what information will appear where and when they click a link?

If you're testing a Web site, take advantage of your tester's license to report bugs on usability. Read up on basic user interface design techniques and learn what makes for good usability. A good source of information is a Microsoft research document titled, "Improving Web Site Usability and Appeal." Its Web address is `msdn.microsoft.com/workshop/management/planning/improvingsiteusa.asp`. This document provides a list of best practices that Microsoft discovered while designing content for its MSN Web sites. Don't be put off by the date, 1997, on the document. Good design is timeless.

Introducing Automation

The last part of this chapter is somewhat a lead-in to the next chapter of the book, Chapter 14, "Automated Testing and Test Tools."

You may have wondered as you read this chapter how you could possibly have enough time to thoroughly test a large and complex Web site. The simple act of clicking all the hyperlinks to make sure that they're valid could take a great deal of time. Add in testing the basic functionality of the Web site's features, doing configuration and compatibility testing, and figuring out a way to test performance and loading by simulating thousands or even millions of users, and you have a big job.

Thankfully, you don't have to do all this testing manually. Testing tools are available, both free and for purchase, that will make your job much easier. Two free ones are located at `www.netmechanic.com` and `websitegarage.netscape.com`. Both sites provide easy-to-use tools that will automatically examine your Web site and test it for things such as browser compatibility, performance problems, broken hyperlinks, HTML standard adherence, and spelling. They can even tell you what graphics on your site are possibly too large and are causing it to be slow. Such tools can save you many hours of what would normally be manual work. Look at them for an idea of what you'll learn about in Chapter 14.

Summary

This chapter wraps up Part III, "Applying Your Testing Skills." Part III has covered a lot of ground—from video card settings to Hungarian localization to ugly Web sites. These topics are just a small piece of the total software world. That diversity is what makes software testing a limitless challenge. Every day new and exciting types of software are released, always pushing the technology forward and creating unique and interesting testing problems to solve. Web site testing is a good topic for this chapter, today, but who knows what it will be in the future.

Hopefully in reading the chapters in Part III you realized that you or a small test team could easily be overwhelmed by the magnitude of testing even a small software product or Web site. A few hundred lines of code written by a single programmer with all its possible platforms, configurations, languages, and users could require dozens or even hundreds of testers to thoroughly test them. The combinations and permutations are endless and, even with careful equivalence partitioning to reduce the number of cases, the job can still seem too big to handle.

In the next two chapters, you'll learn how to leverage both tools and people to bring this huge task down to a manageable size.

Quiz

These quiz questions are provided for your further understanding. See Appendix A, "Answers to Quiz Questions," for the answers—but don't peek!

1. What basic elements of a Web page can easily be tested with a black-box approach?

2. What is gray-box testing?

3. Why is gray-box testing possible with Web site testing?

4. Why can't you rely on a spell checker to check the spelling on a Web page?

5. Name a few areas that you need to consider when performing configuration and compatibility testing of a Web site.

6. Which of Jakob Neilsen's 10 common Web site mistakes would cause configuration and compatibility bugs?

Supplementing Your Testing

PART
IV

If an army of monkeys were strumming on typewriters, they might write all the books in the British Museum.

—Sir Arthur Eddington, British astronomer and physicist

IN THIS PART

Automated Testing and Test Tools

IN THIS CHAPTER

Testing software is hard work. If you've done some testing on your own while reading this book, you've seen that the physical task of performing the tests can take a great deal of time and effort. Sure, you could spend more time equivalence partitioning your test cases, reducing the number that you run, but then you take on more risk because you're reducing coverage, choosing not to test important features. You need to test more, but you don't have the time. What can you do?

The answer is to do what people have done for years in every other field and industry— develop and use tools to make the job easier and more efficient. That's what this chapter is all about.

Highlights of this chapter include

- Why test tools and automation are necessary
- Examples of simple test tools you can use
- How using tools migrates to test automation
- How to feed and care for "monkeys"
- Why test tools and automation aren't a panacea

The Benefits of Automation and Tools

Think back to what you've learned about how software is created. In most software development models, the code-test-fix loop can repeat several times before the software is released. If you're testing a particular feature, that means you may need to run your tests not once, but potentially dozens of times. You'll check that the bugs you found in previous test runs were indeed fixed and that no new bugs were introduced. This process of rerunning your tests is known as *regression testing*.

If a small software project had several thousand test cases to run, there might be barely enough time to execute them just once. Running them numerous times might be impossible, let alone monotonous. Software test tools and automation help solve this problem by providing a better means to run your tests than by manual testing.

The principal attributes of tools and automation are

- **Speed.** Think about how long it would take you to manually try a few thousand test cases for the Windows Calculator. You might average a test case every 5 seconds or so. Automation might be able to run 10, 100, even 1000 times that fast.
- **Efficiency.** While you're busy running test cases, you can't be doing anything else. If you have a test tool that reduces the time it takes for you to run your tests, you have more time for test planning and thinking up new tests.

- **Accuracy and Precision.** After trying a few hundred cases, your attention span will wane and you'll start to make mistakes. A test tool will perform the same test and check the results perfectly, each and every time.

- **Relentlessness.** Test tools and automation never tire or give up. They're like that battery-operated bunny of the TV commercials—they can keep going and going and....

All this probably sounds like great news. You could have test tools do all the work for you—turn them loose and wait for the results. Unfortunately, it's not that easy. Houses aren't built automatically, even though carpenters have power saws and nail guns. The tools just make it easier for them to do their work and for the resulting work to be of higher quality. Software test tools operate the same way.

> **Reminder**
>
> Software test tools aren't a substitute for software testers—they just help software testers perform their jobs better.

It's important to note that using test tools isn't always the right answer. Sometimes there's no substitute for manual testing. For now, take in the information about what tests tools can do and how they work. Think about how you might use them to complement your testing tasks. At the end of this chapter, you'll learn about a few limitations and cautions to consider before you embark on using tools on your projects.

Test Tools

As a software tester you'll be exposed to a wide range of testing tools. The types of tools that you'll use are based on the type of software that you're testing and whether you're performing black-box or white-box tests.

The beauty of test tools is that you don't always need to be an expert in how they work or exactly what they do to use them. Suppose that you're testing networking software that allows a computer to simultaneously communicate with up to 1 million other computers. It would be difficult, if not impossible, to perform a controlled test with 1 million real connections. But, if someone gave you a special tool that simulated those connections, maybe letting you dial up the number from one to a million, you could perform your tests without having to set up a real-world scenario. You don't need to understand how the tool works, just that it does—that's black-box testing.

On the other hand, a tool could be set up to monitor and modify the raw communications that occurs among those million computers. You'd likely need some white-box skills and knowledge of the low-level protocol to effectively use this tool.

> **NOTE**
>
> This example brings up an important distinction between two types of tools—*non-invasive* and *invasive*. If a tool is used only to monitor and examine the software without modifying it, it's considered non-invasive. If, however, the tool modifies the program code or manipulates the operating environment in any way, it's invasive. There are varying degrees of invasiveness and testers usually try to use tools that are as non-invasive as possible to reduce the possibility that their tools are affecting the test results.

The next few pages will discuss the major classes of testing tools and how they're used. Some examples are based on tools that are included with most programming languages; others are commercial tools sold individually. You may find, however, that your software or hardware is unique enough that you'll have to develop or have someone else develop custom tools that fit your specific needs. They will likely, though, still fall into one of these categories.

Viewers and Monitors

A *viewer* or *monitor* test tool allows you to see details of the software's operation that you wouldn't normally be able to see. In Chapter 7, "Testing the Software with X-Ray Glasses," you learned how code coverage analyzers provide a means for you to see what lines of code are executed, what functions are run, and what code paths are followed when you run your tests. A code coverage analyzer is an example of a viewing tool. Most code coverage analyzers are invasive tools because they need to be compiled and linked into the program to access the information they provide.

Figure 14.1 shows an example of another type of viewer—a *communications analyzer* (or *comm analyzer*, for short). This tool allows you to see the raw protocol data moving across a network or other communications cable. It simply taps into the line, pulls off the data as it passes by, and displays it on another computer. If you're testing such a system, you could enter a test case on Computer #1, confirm that the resulting communications data is correct on Computer #3, and check that the appropriate results occurred on Computer #2. You might also use this system to investigate why a bug occurs. By looking at the data pulled off the wire, you could determine if the problem lies in creating the data (Computer #1) or interpreting the data (Computer #2). This type of system is non-invasive to the software.

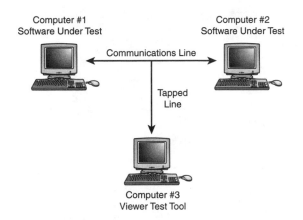

FIGURE 14.1

A communications analyzer provides a view into the raw data being transferred between two systems.

The code debuggers that come with most compilers are also considered viewers because they allow programmers or white-box testers to view internal variable values and program states. Anything that lets you see into the system and look at data that the average user wouldn't be able to see can be classified as a viewer test tool.

Drivers

Drivers are tools used to control and operate the software being tested. One of the simplest examples of a driver is a *batch file*, a simple list of programs or commands that are executed sequentially. In the days of MS-DOS, this was a popular means for testers to execute their test programs. They'd create a batch file containing the names of their test programs, start the batch running, and go home. With today's operating systems and programming languages, there are much more sophisticated methods for executing test programs. For example, a complex Perl script can take the place of an old MS-DOS batch file, and the Windows Task Scheduler (see Figure 14.2) can execute various test programs at certain times throughout the day.

Figure 14.3 shows another example of a driver tool. Suppose that the software you're testing requires large amounts of data to be entered for your test cases. With some hardware modifications and a few software tools, you could replace the keyboard and mouse of the system being tested with an additional computer that acts as a driver. You could write simple programs on this driver computer that automatically generate the appropriate keystrokes and mouse movements to test the software.

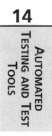

FIGURE 14.2

The Windows Task Scheduler allows you to schedule when programs or batch files are to run on your PC.

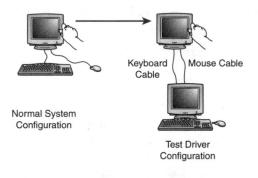

Normal System
Configuration

Keyboard Cable   Mouse Cable

Test Driver
Configuration

FIGURE 14.3

A computer can act as a driver test tool to replace the keyboard and mouse of a system being tested.

You might be thinking, why bother with such a complicated setup? Why not simply run a program on the first system that sends keystrokes to the software being tested? There are potentially two problems with this:

- It's possible that the software or operating system isn't multitasking, making it impossible to run another driver program concurrently.

- By sending keystrokes and mouse movements from an external computer, the test system is non-invasive. If a driver program is running on the same system as the software being tested, it's invasive and may not be considered an acceptable test scenario.

When considering ways to drive the software that you're testing, think of all the possible methods by which your program can be externally controlled. Then find ways to replace that external control with something that will automatically provide test input to it.

Stubs

Stubs, like drivers, were mentioned in Chapter 7 as white-box testing techniques. Stubs are essentially the opposite of drivers in that they don't control or operate the software being tested; they instead receive or respond to data that the software sends. Figure 14.4 shows an example that helps to clarify this.

Normal System
Configuration

Test Stub
Configuration

FIGURE 14.4
A computer can act as a stub, replacing a printer and allowing more efficient analysis of the test output.

If you're testing software that sends data to a printer, one way to test it is to enter data, print it, and look at the resulting paper printout. That would work, but it's fairly slow, inefficient, and error prone. Could you tell if the output had a single missing pixel or if it was just slightly off in color? If you instead replaced the printer with another computer that was running stub software that could read and interpret the printer data, it could much more quickly and accurately check the test results.

Stubs are frequently used when software needs to communicate with external devices. Often during development these devices aren't available or are scarce. A stub allows testing to occur despite not having the hardware and it makes testing more efficient.

> **NOTE**
>
> You may have heard the term *emulator* used to describe a device that's a plug-in replacement for the real device. A PC acting as a printer, understanding the printer codes and responding to the software as though it were a printer, is an emulator. The difference between an emulator and a stub is that the stub also provides a means for a tester to view and interpret the data sent to it.

Stress and Load Tools

Stress and *load* tools induce stresses and loads to the software being tested. A word processor running as the only application on the system, with all available memory and disk space, probably works just fine. But, if the system runs low on these resources, you'd expect a greater potential for bugs. You could copy files to fill up the disk, run lots of programs to eat up memory, and so on, but these methods are inefficient and non-exact. A stress tool specifically designed for this would make testing much easier.

Figure 14.5 shows the Microsoft Stress utility that comes with its programming language development software. Other operating systems and languages have similar utilities. The Stress program allows you to individually set the amounts of memory, disk space, files, and other resources available to the software running on the machine.

Resource	Remaining	
Global	97816.00	KB
User	21	%
GDI	43	%
Disk Space	2047.69	MB
File Handles	120	
Wnd32	1943.03	KB
Menu32	1925.17	KB
GDI32	1930.84	KB

FIGURE 14.5
The Microsoft Stress utility allows you to set the system resources available to the software you're testing.

Setting the values to zero, or near zero, will make the software execute different code paths as it attempts to handle the tight constraints. Ideally, the software will run without crashing or losing data. It may run more slowly, or tell you that it's running low on memory, but it should otherwise work properly or degrade gracefully.

Load tools are similar to stress tools in that they create situations for your software that might otherwise be difficult to create. For example, commercially available programs can be run on Web servers to load them down by simulating a set number of connections and hits. You might want to check that 10,000 simultaneous users and 1 million hits a day can be handled without slowing response times. With a load tool, you can simply dial in that level, run your tests, and see what happens.

Interference Injectors and Noise Generators

Another class of tools is *interference injectors* and *noise generators*. They're similar to stress and load tools but are more random in what they do. The Stress tool, for example, has an executor mode that randomly changes the available resources. A program might run fine with lots of memory and might handle low memory situations, but it could have problems if the amount of available memory is constantly changing. The executor mode of stress would uncover these types of bugs.

Similarly, you could make a slight change to the viewer tool setup shown in Figure 14.1 to create a test configuration as shown in Figure 14.6. In this scenario, the viewer is replaced with hardware and software that allows not only viewing the data on the communications line, but also modifying it. Such a setup could simulate all types of communications errors caused by data dropouts, noisy or bad cables, and so on.

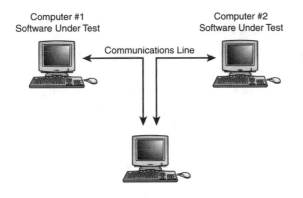

FIGURE 14.6
An interference injector hooked into a communications line could test that the software handles error conditions due to noise.

When deciding where and how to use interference injectors and noise generators, think about what external influences affect the software you're testing, and then figure out ways to vary and manipulate those influences to see how the software handles it.

Analysis Tools

You might call this last category of tools *analysis tools*, a best-of-the-rest group. Most software testers use the following common tools to make their everyday jobs easier. They're not necessarily as fancy as the tools discussed so far. They're often taken for granted, but they get the job done and can save you a great deal of time.

- Word processing software
- Spreadsheet software
- Database software
- File comparison software

- Screen capture and comparison software
- Debugger
- Binary-hex calculator
- Stopwatch
- VCR or camera

Of course, software complexity and direction change all the time. You need to look at your individual situation to decide what the most effective tools would be and how best to apply them.

Software Test Automation

Although *test automation* is just another class of software testing tools, it's one that deserves special consideration. The software test tools that you've learned about so far are indeed effective, but they still must be operated or monitored manually. What if those tools could be combined, started, and run with little or no intervention from you? They could run your test cases, look for bugs, analyze what they see, and log the results. That's software test automation.

The next few sections of this chapter will walk you through the different types of automation, progressing from the simplest to the most complex.

Macro Recording and Playback

The most basic type of test automation is recording your keyboard and mouse actions as you run your tests for the first time and then playing them back when you need to run them again. If the software you're testing is for Windows or the Mac, recording and playing back macros is a fairly easy process. On the Mac you can use QuicKeys; on Windows the shareware program Macro Magic is a good choice. Many macro record and playback programs are available, so you might want to scan your favorite shareware supplier and find one that best fits your needs.

Macro recorders and players are a type of driver tool. As mentioned earlier, drivers are tools used to control and operate the software being tested. With a macro program you're doing just that—the macros you record are played back, repeating the actions that you performed to test the software.

Figure 14.7 shows a screen from the Macro Setup Wizard, which walks you through the steps necessary to configure and capture your macros.

FIGURE 14.7

The Macro Setup Wizard allows you to configure how your recorded macros are triggered and played back. (Figure courtesy of Iolo Technologies, www.iolo.com.)

The Macro Setup Wizard allows you to set the following options for your macros:

- **Name.** Giving the macro a name provides a way to identify it later. Even for a small software project you could write hundreds of macros.

- **Repetitions.** Repetition testing is a great way to find bugs. You can set the number of times the macro will repeat or loop when it runs.

- **Triggers.** You can set how the macro is started. This can be by a hot key (for example, Ctrl+Shift+T), by a set of typed-in characters (maybe `run macro 1`), by clicking a short-cut, when a certain window is displayed (whenever Calculator is started, for example), or when the system has idled unused for a certain length of time.

- **What's captured.** You can select to capture (record) just keystrokes or both keystrokes and mouse actions such as moving and clicking.

- **Playback speed.** The macro can play back from up to 20 percent slower to 500 percent faster than how you originally recorded it. This is important if your software's perfor-mance can vary. What would happen if the software you're testing became a bit slower and the button the macro was to click on wasn't yet onscreen?

- **Playback position.** This option determines if the mouse movements and clicks should be absolute or relative to a certain window onscreen. If you're testing an application that might change onscreen positions, making your movements relative to that application is a good idea; otherwise, the mouse may not click where you would expect.

Now's a good time to experiment with recording and playing back macros. Find and download some macro software, try it out on a few simple programs such as Calculator or Notepad, and see what you think. Think like a tester!

14

AUTOMATED
TESTING AND TEST
TOOLS

What you'll find is that although macros can do some automated testing for you, making it much easier and faster to rerun your tests, they're not perfect. The biggest problem is lack of verification. The macros can't check that the software does what it's supposed to do. The macro could type 100–99 into the Calculator, but it can't test that the result is 1—you still need to do that. This is an issue, sure, but many testers are happy just eliminating all the repetitive typing and mouse moving. It's a much easier job to simply watch the macros run and confirm that the results are what's expected.

Playback speed can be another difficulty with macros. Even if you can adjust the speed of playback, it may not always be enough to keep the macros in sync. A Web page may take 1 second or 10 seconds to load. You could slow down your macros to account for the expected worst case, but then they'd run slowly even if the software was running fast. And, if the Web page unexpectedly took 15 seconds to load, your macros would still get confused—clicking the wrong things at the wrong time.

> **NOTE**
>
> Be careful if you use a macro recorder to capture mouse movements and clicks. Programs don't always start up or appear in the same place onscreen. Setting the playback position to be relative to the program's window rather than absolute to the screen can help, but even then just a slight change in the GUI could throw off your captured steps.

Despite these limitations, recording and playing back macros is a popular means to automate simple testing tasks. It's also a good place to start for testers learning how to automate their testing.

Programmed Macros

Programmed macros are a step up in evolution from the simple record and playback variety. Rather than create programmed macros by recording your actions as you run the test for the first time, create them by programming simple instructions for the playback system to follow. A very simple macro program might look like the one in Listing 14.1 (created with the Macro Setup Wizard). This type of macro can be programmed by selecting individual actions from a menu of choices—you don't even need to type in the commands.

LISTING 14.1   A Simple Macro That Performs a Test on the Windows Calculator

```
1: Calculator Test #2
2: <<EXECUTE:C:\WINDOWS\Calc.exe~~~~>>
3: <<LOOKFOR:Calculator~~SECS:5~~>>
4: 123-100=
5: <<PROMPT:The answer should be 23>>
6: <<CLOSE:Calculator>>
```

Line 1 is a comment line identifying the test. Line 2 executes calc.exe, the Windows calcula-tor. Line 3 waits up to 5 seconds for Calculator to start. It does this by pausing until a window appears with the word Calculator in its title bar. Line 4 types the keys 123–100=. Line 5 dis-plays a message prompt stating that the answer should be 23. Line 6 closes the Calculator win-dow and ends the test.

Notice that programmed macros such as this one have some real advantages over recorded macros. Although they still can't perform verification of the test results, they can pause their execution to prompt the tester (see Figure 14.8) with an expected result and a query for him to okay whether the test passed or failed.

FIGURE 14.8
Simple programmed macros can't verify the results of a test but can prompt the tester for confirmation. (Figure cour-tesy of Iolo Technologies, www.iolo.com.)

Programmed macros can also solve many timing problems of recorded macros by not relying on absolute delays but instead waiting for certain conditions to occur before they go on. In the Calculator example, the macro waits for the program to load before it continues with the test—a much more reliable approach.

So far, so good. With programmed macros you can go a long way toward automating your test-ing. You have a simple macro language to use, generic commands for driving your software, and a means to prompt you for information. For many testing tasks, this is more than sufficient and you'll save a great deal of time automating your tests this way.

You're still missing two important pieces, though, to perform complex testing. First, pro-grammed macros are limited to straight-line execution—they can only loop and repeat. Variables and decision statements that you'd find in a regular programming language aren't available. You also don't have the ability to automatically check the results of your test. For these, you need to move to a comprehensive automated testing tool.

14

AUTOMATED TESTING AND TEST TOOLS

Fully Programmable Automated Testing Tools

What if you had the power of a full-fledged programming language, coupled with macro commands that can drive the software being tested, with the additional capacity to perform verification? You'd have the ultimate bug-finding tool! Figure 14.9 shows an example of such a tool.

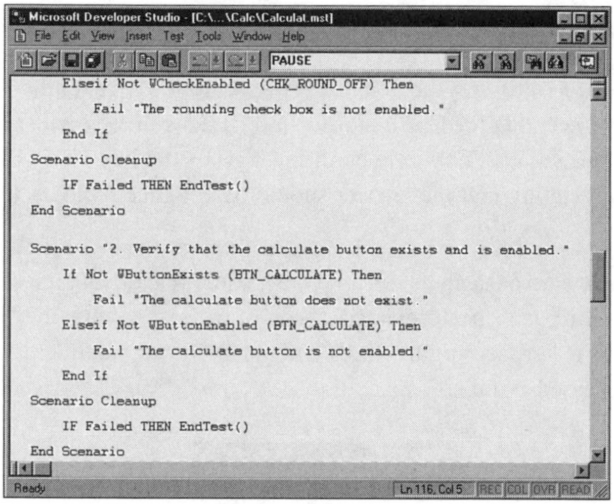

FIGURE 14.9

Visual Test, originally developed by Microsoft and now sold by Rational Software, is an example of a tool that provides a programming environment, macro commands, and verification capabilities in a single package.

Automated testing tools such as Visual Test provide the means for software testers to create very powerful tests. Many are based on the BASIC programming language, making it very easy for even non-programmers to write test code.

If you wanted to try typing the string **Hello World!** 10,000 times, you'd write a few lines of code such as this:

```
FOR i=1 TO 10000
PLAY "Hello World!"
NEXT I
```

If you wanted to move your mouse pointer from the upper left of your 640×480 screen to the lower right and then double-click, you could do it like this:

```
PLAY "{MOVETO 0,0}"
PLAY "{MOVETO 640,480}"
PLAY "{DBLCLICK}"
```

A testing language can also give you better control features than just clicking specific screen areas or sending individual keystrokes. For example, to click an OK button, you could use the command

```
wButtonClick ("OK")
```

You don't need to know where onscreen the OK button is located. The test software would look for it, find it, and click it—just like a user would. Similarly, there are commands for menus, check boxes, option buttons, list boxes, and so on. Commands such as these provide great flexibility in writing your tests, making them much more readable and reliable.

The most important feature that comes with these automation tools is the ability to perform verification, actually checking that the software is doing what's expected. There are several ways to do this:

- **Screen captures.** The first time you run your automated tests, you could capture and save screen images at key points that you know are correct. On future test runs, your automation could then compare the saved screens with the current screens. If they're different, something unexpected happened and the automation could flag it as a bug.

- **Control values.** Rather than capture screens, you could check the value of individual controls in the software's window. If you're testing Calculator, your automation could read the value out of the display field and compare it with what you expected. You could also determine if a button was pressed or a check box was selected. Automation tools provide the means to easily do this within your test program.

- **File and other output.** Similarly, if your program saves data to a file—for example, a word processor—your automation could read it back after creating it and compare it to a known good file. The same techniques would apply if the software being tested sent data over a modem or a network. The automation could be configured to read the data back in and compare it with the data that it expects.

Verification is the last big hurdle to overcome with automated software testing. Once you have that, you can take nearly any test case and create automation that will make trying that case either much easier or completely automatic.

To get more information about the popular test automation products available, visit the following Web sites:

- Mercury Interactive at `www.merc-int.com`
- Rational Software Corporation at `www.rational.com`
- Segue Software at `www.segue.com`

14

AUTOMATED
TESTING AND TEST
TOOLS

These packages can be a bit pricey for individuals since they're targeted mainly at corporate testing teams. But, if you're interested in gaining some experience with them, contact the company and ask for an evaluation copy or, if you're a student, ask for a student discount. Most software tool companies will help you out in hopes that you'll like their product and eventually recommend it to others.

Random Testing: Monkeys and Gorillas

The test automation tools and techniques that you've learned about so far have concentrated on making your job as a software tester easier and more efficient. They're designed to help you in running your test cases or, ideally, running your test cases automatically without the need for constant attention.

Using tools and automation for this purpose will help you find bugs; while the tools are busy doing regression testing, you'll have more time to plan new tests and design new and interesting cases to try. Another type of automated testing, though, isn't designed to help run or automatically run test cases. Its goal is to simulate what your users might do. That type of automation tool is called a *test monkey*.

The term *test monkey* comes from the idea that if you had a million monkeys typing on a million keyboards for a million years, statistically, they might eventually write a Shakespearean play, *Curious George*, or some other great work. All that random pounding of keys could accidentally hit the right combination of letters and the monkeys would, for a moment, look brilliant—much like the one in Figure 14.10.

FIGURE 14.10
Test monkeys will test forever as long as they have electricity and the occasional banana.

When your software is released to the public, it will have thousands or possibly millions of people randomly pounding away on it. Despite your best efforts at designing test cases to find bugs, some bugs will slip by and be found by those users. What if you could supplement your test case approach with a simulation of what all those users would do, before you released your product? You could potentially find bugs that would have otherwise made it past your testing. That's what a test monkey can do.

> **NOTE**
>
> The use of a test monkey to simulate how your customers will use your software in no way insinuates that computer users are related to apes.

Dumb Monkeys

The easiest and most straightforward type of test monkey is a *dumb monkey*. A dumb monkey doesn't know anything about the software being tested; it just clicks or types randomly. Listing 14.2 shows an example of Visual Test code that will randomly click and type 10,000 times.

LISTING 14.2   Just a Few Lines of Code Can Create a Dumb Monkey

```
1: RANDOMIZE TIMER
2: FOR i=1 TO 10000
3: PLAY "{CLICK "+STR$(INT(RND*640))+", "+STR$(INT(RND*480))+" }"
4: PLAY CHR$(RND*256)
5: NEXT i
```

Line 1 initializes the random numbers. Line 2 starts looping from 1 to 10,000 times. Line 3 selects a random point onscreen between 0,0 and 640,480 (VGA resolution) and clicks it. Line 4 picks a random character between 0 and 255 and types it in.

The software running on the PC doesn't know the difference between this program and a real person—except that it happens much more quickly. On a reasonably speedy PC it'll run in just a few seconds. Imagine how many random inputs you'd get if it ran all night!

Remember, this monkey is doing absolutely no verification. It just clicks and types until one of two things happens—either it finishes its loop or the software or the operating system crashes.

> **NOTE**
>
> If you don't believe that a dumb monkey can possibly find a serious bug, try running one on your favorite computer game or multimedia program. It's very likely that it won't last more than a few hours before crashing.

It doesn't seem to make sense that simple random clicking and typing could find a bug, but it does for a couple reasons:

- Given enough time and attempts, just like the monkeys writing Shakespeare, the random inputs will eventually stumble onto a magic sequence that the programmers and testers didn't think of. Maybe the monkey enters some data and immediately deletes it or types in a huge string where a short one was expected. Who knows? It will find it, though.

- A dumb monkey, with its continuous repetition and use, can expose bugs such as memory leaks that might not occur until many hours or days of normal use. If you've ever used software that seemed to become less and less stable the longer you used it, you've seen a problem that could have been found with a dumb monkey.

Semi-Smart Monkeys

Dumb monkeys can be extremely effective. They're easy to write and can find serious, crashing bugs. They lack a few important features, though, that would make them even more effective. Adding these features raises your monkey's IQ a bit, making him semi-smart.

Say that your monkey ran for several hours, logging thousands of random inputs before the software crashed. You'd know there was a problem but you couldn't show the programmer exactly how to re-create it. You could rerun your monkey with the same random seed but if it took several hours again to fail, you'd be wasting a lot of time. The solution is to add logging to your monkey so that everything it does is recorded to a file. When the monkey finds a bug, you need only to look at the log file to see what it was doing before the failure.

It's also a good idea to program your monkey to operate only on the software you're testing. If it's randomly clicking all over the screen, it could (and will eventually) click the exit command and stop the program. Since the monkey doesn't know that the program closed, it'll keep on going. Think about what would happen if the monkey was clicking all over your computer's screen—ouch! Most programmable automation tools provide a way to always target a specific application, or to stop working if the application is no longer present.

Another good feature to make your monkey semi-smart is crash recognition. If you started your monkey running for the night and it found a bug as soon as you walked out the door, you'd lose many hours of valuable test time. If you can add programming to your monkey to recognize that a crash has occurred, restart the computer, and start running again, you could potentially find several bugs each night.

Smart Monkeys

Moving up on the evolutionary scale is the smart monkey. Such a monkey takes the effectiveness of random testing from his less-intelligent brothers and adds to that an awareness of his surroundings. He doesn't just pound on the keyboard randomly—he pounds on it with a purpose.

A true smart monkey knows

- Where he is
- What he can do there
- Where he can go
- Where he's been
- If what he's seeing is correct

Does this list sound familiar? It should. A smart monkey can read the software's state transition map—the type of map described in Chapter 5, "Testing the Software with Blinders On." If all the state information that describes the software can be read by the monkey, it could bounce around the software just like a user would, only much more quickly, and be able to verify things as it went.

A smart monkey testing the Windows Calculator (see Figure 14.11) would know what buttons are available to press, what menu items are present, and where to type in the numbers. If it clicked the Help menu's About Calculator option, it would know that the only ways out were to click OK or the Close button. It wouldn't randomly click all over the screen, eventually stumbling onto one of them.

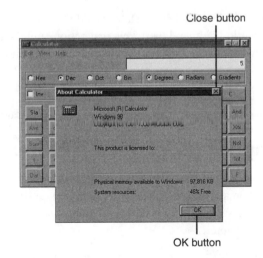

FIGURE 14.11

A smart monkey would know how to close the Calculator About dialog box.

A smart monkey isn't limited to just looking for crashing bugs, either. It can examine data as it goes, checking the results of its actions and looking for differences from what it expects. If you programmed in your test cases, the smart monkey could randomly execute them, look for bugs, and log the results. Very cool!

Figure 14.12 shows a smart monkey called Koko, named after the gorilla that could speak in sign language. To program Koko, you feed it the state table that describes your software by defining each state, the actions that can be performed in that state, and claims that determine whether the result of executing an action is right or wrong.

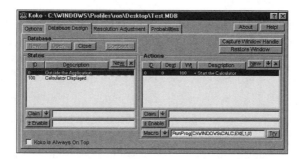

FIGURE 14.12

The Koko smart monkey can be programmed to know where it is and what it can do.

When Koko runs, it drives the software to a known state, randomly selects an action based on a weighting that simulates real-world likelihood, performs that action, and then checks the result. If the action results in the software changing states, Koko knows that and uses a new set of actions that apply to that new state.

With such a system, you could simulate real-world usage of your software, compressing thousands of hours of use into just a few hours. Smart monkeys are truly bug-finding machines!

Realities of Using Test Tools and Automation

Before you get all excited and want to run out and start using tools and automation on your tests, you need to read this section and take it to heart. Test automation isn't a panacea. You should consider some important issues that can make it difficult to use before you begin using the techniques described in this chapter:

- The software changes. Specifications are never fixed. New features are added late. The product name can change at the last minute. What if you recorded thousands of macros to run all your tests and a week before the product was to be released, the software was changed to display an extra screen when it started up? All of your recorded macros would fail to run because they wouldn't know the extra screen was there. You need to write your automation so that it's flexible and can easily and quickly be changed if necessary.

- There's no substitute for the human eye and intuition. Smart monkeys can be programmed to be only so smart. They can test only what you tell them to test. They can never see something and say, "Gee, that looks funny. I should do some more checking"—at least, not yet.

- Verification is hard to do. If you're testing a user interface, the obvious and simplest method to verify your test results is capturing and comparing screens. But, captured screens are huge files and those screens can be constantly changing during the product's development. Make sure that your tools check only what they need to and can efficiently handle changes during product development.

- It's easy to rely on automation too much. Don't ever assume that because all your automation runs without finding a bug that there are no more bugs to find. They're still in there. It's the pesticide paradox.

- Don't spend so much time working on tools and automation that you fail to test the software. It's easy and fun to start writing macros or programming a smart monkey, but that's not testing. These tools may help you be more efficient, but you'll need to use them on the software and do some real testing to find bugs.

- If you're writing macros, developing a tool, or programming a monkey, you're doing development work. You should follow the same standards and guidelines that you ask of your programmers. Just because you're a tester doesn't mean you can break the rules.

- Some tools are invasive and can cause the software being tested to improperly fail. If you use a tool that finds a bug, try to re-create that bug by hand without using the tool. It might turn out to be a simple reproducible bug, or the tool might be the cause of the problem.

Summary

Software test tools and automation can work for any type of software. Most examples presented in this chapter dealt with user interface testing but the same techniques can apply to testing compilers to networks to Web servers. Just think about the testing tasks you need to perform and how you could use software to make it easier and faster—those are the areas to automate.

Sometimes you use your bare hand, sometimes you use a flyswatter, sometimes you (maybe inappropriately) use a hammer. Knowing when to use a test tool and which one to use is an important skill for a software tester. Creating and using tools and test automation can be a fun job. It's very cool to see your computer running on its own, cursor flying around, characters being entered automatically. You'll get lots of satisfaction while you're home in bed or out sipping a latté that your automation is chugging along at work, finding bugs.

Quiz

These quiz questions are provided for your further understanding. See Appendix A, "Answers to Quiz Questions," for the answers—but don't peek!

1. Name a few benefits of using software test tools and automation.

2. What are a few drawbacks or cautions to consider when deciding to use software test tools and automation?

3. What's the difference between a tool and automation?

4. How are viewer tools and injector tools similar and different?

5. **True or False:** An invasive tool is the best type because it operates closest to the software being tested.

6. What's one of the simplest, but effective, types of test automation?

7. Name a few features that could be added to test automation you described in question 6 to make it even more effective.

8. What advantages do smart monkeys have over macros and dumb monkeys?

Bug Bashes and Beta Testing

In Chapter 14, "Automated Testing and Test Tools," you learned how technology in the form of tools and automation can help make your testing more efficient. Using software to test software is a great way to speed up your work and to help find bugs that might otherwise be missed.

Another means to be a more effective tester is to leverage other people. If you could get more people, even if they aren't professional testers, looking at your software before it's released, they may be able to find bugs that you and your fellow testers failed to see.

Highlights of this chapter include

- Why it's important to have other people test
- How you can get others looking at your software
- What beta testing is and how testers are involved
- How to effectively outsource your test work

Only As Far As the Eye Can See

Figure 15.1 shows two almost identical views of the same scene. Get out your egg timer, set it for one minute, and carefully examine both pictures looking for differences between the two. Keep a list of the differences you find in the order that you discover them.

FIGURE 15.1

In one minute, try to find as many differences between the two scenes as you can. Figure courtesy of www. cartoonworks.com.

After you finish looking, have several friends do the same search and compare your lists. What you'll find is that everyone has very different results. The number of differences found, the order that they were found, even which ones were found will be different. Hopefully, if you combine all the lists and throw out the duplicates, you'll have a complete list of all the differences—but even then, there still may be a few that were missed.

Software testing works exactly the same way. You're likely under a tight schedule, you find as many bugs as possible in the time you have, but someone else can come in, test the same code, and find additional bugs. It can be discouraging to see this happen. After all your hard work, you'll think, "How could I have missed such an obvious bug?" Don't worry, it's normal, and there are several reasons and solutions for it:

- Having another set of eyes look at the software helps break the pesticide paradox. As Figure 15.1 demonstrates, people notice different things. Bugs that were always present that built up immunity to your view can be readily seen by a new person on the project. It's the "Emperor Has No Clothes" dilemma.

- Similarly, people don't just see differently from each other, they go about their testing differently, too. Despite your best efforts in reviewing the software's specification and deciding on your test cases, a new person can come in and find a bug by trying something that you never even considered—hitting a different key, clicking the mouse faster, starting a function in a different way, and so on. It's that pesticide paradox again.

- Having someone assist you in your testing helps eliminate boredom. It can get pretty monotonous running the same tests over and over, using the same software features again and again. The boredom will also cause your attention to wane and you might start missing obvious bugs.

- Watching how someone else approaches a problem is a great way to learn new testing techniques. There are always new and different approaches to testing that you can add to your bag of testing tricks.

It's easy to fall into the trap of wanting to be solely responsible for testing your own piece of the software, but don't do it. There's too much to gain by having others help you out.

Test Sharing

The odds are, unless your project is very small, there will be at least several testers testing the software. Even if there are just a few, there are things you can do to get more than your eyes looking at the code.

One common approach is to simply swap test responsibilities with another tester for a few hours or a few days. Think of it as "You run my tests and I'll run yours." You'll both gain an independent look at the software while still having the basic testing tasks completed. Each of

15

you will also learn about an area of the software that you might not be familiar with—which could lead to you thinking up additional test cases to try. At a minimum, get someone else to spend time reviewing your equivalence classes and test cases. Based on their experience, they may be able to offer ideas of new and different areas to test.

A fun way to share the testing tasks is to schedule a *bug bash*. A bug bash is a period of time (usually a couple hours) in which the entire test team stops their normally assigned testing tasks to participate in the bash. In a bug bash, a specific area of the software is selected and all the testers concentrate their testing on that one area or set of features. The selection might be an area that's been especially buggy to see if there are still more problems lurking about. Or, it might be an area that's suspiciously bug free. A bug bash could determine if the bugs have been missed by normal testing or if it's just well written code. There are lots of potential criteria for choosing the area, but ultimately a bug bash gets many different people looking at one particular area of the software for bugs.

One of your greatest allies in your quest to find bugs is your product support or customer service team—the people who will talk with customers when they call or email with questions and problems. These people are obviously very sensitive to bugs and are a great resource to leverage for helping you test. Find out who will be supporting your product once it's released and ask them to participate in your test sharing activities. You'll be amazed at the bugs they'll find for you.

> **NOTE**
>
> Probably the most common class of calls that product support people take is in the area of usability problems. Many of the calls are from people simply trying to figure out how to use the software. For this reason, it's a good idea to get your product support team helping you test the product early in the design cycle to help identify and fix usability bugs.

Beta Testing

The test sharing ideas presented so far have been internal methods—that is, the people that would help you share the testing are either from your test team or the project development team. Another common method for having others verify and validate the software is a process called *beta testing*.

Beta testing is the term used to describe the external testing process in which the software is sent out to a select group of potential customers who use it in a real-world environment. Beta testing usually occurs toward the end of the product development cycle and ideally should just be a validation that the software is ready to release to real customers.

The goals of a beta test can vary considerably from getting the press to write early reviews of the software to user interface validation to a last-ditch effort in finding bugs. As a tester, you need to make it known to the person managing the beta testing what, if anything, you want to achieve from it.

From a test standpoint, there are several things to think about when planning for or relying on a beta test:

- Who are the beta testers? Since a beta test can have different goals, it's important to understand who the beta participants are. For example, you may be interested in identifying any remaining usability bugs left in the software, but the beta testers may all be experienced techies who are more concerned with the low-level operation and not usability. If your area of the software is to be beta tested, make sure that you define what types of beta testers you need in the program so that you can receive the most benefit out of it.

- Similarly, how will you know if the beta testers even use the software? If 1,000 beta testers had the software for a month and reported no problems, would that mean there were no bugs, that they saw bugs but didn't report them, or that the disks were lost in the mail? It's not uncommon for beta testers to let the software sit for days or weeks before they try to use it, and when they do, only use it for a limited time and a limited set of features. Make sure that you or someone running the beta program follows up with the participants to make sure that they're using the software and meeting the plan's goals.

- Beta tests can be a good way to find compatibility and configuration bugs. As you learned in Chapters 8, "Configuration Testing," and 9, "Compatibility Testing," it's difficult to identify and test a representative sample of all the real-world hardware and software setups. If your beta test participants have been wisely chosen to represent your target customers, they should do a good job finding configuration and compatibility problems for you.

- Usability testing is another area that beta testing can contribute to if the participants are well chosen a good mix of experienced and inexperienced users. They'll be seeing the software for the first time and will readily find anything that's confusing or difficult to use.

- Besides configuration, compatibility, and usability, beta tests are surprisingly poor ways to find bugs. The participants often don't have a lot of time to use the software, so they won't find much more than superficial, obvious problems—ones that you likely already know about. And, because beta testing usually occurs near the end of the development cycle, there's not much time to fix bugs that are found.

> **NOTE**
>
> Trying to rely on beta testing as a substitute for real testing is one of the major pit-falls of software product development. *Don't do it!* If such a process would work, why not do the same with the software design and programming?

- A beta test program can take up a lot of a tester's time. A common job for a new tester is to work with the beta customers to help solve their problems, answer their questions, and confirm the bugs they find. If you're assigned this task, you'll also need to work with your fellow testers to understand how the bugs slipped through to the beta testers and how to improve the test cases so that the bugs are found internally in the future. All this can be a full-time job, leaving little room to do any real testing yourself.

If you and your team plan on holding a beta test program, make arrangements in advance, preferably when the product's schedule is being defined. Make sure that the beta test's goals mesh with goals that you and your testing team want out of it and work closely with the person (or team) managing the beta program to keep testing's voice heard.

Beta testing can prove to be a valuable method for getting solid, independent test data back on your software, but to be effective it must be properly defined and managed—you could almost say it needs to be tested.

Outsourcing Your Testing

A common practice in many corporations is to outsource or subcontract a portion of the test work to other companies that specialize in various aspects of software testing. Although this may sound more cumbersome and more expensive than having the work done by testers on the product team, it can be an effective way to share the testing if done properly.

Configuration and compatibility testing are typically good choices for outsourcing. They usually require a large test lab containing many different hardware and software combinations and a staff of several people to manage it. Most small software companies can't afford the overhead and expense for maintaining these test labs, so it makes more sense for them to outsource this testing to companies who make it their business to perform configuration and compatibility tests.

Localization testing is another example that often lends itself to outsourcing. Unless you have a very large test team, it would be impossible to staff testers that speak all the different languages that your product supports. It would be beneficial to have a couple of foreign language speaking testers on your team to look for fundamental localization problems, but it's probably more efficient to outsource the testing of the specific languages. A company that specializes in localization testing would have testers on staff that speak many different languages who are also experienced testers.

As a new software tester, you likely won't be asked to make decisions on what testing tasks will be outsourced, but you may need to work with an outsourcing company if it's testing areas of the software that you're responsible for. The success, or failure, of the outsourcing job may well depend on you. Here's a list of things to consider and to discuss with your test manager or project manager to help make the job run more smoothly:

- What exactly are the testing tasks that the testing company is to perform? Who will define them? Who will approve them?

- What schedule will they follow? Who will set the schedule? What happens if the deadline is missed?

- What deliverables are you to provide to the testing company? The software's specification, periodic software updates, and test cases are some examples.

- What deliverables are they to provide to you? A list of the bugs they find would be the minimum.

- How will you communicate with them? Phone, email, Internet, central database, daily visit? Who are the points of contact at both ends?

- How will you know if the testing company is meeting your expectations? How will they know if they're meeting your expectations?

These aren't rocket science issues, but they're unfortunately often overlooked in the rush to outsource a testing task. Throwing software over a wall and telling a company to "just test it" is ripe for disaster. But, spending some time up-front planning the testing can make outsourcing a very effective means to perform tests that you otherwise couldn't handle because of limited resources.

Summary

What you should take away from this chapter and from Chapter 14 is that you should leverage whatever means possible to be an effective tester. One situation might dictate using technology, another might require extra people, another might need just plain old brute force manual testing. Every software testing problem will be unique, and you'll learn something new with each one. Experiment, try different approaches, watch what others do, but always strive to find the best way make your testing more efficient and more likely to locate those bugs.

This chapter wraps up the book's topics on how to perform software testing. It's been fun. You've learned about the software development process, the basic techniques for software testing, how to apply your skills, and how to supplement what you can do. In Part V, "Working with Test Documentation," you'll see how to pull together everything you've learned so far: how to plan and organize your testing tasks, how to properly record and track the bugs you find, and how to make sure those bugs get fixed.

Quiz

These quiz questions are provided for your further understanding. See Appendix A, "Answers to Quiz Questions," for the answers—but don't peek!

1. Describe the pesticide paradox and how bringing in new people to look at the software helps solve it.

2. What are a few positives to having a beta test program for your software?

3. What are a few cautions to consider with a beta test program?

4. If you're testing for a small software company, why would it be a good idea to outsource your configuration testing?

Working with Test Documentation

PART V

Nothing has really happened until it has been recorded.

—Virginia Woolf, British novelist, essayist, and critic

We have a habit in writing articles published in scientific journals to make the work as finished as possible, to cover up all the tracks, to not worry about the blind alleys or describe how you had the wrong idea at first, and so on. So there isn't any place to publish, in a dignified manner, what you actually did in order to get to do the work.

—Richard Feynman, American physicist

IN THIS PART

Planning Your Test Effort

IN THIS CHAPTER

This chapter marks the beginning of Part V, "Working with Test Documentation." The topics covered so far have given you the big picture of software testing and taught you the basics of finding bugs—where to look, how to test, and how to test efficiently. The chapters in Part V will round out your knowledge by showing you how all the tasks associated with software testing are planned, organized, and communicated to your project team.

Remember what the goal of a software tester is:

> *The goal of a software tester is to find bugs, find them as early as possible, and make sure they get fixed.*

Properly communicating and documenting the test effort with well-constructed test plans, test cases, and test reports will make it more likely that you and your fellow testers will achieve this goal.

This chapter focuses on the test plan, the most fundamental test document that you'll encounter in your work. As a new tester you likely won't be assigned to create the comprehensive test plan for your project—your test lead or manager will do that. You will, however, likely assist in its creation, and therefore need to understand what's involved in planning a test effort and what information goes into a test plan. That way, you can contribute to the planning process and use the information you learn to organize your own testing tasks. Besides, it won't be long until you're writing your own software test plans.

Highlights of this chapter include

- The purpose of test planning
- Why it's the planning, not the plan, that matters
- The areas to consider in the planning process
- What a new tester's role is with the test plan

The Goal of Test Planning

The testing process can't operate in a vacuum. Performing your testing tasks would be very difficult if the programmers wrote their code without telling you what it does, how it works, or when it will be complete. Likewise, if you and the other software testers don't communicate what you plan to test, what resources you need, and what your schedule is, your project will have little chance of succeeding. The *software test plan* is the primary means by which software testers communicate to the product development team what they intend to do.

The ANSI/IEEE Standard 829/1983 for Software Test Documentation states that the purpose of a software test plan is as follows:

To prescribe the scope, approach, resources, and schedule of the testing activities. To identify the items being tested, the features to be tested, the testing tasks to be performed, the personnel responsible for each task, and the risks associated with the plan.

If you read that definition and the ANSI/IEEE standard, notice that the form the test plan takes is a written document. That shouldn't be too surprising, but it's an important point because although the end result is a piece of paper (or online document or Web page), that paper isn't what the test plan is all about.

> *The test plan is simply a by-product of the detailed planning process that's undertaken to create it. It's the planning process that matters, not the resulting document.*

The title of this chapter is "Planning Your Test Effort," not "Writing Your Test Plan." The distinction is intentional. Too often a written test plan ends up as *shelfware*—a document that sits on a shelf, never to be read. If the purpose of the planning effort is flipped from the creation of a document to the process of creating it, from writing a test plan to planning the testing tasks, the shelfware problem disappears.

This isn't to say that a final test plan document that describes and summarizes the results of the planning process is unnecessary. To the contrary, there still needs to be a test plan for reference and archiving—and in some industries it's required by law. What's important is that the plan is the by-product of, not the fundamental reason for, the planning process.

> *The ultimate goal of the test planning process is communicating (not recording) the software test team's intent, its expectations, and its understanding of the testing that's to be performed.*

If you spend time with your project team working through the topics presented in the remainder of this chapter, making sure that everyone has been informed and understands what the test team is planning to do, you'll go a long way in meeting this goal.

Test Planning Topics

Many software testing books present a test plan template or a sample test plan that you can easily modify to create your own project-specific test plan. The problem with this approach is that it makes it too easy to put the emphasis on the document, not the planning process. Test leads and managers of large software projects have been known to take an electronic copy of a test plan template or an existing test plan, spend a few hours cutting, copying, pasting, searching, and replacing, and turn out a "unique" test plan for their project. They felt they had done a great thing, creating in a few hours what other testers had taken weeks or months to create. They missed the point, though, and their project showed it when no one on the product team knew what the heck the testers were doing or why.

For that reason, you won't see a test plan template in this book. What follows, instead, is a list of important topics that should be thoroughly discussed, understood, and agreed to among your entire project team—including all the testers. The list may not map perfectly to all projects, but because it's a list of common and important test-related concerns, it's likely more applicable than a test plan template. By its nature, planning is a very dynamic process, so if you find yourself in a situation where the listed topics don't apply, feel free to adjust them to fit.

Of course, the result of the test planning process will be a document of some sort. The format may be predefined—if the industry or the company has a standard. The *ANSI/IEEE Standard 829/1983 for Software Test Documentation* suggests a common form. Otherwise, the format will be up to your team and should be what's most effective in communicating the fruits of your work.

High-Level Expectations

The first topics to address in the planning process are the ones that define the test team's high-level expectations. They're fundamental topics that must be agreed to by everyone on the project team, but they're often overlooked. They might be considered "too obvious" and assumed to be understood by everyone—but a good tester knows never to assume anything!

- What's the purpose of the test planning process and the software test plan? You know the reasons for test planning—okay, you will soon—but do the programmers know, do the technical writers know, does management know? More importantly, do they agree with and support the test planning process?

- What product is being tested? Of course you believe it's the Ginsumatic v8.0, but is it, for sure? Is this v8.0 release planned to be a complete rewrite or a just a maintenance update? Is it one standalone program or thousands of pieces? Is it being developed in house or by a third party? And what is a Ginsumatic anyway?

  For the test effort to be successful, there must be a complete understanding of what the product is, its magnitude, and its scope. The product description taken from the specification is a good start, but you might be surprised if you show it to several people on the team. It wouldn't be the first programmer who proclaims, "The code I'm writing won't do that!"

- What are the quality and reliability goals of the product? This area generates lots of discussion, but it's imperative that everyone agrees to what these goals are. A sales rep will tell you that the software needs to be as fast as possible. A programmer will say that it needs to have the coolest technology. Product support will tell you that it can't have any crashing bugs. They can't all be right. How do you measure fast and cool? And how do you tell the product support engineer that the software *will* ship with crashing bugs? Your team will be testing the product's quality and reliability, so you need to know what your target is; otherwise, how will you know if the software is hitting it?

A result of the test planning process must be a clear, concise, agreed-on definition of the product's quality and reliability goals. The goals must be absolutes so that there's no dispute on whether they were achieved. If the salespeople want fast, have them define the benchmark—able to process 1 million transactions per second or twice as fast as competitor XYZ running similar tasks. If the programmers want whiz-bang technology, state exactly what the technology is and remember, gratuitous technology is a bug. As for bugs, you can't guarantee that they'll all be found—you know that's impossible. You can state, however, that the goal is for the test automation monkey to run 24 hours without crashing or that all test cases will be run without finding a new bug, and so on. Be specific. As the product's release date approaches, there should be no disagreement about what the quality and reliability goals are. Everyone should know.

People, Places, and Things

Test planning needs to identify the people working on the project, what they do, and how to contact them. If it's a small project this may seem unnecessary, but even small projects can have team members scattered across long distances or undergo personnel changes that make tracking who does what difficult. A large team might have dozens or hundreds of points of contact. The test team will likely work with all of them and knowing who they are and how to contact them is very important. The test plan should include names, titles, addresses, phone numbers, email addresses, and areas of responsibility for all key people on the project.

Similarly, where documents are stored (what shelf the test plan is sitting on), where the software can be downloaded from, where the test tools are located, and so on need to be identified. Think email aliases, servers, and Web site addresses.

If hardware is necessary for running the tests, where is it stored and how is it obtained? If there are external test labs for configuration testing, where are they located and how are they scheduled?

This topic is best described as "pointers to everything that a new tester would ask about." It's often a good test planning area for a new tester to be responsible for. As you find the answers to all your questions, simply record what you discover. What you want to know is probably what everyone will want to know, too.

Definitions

Getting everyone on the project team to agree with the high-level quality and reliability goals is a difficult task. Unfortunately, those terms are only the beginning of the words and concepts that need to be defined for a software project. Recall the definition of a bug from Chapter 1, "Software Testing Background":

1. The software doesn't do something that the product specification says it should do.

2. The software does something that the product specification says it shouldn't do.

3. The software does something that the product specification doesn't mention.

4. The software doesn't do something that the product specification doesn't mention but should.

Would you say that every person on the team knows, understands, and—more importantly—agrees with that definition? Does the project manager know what your goal as a software tester is? If not, the test planning process should work to make sure they do.

This is one of the largest problems that occurs within a project team—the ignorance of what common terms mean as they apply to the project being developed. The programmers think a term means one thing, the testers another, management another. Imagine the contention that would occur if the programmers and testers didn't have the same understanding of something as fundamental as what a bug is.

The test planning process is where the words and terms used by the team members are defined. Differences need to be identified and consensus obtained to ensure that everyone is on the same page.

Here's a list of a few common terms and very loose definitions. Don't take the list to be complete nor the definitions to be fact. They are very dependent on what the project is, the development model the team is following, and the experience level of the people on the team. The terms are listed only to start you thinking about what should be defined for your projects and to show you how important it is for everyone to know the meanings.

- **Build.** A compilation of code and content that the programmers put together to be tested. The test plan should define the frequency of builds (daily, weekly) and the expected quality level.

- **Test release document (TRD).** A document that the programmers release with each build stating what's new, different, fixed, and ready for testing.

- **Alpha release.** A very early build intended for limited distribution to a few key customers and to marketing for demonstration purposes. It's not intended to be used in a real-world situation. The exact contents and quality level must be understood by everyone who will use the alpha release.

- **Beta release.** The formal build intended for widespread distribution to potential customers. Remember from Chapter 15, "Bug Bashes and Beta Testing," that the specific reasons for doing the beta need to be defined.

- **Spec complete.** A schedule date when the specification is supposedly complete and will no longer change. After you work on a few projects, you may think that this date occurs only in fiction books, but it really should be set, with the specification only undergoing minor and controlled changes after that.

- **Feature complete.** A schedule date when the programmers will stop adding new features to the code and concentrate on fixing bugs.

- **Bug committee.** A group made up of the test manager, project manager, development manager, and product support manager that meets weekly to review the bugs and determine which ones to fix and how they should be fixed. The bug committee is one of the primary users of the quality and reliability goals set forth in the test plan.

Inter-Group Responsibilities

Inter-group responsibilities identify tasks and deliverables that potentially affect the test effort. The test team's work is driven by many other functional groups—programmers, project managers, technical writers, and so on. If the responsibilities aren't planned out, the project—specifically the testing—can become a comedy show of "I've got it, no, you take it, didn't you handle, no, I thought you did," resulting in important tasks being forgotten.

The types of tasks that need to be defined aren't the obvious ones—testers test, programmers program. The troublesome tasks potentially have multiple owners or sometimes no owner or a shared responsibility. The easiest way to plan these and communicate the plan is with a simple table (see Figure 16.1).

The tasks run down the left side and the possible owners are across the top. An × denotes the owner of a task and a dash (—) indicates a contributor. A blank means that the group has nothing to do with the task.

Deciding which tasks to list comes with experience. Ideally, several senior members of the team can make a good first pass at a list, but each project is different and will have its own unique inter-group responsibilities and dependencies. A good place to start is to question people about past projects and what they can remember of neglected tasks.

What Will and Won't Be Tested

You might be surprised to find that everything included with a software product isn't necessarily tested. There may be components of the software that were previously released and have already been tested. Content may be taken as is from another software company. An outsourcing company may supply pre-tested portions of the product.

Task	Program Management	Programmers	Test	Tech Writers	Marketing	Product Support
Write vision statement for product	---				X	
Create list of product components	X					
Create Contracts	X				---	
Product design/features	X			---	---	
Master project schedule	X	---		---	---	
Produce and maintain product spec	X					
Review product spec	---	---	---	---	---	---
Internal product architecture	---	X				
Design and code product		X				
Test planning			X			
Review test plan		---	X	---	---	---
Unit testing		X				
General testing			X			
Create configuration list		---	X		---	---
Config testing			X			
Define performance benchmarks	X		---			
Run benchmark tests			X			
Content testing			---	X		
Test code from external groups			---			
Automate/maintain build process		X				
Disk building/duplication		X				
Disk QA			X			
Create beta list					X	---
Manage beta program	---		---		X	---
Review printed material	---	---	---	X	---	---
Define demo version	---				X	
Produce demo version	---				X	
Test demo version			X			
Bug Committee	X	---	---		---	---

FIGURE 16.1

Use a table to help organize inter-group responsibilities.

The planning process needs to identify each component of the software and make known whether it will be tested. If it's not tested, there needs to be a reason it won't be covered. It would be a disaster if a piece of code slipped through the development cycle completely untested because of a misunderstanding.

Test Phases

To plan the test phases, the test team will look at the proposed development model and decide whether unique phases, or stages, of testing should be performed over the course of the project. In a code-and-fix model, there's probably only one test phase—test until someone yells stop. In the waterfall and spiral models, there can be several test phases from examining the product spec to acceptance testing. Yes, test planning is one of the test phases.

The test planning process should identify each proposed test phase and make each phase known to the project team. This process often helps the entire team form and understand the overall development model.

NOTE

Two very important concepts associated with the test phases are the entrance and exit criteria. The test team can't just walk in to work on Monday morning, look at the calendar and see that they're now in the next phase. Each phase must have criteria defined for it that objectively and absolutely declares if the phase is over and the next one has begun.

For example, the spec review stage might be over when the minutes to the formal spec review have been published. The beta test stage might begin when the testers have completed an acceptance test pass with no new bugs found on the proposed beta release build.

Without explicit entrance and exit criteria, the test effort will dissolve into single, undirected test effort—much like the code-and-fix development model.

Test Strategy

An exercise associated with defining the test phases is defining the test strategy. The test strategy describes the approach that the test team will use to test the software both overall and in each phase. Think back to what you've learned so far about software testing. If you were presented with a product to test, you'd need to decide if it's better to use black-box testing or white-box testing. If you decide to use a mix of both techniques, when will you apply each and to which parts of the software?

It might be a good idea to test some of the code manually and other code with tools and automation. If tools will be used, do they need to be developed or can existing commercial solutions be purchased? If so, which ones? Maybe it would be more efficient to outsource the entire test effort to a specialized testing company and require only a skeleton testing crew to oversee their work.

Deciding on the strategy is a complex task—one that needs to be made by very experienced testers because it can determine the success or failure of the test effort. It's vitally important for everyone on the project team to understand and be in agreement with the proposed plan.

Resource Requirements

Planning the resource requirements is the process of deciding what's necessary to accomplish the testing strategy. Everything that could possibly be used for testing over the course of the project needs to be considered. For example:

- **People.** How many, what experience, what expertise? Should they be full-time, part-time, contract, students?
- **Equipment.** Computers, test hardware, printers, tools.
- **Office and lab space.** Where will they be located? How big will they be? How will they be arranged?
- **Software.** Word processors, databases, custom tools. What will be purchased, what needs to be written?
- **Outsource companies.** Will they be used? What criteria will be used for choosing them? How much will they cost?
- **Miscellaneous supplies.** Disks, phones, reference books, training material. What else might be necessary over the course of the project?

The specific resource requirements are very project-, team-, and company-dependent, so the test plan effort will need to carefully evaluate what will be needed to test the software. It's often difficult or even impossible to obtain resources late in the project that weren't budgeted for at the beginning, so it's imperative to be thorough when creating the list.

Tester Assignments

Once the test phases, test strategy, and resource requirements are defined, that information can be used with the product spec to break out the individual tester assignments. The *inter*-group responsibilities discussed earlier dealt with what functional group (management, test, programmers, and so on) is responsible for what high-level tasks. Planning the tester assignments identifies the testers (this means you) responsible for each area of the software and for each testable feature. Table 16.1 shows a greatly simplified example of a tester assignments table for Windows WordPad.

TABLE 16.1   High-Level Tester Assignments for WordPad

Tester	Test Assignments
Al	Character formatting: fonts, size, color, style
Sarah	Layout: bullets, paragraphs, tabs, wrapping
Luis	Configuration and compatibility
Jolie	UI: usability, appearance, accessibility
Valerie	Documentation: online help, rollover help
Ron	Stress and load

A real-world responsibilities table would go into much more detail to assure that every part of the software has someone assigned to test it. Each tester would know exactly what they were responsible for and have enough information to go off and start designing test cases.

Test Schedule

The test schedule takes all the information presented so far and maps it into the overall project schedule. This stage is often critical in the test planning effort because a few highly desired features that were thought to be easy to design and code may turn out to be very time consuming to test. An example would be a program that does no printing except in one limited, obscure area. No one may realize the testing impact that printing has, but keeping that feature in the product could result in weeks of printer configuration testing time. Completing a test schedule as part of test planning will provide the product team and project manager with the information needed to better schedule the overall project. They may even decide, based on the testing schedule, to cut certain features from the product or postpone them to a later release.

An important consideration with test planning is that the amount of test work typically isn't distributed evenly over the entire product development cycle. Some testing occurs early in the form of spec and code reviews, tool development, and so on, but the number of testing tasks and the number of people and amount of time spent testing often increases over the course of the project, with the peak being a short time before the product is released. Figure 16.2 shows what a typical test resource graph may look like.

The effect of this gradual increase is that the test schedule is increasingly influenced by what happens earlier in the project. If some part of the project is delivered to the test group two weeks late and only three weeks were scheduled for testing, what happens? Does the three weeks of testing now have to occur in only one week or does the project get delayed two weeks? This problem is known as *schedule crunch*.

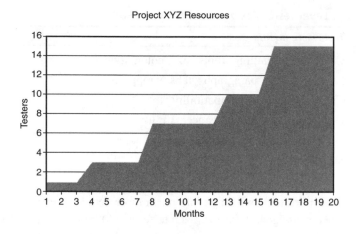

FIGURE 16.2

The amount of test resources on a project typically increases over the course of the development schedule.

One way to help keep the testing tasks from being crunched is for the test schedule to avoid absolute dates for starting and stopping tasks. Table 16.2 is a test schedule that would surely get the team into a schedule crunch.

TABLE 16.2   A Test Schedule Based on Fixed Dates

Testing Task	Date
Test Plan Complete	3/5/2001
Test Cases Complete	6/1/2001
Test Pass #1	6/15/2001–8/1/2001
Test Pass #2	8/15/2001–10/1/2001
Test Pass #3	10/15/2001–11/15/2001

If the test schedule instead uses relative dates based on the entrance and exit criteria defined by the testing phases, it becomes clearer that the testing tasks rely on some other deliverables being completed first. It's also more apparent how much time the individual tasks take. Table 16.3 shows an example of this.

TABLE 16.3   A Test Schedule Based on Relative Dates

Testing Task	Start Date	Duration
Test Plan Complete	7 days after spec complete	4 weeks
Test Cases Complete	Test plan complete	12 weeks
Test Pass #1	Code complete build	6 weeks
Test Pass #2	Beta build	6 weeks
Test Pass #3	Release build	4 weeks

Many software scheduling products will make this process easier to manage. Your project manager or test manager is ultimately responsible for the schedule and will likely use such software, but you will be asked to contribute to it to schedule your specific tasks.

Test Cases

You already know what test cases are from what you've learned in this book. Chapter 17, "Writing and Tracking Test Cases," will go further into detail about them. The test planning process will decide what approach will be used to write them, where the test cases will be stored, and how they'll be used and maintained.

Bug Reporting

Chapter 18, "Reporting What You Find," will describe the techniques that can be used to record and track the bugs you find. The possibilities range from shouting over a cubical wall to sticky notes to complex bug-tracking databases. Exactly what process will be used to manage the bugs needs to be planned so that each and every bug is tracked from when it's found to when it's fixed—and never, ever forgotten.

Metrics and Statistics

Metrics and statistics are the means by which the progress and the success of the project, and the testing, are tracked. They're discussed in detail in Chapter 19, "Measuring Your Success." The test planning process should identify exactly what information will be gathered, what decisions will be made with them, and who will be responsible for collecting them.

Examples of test metrics that might be useful are

- Total bugs found daily over the course of the project
- List of bugs that still need to be fixed
- Current bugs ranked by how severe they are

- Total bugs found per tester
- Number of bugs found per software feature or area

Risks and Issues

A common and very useful part of test planning is to identify potential problem or risky areas of the project—ones that could have an impact on the test effort.

Suppose that you and 10 other new testers, whose total software test experience was reading this book, were assigned to test the software for a new nuclear power plant. That would be a risk. Maybe no one realizes that some new software has to be tested against 1,500 modems and there's no time in the project schedule for it. Another risk.

As a software tester, you'll be responsible for identifying risks during the planning process and communicating your concerns to your manager and the project manager. These risks will be identified in the software test plan and accounted for in the schedule. Some will come true, others will turn out to be benign. The important thing is to identify them early so that they don't appear as a surprise late in the project.

Summary

Developing a test plan, even for a small project, is a large task that can't be taken lightly. Sure, it would be easy to fill in a template's blanks and in a few hours be printing out copies of a test plan, but that's missing the point. Test planning is a job that should involve all testers and key players from across the entire product team. Taking the time to do it properly may take many weeks or even months. But, building a comprehensive understanding and an agreement of what's to be tested, why it's to be tested, and how it's to be tested early in the product development cycle will make the test effort run much more smoothly than if the process is rushed.

If you're new to testing—and you probably are if you're reading this book—you likely won't be responsible for developing an overall software test plan. You should, however, be prepared to provide input on all the topics presented in this chapter to your test lead or manager. You'll be responsible for testing certain aspects and features of the software; the schedule you make, the resources you need, and the risks you take will all eventually bubble up to the master test plan.

Quiz

These quiz questions are provided for your further understanding. See Appendix A, "Answers to Quiz Questions," for the answers—but don't peek!

1. What's the purpose of a test plan?

2. Why is it the process of creating the plan that matters, not the plan itself?

3. Why is defining the software's quality and reliability goals an important part of test planning?

4. What are entrance and exit criteria?

5. Name a few typical testing resources that should be considered when test planning.

6. **True or False:** A schedule should be made to meet absolute dates so that there's no question when a testing task or phase is to start and when it is to end.

Writing and Tracking Test Cases

IN THIS CHAPTER

In Chapter 16, "Planning Your Test Effort," you learned about the test planning process and the creation of a project test plan. The details and information that the test plan communicates are necessary for the project to succeed, but they are a bit abstract and high level for an individual tester's day-to-day testing activities.

The next step down in the test planning process, writing and tracking test cases, is one that more directly influences your typical tasks as a software tester. Initially you may be involved only in running test cases that someone else has written, but you'll very soon be writing them for yourself and for other testers to use. This chapter will teach you how to effectively develop and manage those test cases to make your testing go as efficiently as possible.

Highlights of this chapter include

- Why writing and tracking test cases is important
- What a test design specification is
- What a test case specification is
- How test procedures should be written
- How test cases should be organized

The Goals of Test Case Planning

The early chapters of this book discussed the different software development models and the various testing techniques that can be used, based on those models, to perform effective testing. In a big-bang or code-and-fix model, the testers are at the mercy of the project, often having to guess what testing to perform and whether what they find are indeed bugs. In the more disciplined development models, testing becomes a bit easier because there's formal documentation such as product specs and design specs. The software creation—the design, architecture, and programming—becomes a true process, not just a chaotic race to get a product out the door. Testing in that environment is much more efficient and predictable.

There's the old saying, "What's good for the goose is good for the gander," meaning what's beneficial to one person or group is also beneficial to another. Hopefully, from what you've learned so far, you would think it's heresy for a programmer to take the product spec and immediately start coding without developing a more detailed plan and distributing it for review. A tester, then, taking the test plan and instantly sitting down to think up test cases and begin testing should seem just as wrong. If software testers expect the project managers and the programmers to be more disciplined, instill some methods, and follow some rules to make the development process run more smoothly, they should also expect to do the same.

Carefully and methodically planning test cases is a step in that direction. Doing so is very important for four reasons:

- **Organization.** Even on small software projects it's possible to have many thousands of test cases. The cases may have been created by several testers over the course of several months or even years. Proper planning will organize them so that all the testers and other project team members can review and use them effectively.

- **Repeatability.** As you've learned, it's necessary over the course of a project to run the same tests several times to look for new bugs and to make sure that old ones have been fixed. Without proper planning, it would be impossible to know what test cases were last run and exactly how they were run so that you could repeat the exact tests.

- **Tracking.** Similarly, you need to answer important questions over the course of a project. How many test cases did you plan to run? How many did you run on the last software release? How many passed and how many failed? Were any test cases skipped? And so on. If no planning went into the test cases, it would be impossible to answer these questions.

- **Proof of testing (or not testing).** In a few high-risk industries, the software test team must prove that it did indeed run the tests that it planned to run. It could actually be illegal, and dangerous, to release software in which a few test cases were skipped. Proper test case planning and tracking provides a means for proving what was tested.

> **NOTE**
>
> Don't confuse test case planning with the identification of test cases that you learned in Part II, "Testing Fundamentals." Those chapters taught you how to test and how to select test cases, similar to teaching a programmer how to program in a specific language. Test case planning is the next step up and is similar to a programmer learning how to perform high-level design and properly document his work.

Ad Hoc Testing

One type of software testing, called *ad hoc testing*, describes performing tests without a real plan—no test case planning and sometimes not even a high-level test plan. With ad hoc testing, a tester sits down with the software and starts banging the keys. Some people are naturally good at this and can find bugs right away. It may look impressive and may have some value as a supplement to planned tests—for example, in a bug bash—but it's not organized, it's not repeatable, it can't be tracked, and when it's complete, there's no proof that it was ever done. As a tester you don't want code that was written in an ad hoc manner, nor do your customers want software that was tested exclusively in an ad hoc manner.

Test Case Planning Overview

So where exactly does test case planning fit into the grand scheme of testing? Figure 17.1 shows the relationships among the different types of test plans.

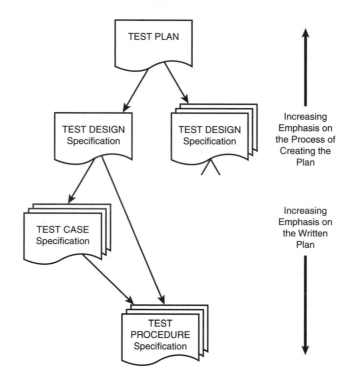

FIGURE 17.1
The different levels of test plans all interact and vary on whether their importance is the plan itself or the process of creating it.

You're already familiar with the top, or project level, test plan and know that the process of creating it is more important than the resulting document. The next three levels, the *test design specification*, the *test case specification*, and the *test procedure specification* are described in detail in the following sections.

As you can see in Figure 17.1, moving further away from the top-level test plan puts less emphasis on the process of creation and more on the resulting written document. The reason is that these plans become useful on a daily, sometimes hourly, basis by the testers performing

Writing and Tracking Test Cases

CHAPTER 17

271

17

WRITING AND
TRACKING TEST
CASES

the testing. As you'll learn, at the lowest level they become step-by-step instructions for executing a test, making it key that they're clear, concise, and organized—how they got that way isn't nearly as important.

The information presented in this chapter is adapted from the *ANSI/IEEE Std 829-1983 Standard for Software Test Documentation* (available from http://standards.ieee.org). This standard is what many testing teams have adopted as their test planning documentation—intentional or not—because it represents a logical and common-sense method for test planning. The important thing to realize about this standard is that unless you're bound to follow it to the letter because of the type of software you're testing or by your corporate or industry policy, you should use it as a guideline and not a standard. The information it contains and approaches it recommends are as valid today as they were when the standard was written in 1983. But, what used to work best as a written document is often better and more efficiently presented today as a spreadsheet or a database. You'll see an example of this later in the chapter.

The bottom line is that you and your test team should create test plans that cover the information outlined in ANSI/IEEE 829. If paper printouts work best (which would be hard to believe), by all means use them. If, however, you think a central database is more efficient and your team has the time and budget to develop or buy one, you should go with that approach. Ultimately it doesn't matter. What does matter is that when you've completed your work, you've met the four goals of test case planning: organization, repeatability, tracking, and proof.

Test Design

The overall project test plan is written at a very high level. It breaks out the software into specific features and testable items and assigns them to individual testers, but it doesn't specify exactly how those features will be tested. There may be a general mention of using automation or black-box or white-box testing, but the test plan doesn't get into the details of exactly where and how they will be used. This next level of detail that defines the testing approach for individual software features is the test design specification.

ANSI/IEEE 829 states that the test design specification "refines the test approach [defined in the test plan] and identifies the features to be covered by the design and its associated tests. It also identifies the test cases and test procedures, if any, required to accomplish the testing and specifies the feature pass/fail criteria."

The purpose of the test design spec is to organize and describe the testing that needs to be performed on a specific feature. It doesn't, however, give the detailed cases or the steps to execute to perform the testing. The following topics, adapted from the ANSI/IEEE 829 standard, address this purpose and should be part of the test design specs that you create:

- **Identifiers.** A unique identifier that can be used to reference and locate the test design spec. The spec should also reference the overall test plan and contain pointers to any other plans or specs that it references.

- **Features to be tested.** A description of the software feature covered by the test design spec—for example, "the addition function of Calculator," "font size selection and display in WordPad," and "video card configuration testing of QuickTime."

  This section should also identify features that may be indirectly tested as a side effect of testing the primary feature. For example, "Although not the target of this plan, the UI of the file open dialog box will be indirectly tested in the process of testing the load and save functionality."

  It should also list features that won't be tested, ones that may be misconstrued as being covered by this plan. For example, "Because testing Calculator's addition function will be performed with automation by sending keystrokes to the software, there will be no indirect testing of the onscreen UI. The UI testing is addressed in a separate test design plan—CalcUI12345."

- **Approach.** A description of the general approach that will be used to test the features. It should expand on the approach, if any, listed in the test plan, describe the technique to be used, and explain how the results will be verified.

  For example, "A testing tool will be developed to sequentially load and save pre-built data files of various sizes. The number of data files, the sizes, and the data they contain will be determined through black-box techniques and supplemented with white-box examples from the programmer. A pass or fail will be determined by comparing the saved file bit-for-bit against the original using a file compare tool."

- **Test case identification.** A high-level description and references to the specific test cases that will be used to check the feature. It should list the selected equivalence partitions and provide references to the test cases and test procedures used to run them. For example,

  Check the highest possible value   Test Case ID# 15326

  Check the lowest possible value   Test Case ID# 15327

  Check several interim powers of 2   Test Case ID# 15328

  It's important that the actual test case values aren't defined in this section. For someone reviewing the test design spec for proper test coverage, a description of the equivalence partitions is much more useful than the specific values themselves.

- **Pass/fail criteria.** Describes exactly what constitutes a pass and a fail of the tested feature. This may be very simple and clear—a pass is when all the test cases are run without finding a bug. It can also be fuzzy—a failure is when 10 percent or more of the test cases fail. There should be no doubt, though, what constitutes a pass or a fail of the feature.

Yes, a Crash Is a Failure

I was involved in a project that used an outsourced testing company for configuration testing of a multimedia program. They weren't the best choice but were the only ones available at the time. To make sure the job went smoothly, detailed test design specs, test case specs, and test procedures were submitted to the testing company so that there would be no question as to what would and wouldn't be tested.

Several weeks passed and the testing seemed to be going smoothly—*too* smoothly— when one day the lead tester on the project called. He reported on what his team had found for the week, which wasn't much, and just before hanging up asked if he should be reporting bugs on things that weren't listed in the documentation. When asked why, he said that since the first day they started testing his team had occasionally seen these big white boxes that said something about a "general protection fault." They would dismiss them but eventually their PC screens would turn bright blue with another cryptic serious failure error message and they would be forced to reboot their machines. Since that specific error wasn't listed as one of the fail criteria, he wasn't sure if it was important and thought he should check.

Test Cases

Chapters 4 through 7 described the fundamentals of software testing—dissecting a specification, code, and software to derive the minimal amount of test cases that would effectively test the software. What wasn't discussed in those chapters is how to record and document the cases you create. If you've already started doing some software testing, you've likely experimented with different ideas and formats. This section on documenting test cases will give you a few more options to consider.

ANSI/IEEE 829 states that the test case specification "documents the actual values used for input along with the anticipated outputs. A test case also identifies any constraints on the test procedure resulting from use of that specific test case."

Essentially, the details of a test case should explain exactly what values or conditions will be sent to the software and what result is expected. It can be referenced by one or more test design specs and may reference more than one test procedure. The ANSI/IEEE 829 standard also lists some other important information that should be included:

- **Identifiers.** A unique identifier is referenced by the test design specs and the test procedure specs.

- **Test item.** This describes the detailed feature, code module, and so on that's being tested. It should be more specific than the features listed in the test design spec. If the test design spec said "the addition function of Calculator," the test case spec would say "upper limit overflow handling of addition calculations." It should also provide references to product specifications or other design docs from which the test case was based.

- **Input specification.** This specification lists all the inputs or conditions given to the software to execute the test case. If you're testing Calculator, this may be as simple as 1+1. If you're testing cellular telephone switching software, there could be hundreds or thousands of input conditions. If you're testing a file-based product, it would be the name of the file and a description of its contents.

- **Output specification.** This describes the result you expect from executing the test case. Did 1+1 equal 2? Were the thousands of output variables set correctly in the cell software? Did all the contents of the file load as expected?

- **Environmental needs.** Environmental needs are the hardware, software, test tools, facilities, staff, and so on that are necessary to run the test case.

- **Special procedural requirements.** This section describes anything unusual that must be done to perform the test. Testing WordPad probably doesn't need anything special, but testing nuclear power plant software might.

- **Intercase dependencies.** Chapter 1, "Software Testing Background," included a description of a bug that caused NASA's Mars Polar Lander to crash on Mars. It's a perfect example of an undocumented intercase dependency. If a test case depends on another test case or might be affected by another, that information should go here.

Are you panicked yet? If you follow this suggested level of documentation to the letter, you could be writing at least a page of descriptive text for each test case you identify! Thousands of test cases could take thousands of pages of documentation. The project could be outdated by the time you finish writing.

This is another reason why you should take the ANSI/IEEE 829 standard as a guideline and not follow it to the letter—unless you have to. Many government projects and certain industries are required to document their test cases to this level, but in most other instances you can take some shortcuts.

Taking a shortcut doesn't mean dismissing or neglecting important information—it means figuring out a way to condense the information into a more efficient means of communicating it. For example, there's no reason that you're limited to presenting test cases in written paragraph form. Figure 17.2 shows an example of a printer compatibility matrix.

Test Case ID	Printer Mfg	Model	Mode	Options
WP0001	Canon	BJC-7000	B/W	Text
WP0002	Canon	BJC-7000	B/W	Superphoto
WP0003	Canon	BJC-7000	B/W	Auto
WP0004	Canon	BJC-7000	B/W	Draft
WP0005	Canon	BJC-7000	Color	Text
WP0006	Canon	BJC-7000	Color	Superphoto
WP0007	Canon	BJC-7000	Color	Auto
WP0008	Canon	BJC-7000	Color	Draft
WP0009	HP	LaserJet IV	High	
WP0010	HP	LaserJet IV	Medium	
WP0011	HP	LaserJet IV	Low	

FIGURE 17.2

Test cases can be presented in the form of matrix or table.

Each line of the matrix is a specific test case and has its own identifier. All the other information that goes with a test case—test item, input spec, output spec, environmental needs, special requirements, and dependencies—are most likely common to all these cases and could be written once and attached to the table. Someone reviewing your test cases could quickly read that information and then review the table to check its coverage.

Other options for presenting test cases are simple lists, outlines, or even graphical diagrams such as state tables or data flow diagrams. Remember, you're trying to communicate your test cases to others and should use whichever method is most effective. Be creative, but stay true to the purpose of documenting your test cases.

Test Procedures

After you document the test designs and test cases, what remains are the procedures that need to be followed to execute the test cases. ANSI/IEEE 829 states that the *test procedure* specification "identifies all the steps required to operate the system and exercise the specified test cases in order to implement the associated test design."

The test procedure or *test script* spec defines the step-by-step details of exactly how to perform the test cases. Here's the information that needs to be defined:

- **Identifier.** A unique identifier that ties the test procedure to the associated test cases and test design.
- **Purpose.** The purpose of the procedure and reference to the test cases that it will execute.
- **Special requirements.** Other procedures, special testing skills, or special equipment needed to run the procedure.
- **Procedure steps.** Detailed description of how the tests are to be run:

- **Log.** Tells how and by what method the results and observations will be recorded.
- **Setup.** Explains how to prepare for the test.
- **Start.** Explains the steps used to start the test.
- **Procedure.** Describes the steps used to run the tests.
- **Measure.** Describes how the results are to be determined—for example, with a stopwatch or visual determination.
- **Shut down.** Explains the steps for suspending the test for unexpected reasons.
- **Restart.** Tells the tester how to pick up the test at a certain point if there's a failure or after shutting down.
- **Stop.** Describes the steps for an orderly halt to the test.
- **Wrap up.** Explains how to restore the environment to its pre-test condition.
- **Contingencies.** Explains what to do if things don't go as planned.

It's not sufficient for a test procedure to just say, "Try all the following test cases and report back on what you see…." That would be simple and easy but wouldn't tell a new tester anything about how to perform the testing. It wouldn't be repeatable and there'd be no way to prove what steps were executed. Using a detailed procedure makes known exactly what will be tested and how. Figure 17.3 shows an excerpt from a fictional example of a test procedure for Windows Calculator.

Detail versus Reality

An old saying, "Do everything in moderation," applies perfectly well to test case planning. Remember the four goals: organization, repeatability, tracking, and proof. As a software tester developing test cases, you need to work toward these goals—but their level is determined by your industry, your company, your project, and your team. It's unlikely that you'll need to document your test cases down to the greatest level of detail and, hopefully, you won't be working on an ad hoc seat-of-your-pants project where you don't need to document anything at all. Odds are, your work will lie somewhere in between.

The trick is finding the right level of moderation. Consider the test procedure shown in Figure 17.3 that requires Windows 98 to be installed on a PC to run the tests. The procedure states in its setup section that Windows 98 is required—but it doesn't state what version of Windows 98. What happens in a year or two when the next version comes out? Does the test procedure need to be updated to reflect the change? To avoid this problem, the version could be omitted and replaced with "latest available," but then what happens if a new release comes out during the product cycle? Should the tester switch OS releases in the middle of the project?

Identifier: WinCalcProc98.1872

Purpose: This procedure describes the steps necessary to execute the Addition function test cases WinCalc98.0051 through WinCalc98.0185.

Special Requirements: No special hardware or software is required to run this procedure other than what is outlined in the individual test cases.

Procedure Steps:

    Log: The tester will use WordPad with the Testlog template as the means for taking notes while performing this procedure. All the fields marked as required must be filled in. The Mantis bug tracking system will be used to record any problems found while running the procedure.

    Setup: The tester must install a clean copy of Windows 98 on his or her machine prior to running this procedure. Use the test tools WipeDisk and Clone before installing the latest version of Windows 98. Refer to the test support doc titled "Starting Fresh" for more information on these tools.

    Start:
        Boot up Windows 98.
        Click the Start Button.
        Select Programs.
        Select Accessories.
        Select Calculator.

    Procedure: For each test case identified above, enter the test input data using the keyboard (not the onscreen numbers) and compare the results to the specified output.

    Measure: …

FIGURE 17.3
A fictional example of a test procedure shows how much detail can be involved.

Another issue is that the procedure tells the tester to simply install a "clean copy" of Win98. What does clean copy mean? The procedure lists a couple of tools, WipeDisk and Clone, to be used in the setup process and refers the tester to a document that explains how to use them. Should the procedure steps be more detailed and explain exactly where to obtain this other document and these tools? If you've ever installed an operating system, you know it's a complex process that requires the installer to answer many questions and decide on many options. Should this procedure or a related procedure go into that level of detail? If it doesn't, how can it be known what configuration the tests were run on? If it does, and the installation process changes, there could be hundreds of test procedures to update. What a mess.

Unfortunately, there is no single, right answer. Highly detailed test case specs reduce ambiguity, make tests perfectly repeatable, and allow inexperienced testers to execute tests exactly as they were intended. On the other hand, writing test case specs to this level takes considerably more time and effort, can make updates difficult, and, because of all the details, bog down the test effort, causing it to take much longer to run.

When you start writing test cases, your best bet is to adopt the standards of the project you're working on. If you're testing a new medical device, your procedures will most likely need to be much more detailed than if you're testing a video game. If you're involved in setting up or recommending how the test design, test cases, and test procedures will be written for a new project, review the formats defined by the ANSI/IEEE 829 standard, try some examples, and see what works best for you, your team, and your project.

Test Case Organization and Tracking

One consideration that you should take into account when creating the test case documentation is how the information will be organized and tracked. Think about the questions that a tester or the test team should be able to answer:

- Which test cases do you plan to run?
- How many test cases do you plan to run? How long will it take to run them?
- Can you pick and choose *test suites* (groups of related test cases) to run on particular features or areas of the software?
- When you run the cases, will you be able to record which ones pass and which ones fail?
- Of the ones that failed, which ones also failed the last time you ran them?
- What percentage of the cases passed the last time you ran them?

These examples of important questions might be asked over the course of a typical project. Chapter 19, "Measuring Your Success," will discuss data collection and statistics in more detail, but for now, consider that some sort of process needs to be in place that allows you to manage your test cases and track the results of running them. There are essentially four possible systems:

- **In your head.** Don't even consider this one, even for the simplest projects, unless you're testing software for your own personal use and have no reason to track your testing. You just can't do it.
- **Paper/documents.** It's possible to manage the test cases for very small projects on paper. Tables and charts of checklists have been used effectively. They're obviously a weak method for organizing and searching the data but they do offer one very important positive—a written checklist that includes a tester's initials or signature denoting that tests were run is excellent proof in a court-of-law that testing was performed.

- **Spreadsheet.** A popular and very workable method of tracking test cases is by using a spreadsheet. Figure 17.4 shows an example of this. By keeping all the details of the test cases in one place, a spreadsheet can provide an at-a-glance view of your testing status. They're easy to use, relatively easy to set up, and provide good tracking and proof of testing.

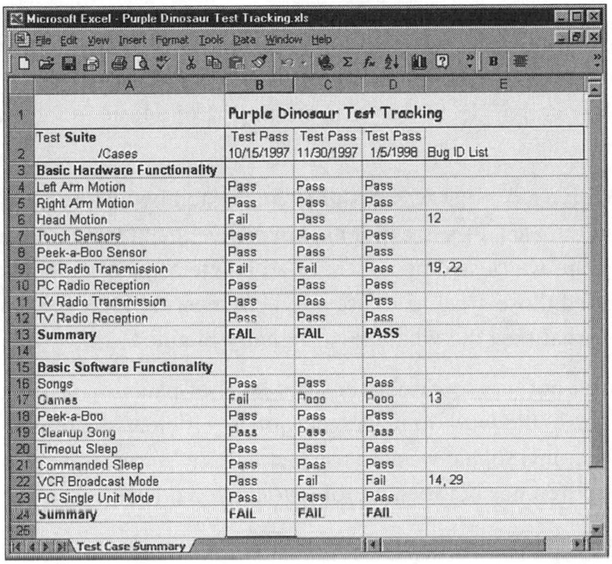

Microsoft Excel - Purple Dinosaur Test Tracking.xls

File Edit View Insert Format Tools Data Window Help

Test Suite /Cases	Test Pass 10/15/1997	Test Pass 11/30/1997	Test Pass 1/5/1998	Bug ID List
Purple Dinosaur Test Tracking				
Basic Hardware Functionality				
Left Arm Motion	Pass	Pass	Pass	
Right Arm Motion	Pass	Pass	Pass	
Head Motion	Fail	Pass	Pass	12
Touch Sensors	Pass	Pass	Pass	
Peek-a-Boo Sensor	Pass	Pass	Pass	
PC Radio Transmission	Fail	Fail	Pass	19, 22
PC Radio Reception	Pass	Pass	Pass	
TV Radio Transmission	Pass	Pass	Pass	
TV Radio Reception	Pass	Pass	Pass	
Summary	FAIL	FAIL	PASS	
Basic Software Functionality				
Songs	Pass	Pass	Pass	
Games	Fail	Pass	Pass	13
Peek-a-Boo	Pass	Pass	Pass	
Cleanup Song	Pass	Pass	Pass	
Timeout Sleep	Pass	Pass	Pass	
Commanded Sleep	Pass	Pass	Pass	
VCR Broadcast Mode	Pass	Fail	Fail	14, 29
PC Single Unit Mode	Pass	Pass	Pass	
Summary	FAIL	FAIL	FAIL	

Test Case Summary

FIGURE 17.4
A spreadsheet can be used to effectively track and manage test suites and test cases.

- **Custom database.** The ideal method for tracking test cases is to use a database programmed specifically to handle test cases. Many commercially available applications are set up to perform just this specific task. Visit some of the Web links listed in Chapter 21, "Your Career as a Software Tester," for more information and recommendations from other testers. If you're interested in creating your own tracking system, database software such as FileMaker Pro, Microsoft Access, and many others provide almost drag-and-drop database creation that would let you build a database that mapped to the ANSI/IEEE 829 standard in just a few hours. You could then set up reports and queries that would allow you to answer just about any question regarding the test cases.

The important thing to remember is that the number of test cases can easily be in the thousands and without a means to manage them, you and the other testers could quickly be lost in a sea of documentation. You need to know, at a glance, the answer to fundamental questions such as, "What will I be testing tomorrow, and how many test cases will I need to run?"

Summary

It's time again to remind you of the four reasons for carefully planning your test cases: organization, repeatability, tracking, and proof of testing. These can't be stressed enough because it's very easy to become lazy and neglect a very important part of a tester's job—to document exactly what you do.

You wouldn't want to drive a car that was designed and tested by an engineering team that scribbled their work on the back of a cocktail napkin or lived next to a nuclear power plant where the control software was tested by a team of ad hoc testers. You would want the engineers who built and tested those systems to use good engineering practices, to document their work, and to make sure that they did what they originally planned.

As a new tester, you may not have control over what level of planning and documentation your project is using, but you should work to make your job as efficient as possible. Find out what's necessary and what's not, investigate ways to use technology to improve the process, but never cut corners. That's the difference between a professional and a hack.

This chapter and Chapter 16 dealt with planning and documenting what you intend to test. The next two chapters will cover how to document the results of your testing and how to tell the world that you found a bug.

Quiz

These quiz questions are provided for your further understanding. See Appendix A, "Answers to Quiz Questions," for the answers—but don't peek!

1. What are the four reasons for test case planning?
2. What is ad hoc testing?
3. What's the purpose of a test design specification?
4. What is a test case specification?
5. Other than a traditional document, what means can you use to present your test cases?
6. What's the purpose of a test procedure specification?
7. At what level of detail should test procedures be written?

Reporting What You Find

IN THIS CHAPTER

If you stand back and look at the big picture of software testing, you'll see that it has three main tasks: test planning, actual testing, and the subject of this chapter—reporting what you find.

On the surface, it may seem as though reporting the problems you discover would be the easiest of the three. Compared to the work involved in planning the testing and the skills necessary to efficiently find bugs, telling the world that you found something wrong would surely be a simpler and less time-consuming job. In reality, it may be the most important—and sometimes most difficult—task that you, as a software tester, will perform.

In this chapter you'll learn why reporting what you find is such a critical task and how to use various techniques and tools to ensure that the bugs you find are clearly communicated and given the best chance of being fixed the way they should.

Highlights of this chapter include

- Why all bugs aren't always fixed
- What you can do to make it more likely that the bugs you find are fixed
- What techniques you can use to isolate and reproduce a bug
- What a bug's life is like from birth to death
- How to track your bugs manually or with a database

Chicken Little Reports a Problem

Chicken Little was in the woods one day when an acorn fell on her head. It scared her so much she trembled all over. She shook so hard, half her feathers fell out.

"Help! Help! The sky is falling! I have to go tell the king!" Chicken Little said.

So she ran in great fright to tell the king. Along the way she met Henny Penny.

"Where are you going, Chicken Little?" asked Henny Penny.

"Oh, help! The sky is falling!" said Chicken Little.

"How do you know?" asked Henny Penny.

"I saw it with my own eyes, and heard it with my own ears, and part of it fell on my head!" said Chicken Little.

"This is terrible, just terrible! We'd better hurry up," said Henny Penny. So they both ran away as fast as they could.

In this excerpt from a popular children's story, Chicken Little is startled when something unexpected occurs and proceeds to run off in hysteria, shouting to the world what she thinks is happening. Imagine what Chicken Little would do if she found a serious software bug! What do you think a project manager or a programmer would do if they saw Chicken Little and Henny Penny running their way? There are lots of interesting parallels between this simple fable and software testing. Keep it in mind as you read the rest of this chapter.

Getting Your Bugs Fixed

Way back in Chapter 3, "The Realities of Software Testing," you learned that despite your best efforts at planning and executing your tests, not all the bugs you find will be fixed. Some may be dismissed completely, and others may be *deferred* or *postponed* for fixing in a subsequent release of the software. At the time, it may have been a bit discouraging or even frightening to think that such a concept was a possibility. Hopefully, now that you know a great deal more about software testing, you can see why not fixing all the bugs is a reality.

The reasons listed in Chapter 3 for not fixing a bug were:

- **There's not enough time.** Every project always has too many software features, too few people to code and test them, and not enough room left in the schedule to finish. If you're working on a tax-preparation program, April 15 isn't going to move—you must have your software ready in time.

- **It's really not a bug.** Maybe you've heard the phrase, "It's not a bug, it's a feature!" It's not uncommon for misunderstandings, test errors, or spec changes to result in would-be bugs being dismissed as features.

- **It's too risky to fix.** Unfortunately, this is all too often true. Software is fragile, inter-twined, and sometimes like spaghetti. You might make a bug fix that causes other bugs to appear. Under the pressure to release a product under a tight schedule, it might be too risky to change the software. It may be better to leave in the known bug to avoid the risk of creating new, unknown ones.

- **It's just not worth it.** This may sound harsh, but it's reality. Bugs that would occur infrequently or appear in little-used features may be dismissed. Bugs that have *workarounds*, ways that a user can prevent or avoid the bug, often aren't fixed. It all comes down to a business decision based on risk.

One more item should be added to this list that can often be the contributing reason for all of them:

- **Bugs are reported ineffectively.** The tester didn't make a strong enough case that a particular bug should be fixed. As a result, the bug was misunderstood as not being a bug, was deemed not important enough to delay the product, was thought to be too risky to fix, or was just plain considered to not be worth fixing.

As in the case with Chicken Little, running around screaming that the sky is falling is usually not an effective approach for communicating a problem (unless, of course, the sky really is falling and it's obvious that it is). Most bugs that you find won't be as dramatic as this. They will require you to clearly and succinctly communicate your findings to the team making the fix/no-fix judgment so that they have all the information they need to decide what to do.

NOTE

Because of all the different software development models and possible team dynamics, it's impossible to tell you exactly how the fix/no-fix decision-making process will work for your team or project. In many cases, the decision lies solely with the project manager, in others it's with the programmer, and in others, it's left to a committee.

What is universal, though, is that some person or group of people will review the bugs you report and determine whether they will be fixed. The information you provide that describes the bug is used to make that decision.

You don't need to be a lawyer or an ex-debate team captain to know how to persuade everyone that your bugs need to be fixed. Common sense and basic communication skills will take you a long way. Later in this chapter you'll learn about the different systems for bug logging and tracking, but for now, consider these fundamental principles for reporting a bug:

- **Report bugs as soon as possible.** This has been discussed many times before, but it can't be emphasized enough. The earlier you find a bug, the more time that remains in the schedule to get it fixed. Suppose that you find an embarrassing misspelling in a Help file a few months before the software is released. That bug has a very high likelihood of being fixed. If you find the same bug a few hours before the release, odds are it won't be fixed. Figure 18.1 shows this relationship between time and bug fixing on a graph.

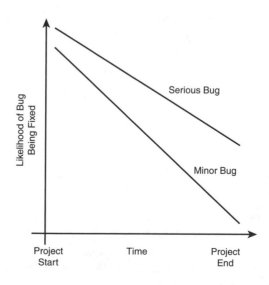

FIGURE 18.1

The later a bug is found, the less likely it is to be fixed, especially if it's a very minor bug.

This may seem strange—the bug is still the same bug whether you find it today or three months from now. Ideally, it shouldn't matter when it's found, just what the bug is. In reality, however, the risks of fixing that bug go up over time and increasingly weigh on the decision-making process.

- **Effectively describe the bugs.** Suppose that you were a programmer and received the following bug report from a tester: "Whenever I type a bunch of random characters in the login box, the software starts to do weird stuff." How would you even begin to fix this bug without knowing what the random characters were, how big a bunch is, and what kind of weird stuff was happening?

An Effective Bug Description

Effective bug descriptions would be as follows:

- **Minimal.** It explains just the facts and the details necessary to demonstrate and describe the bug. Stating "a bunch of random characters" isn't minimal. Give an exact sequence of steps that shows the problem. If more than one set of inputs or actions causes the bug, cite a couple of examples, especially if they show a pattern or a clue that might help the programmer find the cause. Be short and to the point.

- **Singular.** There should be only one bug per report. This sounds obvious, but it's sometimes difficult to differentiate between similar looking bugs and in the rush to get a product out it may seem easier to just lump them together. The problem with reporting more than one bug in a single report is that it's usually only the first bug that gets attention and is fixed—the others become forgotten or ignored. It's also impossible to individually track multiple bugs that are listed on the same report (more on this later).

  It's easy to say that bugs should be reported individually and not grouped together, but it's not always straightforward to do. Consider this bug report: "The following five words are misspelled in the online help file: ...." That, obviously should be reported as five separate bugs. But what about, "The login dialog won't accept passwords or login IDs with uppercase characters"? Is that one bug or two? From the user perspective, it looks like two, one against the passwords and another against the login IDs. But, at the code level, it may be just one where the programmer didn't handle uppercase characters correctly.

  A quick tip: When in doubt, enter individual bugs. You're looking for symptoms, not causes. Several bugs may turn out to have the same cause, but you can't know that until the bug is fixed. It's better to err on the side of individual reports than delay or, worse, forget about fixing a bug because it was lumped in with others.

- **Obvious and general.** A bug described with numerous complex, convoluted steps that shows a very specific instance of a bug is less likely to get fixed than one described with easily performed steps that shows the bug to be very general and readily seen by a user.

  Reporting bugs that your test tools or automation finds is a good example of this. Your automation may have run for six hours before finding a bug. A project manager deciding on a bug would be hesitant to fix one that takes six hours of constant keyboard pounding to occur. If you spend some time analyzing the results of your tool, however, you could find that it doesn't take six hours—it just takes 10 common and likely keystrokes. This process is known as *isolating* a bug. Your automation just happened to stumble upon those keystrokes while it ran. If you want this bug to get serious attention, your bug report should list those 10 magic keystrokes, not the thousands that the automation ran to get there.

- **Reproducible.** To be taken seriously, a bug report must show the bug to be *reproducible*—following a predefined set of steps will cause the software to achieve the same state and the bug to occur again. One of the more difficult, but fun, areas of software testing is trying to isolate and reproduce what seems like random software behavior—occasional crashes, chance data corruption, and so on. Later in this chapter you'll learn a few techniques for doing this. Once you reproduce the bug to its obvious and general steps, you can report it.

- **Be nonjudgmental in reporting bugs.** It's easy for testers and programmers to form an adversarial relationship. Reread Chapter 3 if you forget why. Bug reports can be viewed by the programmers and others on the development team as the tester's "report card" on their work so they need to be nonjudgmental, nonpersonal, and noninflammatory. A bug report that says, "Your code for controlling the printer is terrible, it just plain doesn't work. I can't believe that you even checked it in for testing," would be out of line. Bug reports should be written against the product, not the person, and state only the facts. No gloating, no grandstanding, no personalizing, no egos, no accusations. Tact and diplomacy are what matters.

- **Follow up on your bug reports.** One thing worse than not finding an important bug is finding a bug, reporting it, and then forgetting about it or losing track of it. You've learned that testing software is hard work, so don't let the results of your labor, the bugs you find, become neglected. From the moment you find a bug, it's your responsibility to make sure that it's reported properly and given the attention that it needs to be addressed. A good tester finds and logs lots of bugs. A great tester finds and logs lots of bugs but also continues to monitor them through the process of getting them fixed. You'll learn more about this later in the chapter.

These principles—report bugs as soon as possible, effectively describe them, be nonjudgmental in reporting them, and follow up on them—should be common sense. You could apply these rules to almost any communications task. It's sometimes difficult, though, in the rush to create a product to remember to apply them to your testing. However, if you want to be effective at reporting your bugs and getting them fixed, these are fundamental rules to follow.

Isolating and Reproducing Bugs

You've just learned that to effectively report a bug, you need to describe it as obvious, general, and reproducible. In many cases this is easy. Suppose that you have a simple test case for a painting program that checks that all the possible colors can be used for drawing. If each and every time you select the color red the program draws in the color green, that's an obvious, general, and reproducible bug.

What would you do, though, if this incorrect color bug only occurs after you've run several of your other test cases and doesn't occur if you run the specific failing test case directly after rebooting the machine? What if it seems to occur randomly or only during a full moon? You'd have some sleuthing to do.

Isolating and reproducing bugs is where you get to put on your detective hat and try to figure out exactly what the steps are to narrow down the problem. The good news is that there's no such thing as a random software bug—if you create the exact same situation with the exact same inputs, the bug will reoccur. The bad news is that identifying and setting up that exact situation and the exact same inputs can be tricky and time consuming. Once you know the answer, it looks easy. When you don't know the answer, it looks hard.

18

REPORTING WHAT
YOU FIND

> **NOTE**
>
> Some testers are naturally good at isolating and reproducing bugs. They can discover a bug and very quickly narrow down the specific steps and conditions that cause the problem. For others, this skill comes with practice after finding and reporting many different types of bugs. To be an effective software tester, though, these are skills that you'll need to master, so take every opportunity you can to work at isolating and reproducing bugs.

A few tips and tricks will give you a good start if you find a bug that seems to take numerous steps to reproduce or can't seem to be reproduced at all. If you run into such a situation, try the suggestions in this list as a first step in isolating the bug:

- Don't take anything for granted. Keep notes of everything you do—every step, every pause, everything. It's easy to leave out a step or add one unintentionally. Have a co-worker watch you try the test case. Use a keystroke and mouse recording program so that you can record and playback your steps exactly. Use a video camera to record your test session if necessary. The goal is to make sure that every detail of the steps necessary to cause the bug are visible and can be analyzed from a different view.

- Look for time-dependent and race condition problems. Does the bug occur only at a certain time of day? Maybe it depends on how quickly you enter the data or the fact that you're saving data to a slower floppy instead of a fast hard drive. Was the network busy when you saw the bug? Try your test case on slower or faster hardware. Think timing.

- White-box issues of stress- and load-related boundary condition bugs, memory leaks, and data overflows can be slow to reveal themselves. You might perform a test that causes data to be overwritten but you won't know it until you try to use that data—maybe in a later test. Bugs that don't appear after a reboot but only after running other tests are usually in this category. If this happens, look at the previous tests you've run, maybe by using some dynamic white-box techniques, to see if a bug has gone unnoticed.

- State bugs show up only in certain states of the software. Examples of state bugs would be ones that occur only the first time the software is run or that occur only after the first time. Maybe the bug happens only after the data was saved or before any key was pressed. State bugs may look like a time-dependent or race condition problem but you'll find that time is unimportant—it's the order in which things happen, not when they happen.

- Consider resource dependencies and interactions with memory, network, and hardware sharing. Does the bug occur only on a "busy" system that's running other software and communicating with other hardware? In the end, the bug may turn out to be a race condition, memory leak, or state bug that's aggravated by the software's dependency or interaction with a resource, but looking at these influences may help you isolate it.

- Don't ignore the hardware. Unlike software, hardware can degrade and act unpredictably. A loose card, a bad memory chip, or an overheated CPU can cause failures that look like software bugs but really aren't. Try to reproduce your bugs on different hardware. This is especially important if you're performing configuration or compatibility testing. You'll want to know if the bug shows up on one system or many.

If, after your best attempts at isolating the bug, you can't produce a short, concise set of steps that reproduce it, you still need to log the bug so you don't risk losing track of it. It's possible that with just the information you've learned a programmer may still be able to figure out what the problem is. Since the programmer is familiar with the code, seeing the symptom, the test case steps, and especially the process you took attempting to isolate the problem, may give him a clue where to look for the bug. Of course, a programmer won't want to, nor should he have to, do this with every bug you find, but sometimes those tough ones to isolate require a team effort.

Not All Bugs Are Created Equal

You would probably agree that a bug that corrupts a user's data is more severe than one that's a simple misspelling. But, what if the data corruption can occur only in such a very rare instance that no user is ever likely to see it and the misspelling causes every user to have problems installing the software? Which is more important to fix? The decisions become more difficult.

Of course, if every project had infinite time, both problems would be fixed, but that's never the case. As you learned earlier in this chapter, trade-offs must be made and risks must be taken in every software project to decide what bugs to fix and what bugs not to fix or to postpone to a later release of the software.

When you report your bugs, you'll most often have a say in what should happen to them. You'll classify your bugs and identify in a short, concise way what their impact is. The common method for doing this is to give your bugs a *severity* and a *priority* level. Of course, the specifics of the method vary among companies, but the general concept is the same:

- *Severity* indicates how bad the bug is and reflects its impact to the product and to the user.
- *Priority* indicates how important it is to fix the bug and when it should be fixed.

The following list of common classification of severity and priority should help you better understand the difference between the two. Keep in mind, these are just examples. Some companies use up to ten levels and others use just three. No matter how many levels are used, though, the goals are the same.

Severity

1. System crash, data loss, data corruption
2. Operational error, wrong result, loss of functionality
3. Minor problem, misspelling, UI layout, rare occurrence
4. Suggestion

Priority

1. Immediate fix, blocks further testing, very visible
2. Must fix before the product is released
3. Should fix if time permits
4. Would like fix but can be released as is

A data corruption bug that happens very rarely might be classified as Severity 1, Priority 3. A misspelling in the setup instructions that causes users to phone in for help might be classified as Severity 3, Priority 2.

What about a release of the software for testing that crashes as soon as you start it up? Probably Severity 1, Priority 1. If you think a button should be moved a little further down on the page you might classify it as Severity 4, Priority 4.

This information is vital to the person or team reviewing the bug reports and deciding what bugs should be fixed and in what order. If a programmer has 25 bugs assigned to him, he should probably start working on the Priority 1's first, instead of just fixing the easiest ones. Similarly, two project managers—one working on game software and another on a heart monitor—would use this same information but could make different decisions based on it. One would likely choose to make the software look the best and run the fastest; the other would choose to make the software as reliable as possible. The severity and priority information is what they would use to make these decisions. You'll see later in this chapter how these fields are used in a real bug-tracking system.

> **NOTE**
>
> A bug's priority can change over the course of a project. A bug that you originally labeled as Priority 2 could be changed to Level 4 as time starts to run out and the software release date looms. If you're the software tester who found the bug, you need to continually monitor the bug's status to make sure that you agree with any changes made to it and to provide further test data or persuasion to get it fixed.

A Bug's Life Cycle

In entomology (the study of real, living bugs), the term *life cycle* refers to the various stages that an insect assumes over its life. If you think back to your high school biology class, you'll remember that the life cycle stages for most insects are the egg, larvae, pupae, and adult. It seems appropriate, given that software problems are also called bugs, that a similar life cycle system is used to identify their stages of life. A software bug's stages don't exactly match a real bug's, but the concept is the same. Figure 18.2 shows an example of the simplest, and most optimal, software bug life cycle.

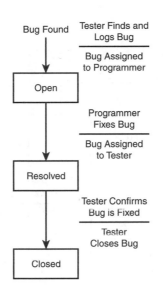

FIGURE 18.2

A state table shows that a software bug has a life cycle similar to an insect.

This example shows that when a bug is first found by a software tester, it's logged and assigned to a programmer to be fixed. This state is called the *open state*. Once the programmer fixes the code, he assigns it back to the tester and the bug enters the *resolved state*. The tester then performs a regression test to confirm that the bug is indeed fixed and, if it is, closes it out. The bug then enters its final state, the *closed state*.

In many instances, this is as complicated as a software bug's life cycle gets: a bug is opened, resolved, and closed. In some situations, though, the life cycle gets a bit more complicated, as shown in Figure 18.3.

In this case, the life cycle starts out the same with the tester opening the bug and assigning it to the programmer, but the programmer doesn't fix it. He doesn't think it's bad enough to fix and assigns it to the project manager to decide. The project manager agrees with the programmer and places the bug in the resolved state as a "won't-fix" bug. The tester disagrees, looks for and finds a more obvious and general case that demonstrates the bug, reopens it, and assigns it to the project manager. The project manager, seeing the new information, agrees and assigns it to the programmer to fix. The programmer fixes the bug, resolves it as fixed, and assigns it to the tester. The tester confirms the fix and closes the bug.

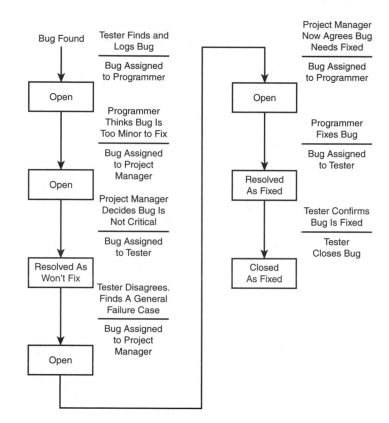

FIGURE 18.3

A bug's life cycle can easily become very complicated if the bug-fixing process doesn't occur as smoothly as expected.

You can see that a bug might undergo numerous changes and iterations over its life, sometimes looping back and starting the life cycle all over again. Figure 18.4 takes the simple model of Figure 18.2 and adds to it the possible decisions, approvals, and looping that can occur in most projects. Of course, every software company and project will have its own system, but this figure is fairly generic and should cover most any bug life cycle that you'll encounter.

This generic life cycle has two additional states and extra connecting lines. The *review state* is where the project manager or the committee, sometimes called a *Change Control Board*, decides whether the bug should be fixed. In some projects all bugs go through the review state before they're assigned to the programmer for fixing. In other projects, this may not occur until near the end of the project, or not at all. Notice that the review state can also go directly to the closed state. This happens if the review decides that the bug shouldn't be fixed—it could be too minor, is really not a problem, or is a testing error. The other added state is *deferred*. The review may determine that the bug should be considered for fixing at some time in the future, but not for this release of the software.

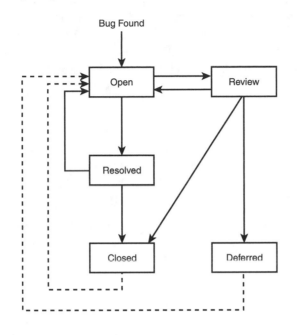

FIGURE 18.4
This generic bug life-cycle state table covers most of the possible situations that can occur.

The additional line from the resolved state back to the open state covers the situation where the tester finds that the bug hasn't been fixed. It gets reopened and the bug's life cycle repeats. The two dotted lines that loop from the closed state and the deferred state back to the open state rarely occur but are important enough to mention. Since a tester never gives up, it's possible that a bug that was thought to be fixed, tested, and closed could reappear. Such bugs are often called *regressions*. It's also possible that a deferred bug could later be proven serious enough to fix immediately. If either of these situations occurs, the bug is reopened and started through the process again.

Most project teams adopt rules for who can change the state of a bug or assign it to someone else. For example, maybe only the project manager can decide to defer a bug or only a tester is permitted to close a bug. What's important is that once you log a bug, you follow it through its life cycle, don't lose track of it, and provide the necessary information to drive it to being fixed and closed.

Bug-Tracking Systems

By now it should be clear that the bug-reporting process is a complex beast that requires a great deal of information, a high level of detail, and a fair amount discipline to be effective. Everything you've learned so far in this chapter sounds good on the surface, but to put it into practice requires some type of system that allows you to log the bugs you find and monitor them throughout their life cycle. A bug-tracking system does just that.

The remainder of this chapter will discuss the fundamentals of a bug-tracking system and give you examples of using a paper-based approach and a full-fledged database. Of course what you use will likely be customized and specific to your company or project, but in general, the concepts are consistent across the software industry so you should be able to apply your skills to just about any system you're asked to use.

The Standard: The Test Incident Report

Your good friend, the ANSI/IEEE 829 Standard for Software Test Documentation (available at `standards.iee.org`), defines a document called the *Test Incident Report* whose purpose is "to document any event that occurs during the testing process which requires investigation." In short, to log a bug.

Reviewing the standard is a good way to distill what you've learned about the bug-reporting process so far and to see it all put into one place. The following list shows the areas that the standard defines, adapted and updated a bit, to reflect more current terminology.

- **Identifier.** Specifies an ID that's unique to this bug report that can be used to locate and refer to it.
- **Summary.** Summarizes the bug into a short, concise statement of fact. References to the software being tested and its version, the associated test procedure, test case, and the test spec should also be included.
- **Incident Description.** Provides a detailed description of the bug with the following information:

  Date and time

  Tester's name

  Hardware and software configuration used

  Inputs

  Procedure steps

  Expected results

  Actual results

  Attempts to reproduce and description of what was tried

Other observations or information that may help the programmer locate the bug

- **Impact.** The severity and priority as well as an indication of impact to the test plan, test specs, test procedures, and test cases.

Manual Bug Reporting and Tracking

The 829 standard doesn't define the format that the bug report should take, but it does give an example of a simple document. Figure 18.5 shows what such a paper bug report can look like.

```
WIDGETS SOFTWARE INC.     BUG REPORT      BUG#:_____
SOFTWARE:_____RELEASE:_____VERSION:_____
TESTER:_____DATE:_____ASSIGNED TO:_____
SEVERITY: 1 2 3 4     PRIORITY: 1 2 3 4   REPRODUCIBLE:   Y   N
TITLE:_____
DESCRIPTION:_____
_____
_____
_____
_____
_____
_____

RESOLUTION: FIXED DUPLICATE NO-REPRO CAN'T FIX DEFERRED WON'T FIX
DATE RESOLVED:_____RESOLVED BY:_____VERSION:_____
RESOLUTION COMMENT:_____
_____
_____

RETESTED BY:_____VERSION TESTED:_____DATE TESTED:_____
RETEST COMMENT:_____
_____
_____

                       SIGNATURES:
ORIGINATOR:_____  TESTER:_____
PROGRAMMER:_____   PROJECT MANAGER:_____
MARKETING:_____   PRODUCT SUPPORT:_____
```

FIGURE 18.5
A sample bug report form shows how the details of a bug can be condensed to a single page of data.

Notice that this one-page form can hold all the information necessary to identify and describe a bug. It also contains fields that you can use to track a bug through its life cycle. Once the form is filed by the tester, it can be assigned to a programmer to be fixed. The programmer has fields where she can enter information regarding the fix, including choices for the possible resolutions. There's also an area where, once the bug is resolved, the tester can supply information about his efforts in retesting and closing out the bug. At the bottom of the form is an area for signatures—in many industries, you put your name on the line to reflect that a bug has been resolved to your satisfaction.

For very small projects, paper forms can work just fine. As recently as the early 1990s, even large, mission-critical projects with thousands of reported bugs used paper forms for bug reporting and tracking. There still may be pockets of this today.

The problem with paper forms is that, well, they're paper, and if you've ever walked into a paper-run office and asked someone to find something, you know how inefficient such a system can be. Think about the complex bug life cycles that can occur (an example of which was shown in Figure 18.3), and you'll wonder how a paper system can work. What if someone wanted to know the status of Bug #6329 or how many Priority 1 bugs were left to fix? Thank goodness for spreadsheets and databases.

Automated Bug Reporting and Tracking

Just as with the test case and test procedure documents described in Chapter 17, there's no reason that the ANSI/IEEE 829 standard can't be brought up-to-date and adapted to work with modern systems. After all, the information for tracking bugs, the data put on the form shown in Figure 18.5, is just text and numbers—a perfect application for a database. Figure 18.6 shows such an automated bug reporting and tracking system that represents the type you might encounter in your work.

Figure 18.6 shows a top-level view of a bug database containing 3,263 bugs. The individual bugs, their IDs, titles, status, priority, severity, and resolution are shown in a simple listing at the top third of the screen. Further information about the selected bug entry is then shown on the bottom part of the screen. At a glance you can see who opened the bug, who resolved it, and who closed it. You can also scroll through details that were entered about the bug as it went through its life cycle.

Notice that at the top of the screen there is a series of buttons that you can click to create (open) a new bug or to edit, resolve, close, or reactivate (reopen) an existing bug. The next few pages will show you the windows that appear when you select each option.

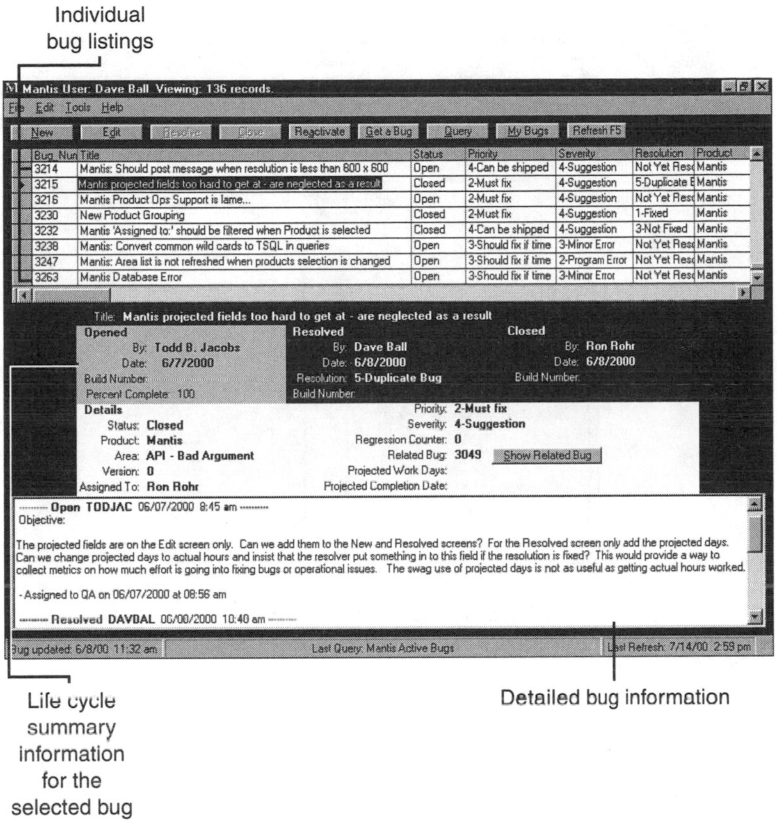

Individual
bug listings

FIGURE 18.6

The main window of a typical bug-reporting database shows what an automated system can provide. (Mantis bug database images in this chapter courtesy of Dave Ball and HBS International, Inc.)

Figure 18.7 shows the New Bug dialog box, in which information is entered to log a new bug into the system. The top-level description of the bug includes its title, severity, priority, software version info, and so on. The comment field is where you would enter the details of how the bug was discovered. This database conveniently prefills the comment area with headers that guide you in providing the necessary information. If you're entering a new bug, all you need to do is follow the prompts—entering your test's objective, the setup steps, the steps that reproduce the bug, what result you expected, what result you saw, and what hardware and software configurations you were using when you saw the bug.

18

REPORTING WHAT
YOU FIND

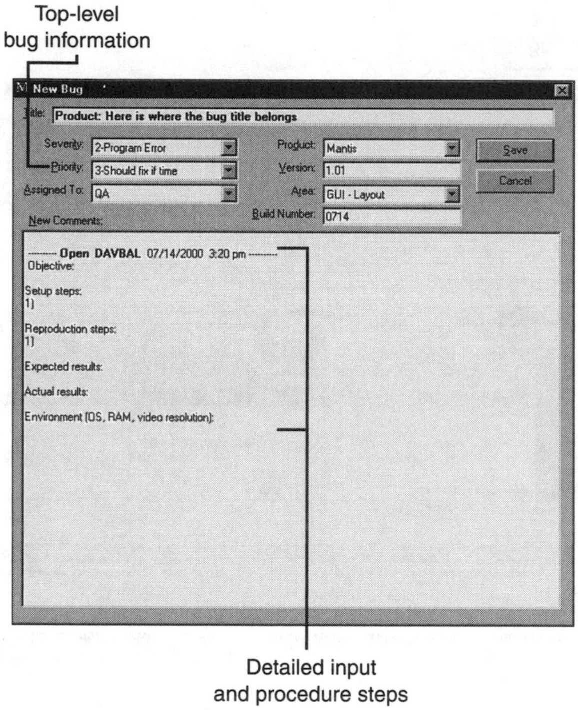

Top-level
bug information

Detailed input
and procedure steps

FIGURE 18.7

A new bug starts its life cycle in the New Bug dialog box.

Once a bug is entered, and really anytime during its life cycle, new information may need to be added to clarify the description, change the priority or severity, or make other minor tweaks to the data. Figure 18.8 shows the window that provides this functionality.

Notice that this dialog box provides additional data fields over what the new bug window provided. Editing a bug allows you to relate this bug to another one if you find one that seems similar. A programmer can add information about how much progress he's made in fixing the bug and how much longer it will take. There's even a field that can put the bug "on hold," sort of freezing it in its current state in the life cycle.

An important feature shown in Figure 18.8 is in the Comments section. Each time a bug is modified, when it's opened, edited, resolved, and closed, that information is recorded in the comment field. At a glance you can see what states the bug has been through over its life.

Additional edit fields

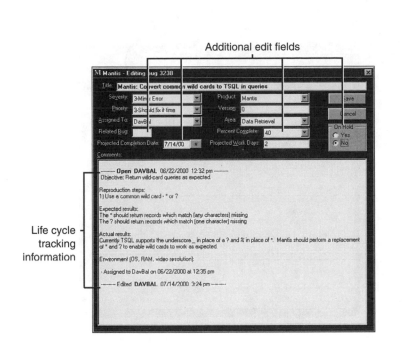

Life cycle
tracking
information

FIGURE 18.8

The Edit window allows you to add more information to an existing bug entry.

Figure 18.9 shows the dialog box used when someone, usually the programmer or project manager, resolves a bug. A drop-down list provides different resolution choices from Fixed to Can't Fix to Duplicate. If the bug is fixed, the build—or version number that will contain the fix—is entered, and information about what was fixed or how the fix was made is added to the comment field. The bug is then reassigned to the tester for closing.

Many bug databases track not just comments about the fix, but also details of exactly what the programmers did to make the fix. The line of code, the module, and even the type of error can be recorded as it often provides useful information to the white-box tester.

After a bug is resolved, it's typically assigned back to you, the tester, for closing. Figure 18.10 shows the bug Closing dialog box. Because the database tracked every modification to the bug report since it was opened, you can see the decisions that were made along the way and what exactly was fixed. It's possible that the bug wasn't fixed the way you expected, maybe a similar bug had been found and added by another tester, or maybe the programmer made a comment about the fix being risky. All this information will assist you when you retest the bug to make sure it's fixed. If it turns out that it's not fixed, you simply reopen the bug to start the life cycle over again.

18

REPORTING WHAT
YOU FIND

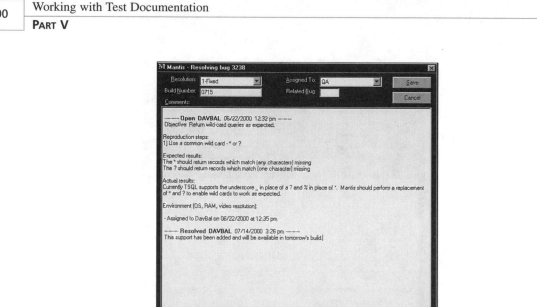

FIGURE 18.9

The Resolving dialog box is typically used by the programmer to record information regarding the bug fix.

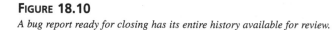

FIGURE 18.10

A bug report ready for closing has its entire history available for review.

Once you use a real bug-tracking database, you'll wonder how a software project's bugs could ever have been managed on paper. A bug-tracking database provides a central point that an entire project team, not just the testers, can use to communicate the status of the project, tell who's assigned what tasks to perform, and, most importantly, assure that no bug falls through the cracks. It's the culmination of everything you've learned in this chapter about how to report the bugs you find.

Summary

This chapter started out with an excerpt from the kids' story about Chicken Little that described her reaction when an acorn unexpectedly fell on her head. She thought she had discovered a serious problem—a Severity 1, Priority 1 bug—and immediately began running around screaming that the sky was falling.

As a software tester, it's sometimes easy to get caught up in the moment when you find that something in the program you're testing doesn't work as expected. What you've learned in this chapter is that there's a formal process that should be followed to properly isolate, categorize, record, and track the problems you find to ensure that they're eventually resolved and, hopefully, fixed.

Chicken Little has never read Chapter 18, so she didn't know what to do other than tell everyone she met what she thought was happening. She was wrong, of course. The sky wasn't falling. If she had at least stopped to isolate and reproduce the problem, she would have discovered that it wasn't really a problem at all—it was by design that the nut fell from the tree. In the end, her panic and naïveté did her in. (If you're unfamiliar with the story, she and her barnyard friends eventually meet a hungry fox who invites them into his den to hear their story.)

The moral of all this is that to be an effective tester, you need to not just plan your testing and find bugs, but also to apply a methodical and systematic approach to reporting them. An exaggerated, poorly reported, or misplaced bug is no bug at all—and surely one that won't be fixed.

Quiz

These quiz questions are provided for your further understanding. See Appendix A, "Answers to Quiz Questions," for the answers—but don't peek!

1. Cite a few reasons that a bug might not be fixed.

2. What basic principles can you apply to your bug reports to give them the best chance of getting the bug fixed?

3. Describe a few techniques for isolating and reproducing a bug.

4. Suppose that you're running tests on the Windows Calculator and find that 1+1=2, 2+2=5, 3+3=6, 4+4=9, 5+5=10, and 6+6=13. Write a bug title and bug description that effectively describes this problem.

5. What severity and priority would you give to a misspelling in a company's logo on the software's startup screen?

6. What are the three basic states of a software bug's life cycle and the two common additional states?

7. List a few reasons that a database bug-tracking system is so much more useful than a paper-based system.

Measuring Your Success

IN THIS CHAPTER

In Chapter 18 you learned the basics of reporting the bugs you find and how a specialized bug database can be used to track them. Although most of your exposure to this database will be in entering bugs, the indirect benefit to using it is the ability to extract all sorts of useful and interesting data that can indicate the success (or failure) of the test effort and the project's progress.

By using the information in the bug-tracking database, you can perform queries that will tell you what types of bugs you're finding, what your bug find rate is, and how many of your bugs have been fixed. Your test manager or the project manager can see if any trends in the data show areas that may need more testing or whether the project is on track for its scheduled release date. The data is all there, it's just a matter of creating reports that will show the information you're after.

This chapter will introduce you to some of the popular queries and reports that you're likely to see as a software tester and give you examples of how they're used in a typical software project. Highlights of this chapter include

- What metrics and statistics can do for you
- Why caution needs to be exercised in data collecting and reporting
- How to use simple bug database queries and reports
- Some frequently used project-level measurements

Using the Information in the Bug Tracking Database

Consider the following questions:

- What areas of the software you're testing have the most bugs? The fewest bugs?
- How many resolved bugs are currently assigned to Martha?
- Bob is leaving for vacation soon. Will he likely have all his bugs fixed by then?
- How many bugs have you found this week? This month? On the entire project?
- Can you please bring a list of all the open Priority 1 bugs to the project review meeting?
- Does the software look like it's on track to meet the scheduled release date?

These fundamental questions are routinely asked over the course of a software project. They aren't rocket science, they're simple, straightforward questions to which you and the rest of your test team and the project team will eventually need to know the answers.

It may be surprising that a bug-tracking database can become such a fundamental means for measuring a project's status and answering such important questions. If you didn't know better, you'd think it would be the master schedule or the project plan or something that the project manager handled. In reality, though, those documents reflect the project's original intentions—the bug database reflects the project's reality. If you want to choose a high-quality restaurant, you could select one based on the chef's résumé or the owner's history. But, if you want to be sure to pick a good one, you'd read the latest food critic review or the history of health inspection reports. The project's bug database works the same way. It tells you what has happened in the past, what's happening now, and allows you to look at the data to make an educated guess of the future.

> **NOTE**
>
> The term used to describe a measurement of a particular attribute of a software project is a *software metric*. The average number of bugs per tester per day is a metric. The number of bugs found per area of the software is a metric. The ratio of Severity 1 bugs to Severity 4 bugs is a metric.

Because the bug database is continually updated with new bugs, bug entry and fix dates, project member names, bug assignments, and so on, it's the natural means to pull all sorts of metrics that describe the project's status—as well as an individual tester's or programmer's status.

Therein lies one of the potential problems with using the bug database for metrics. The same database that can tell everyone how many Priority 1 bugs are still left to fix can also tell management how many bugs were created by a specific programmer. It can also tell your boss how many bugs you entered compared to the other testers on your team. Is that a good thing? Maybe, if the programmer and you are really good at your work, but, what if you're testing that good programmer's code? There would be fewer bugs to find and your bug-find metrics suddenly wouldn't look so hot compared to other testers testing some really bug-ridden code.

It's not the intent of this chapter to get into the moral and interpersonal issues that can arise from how the data in the bug database is used. In general, though, it should primarily be viewed as the means to track project-level metrics, not an individual person's performance, unless the metrics are private, understood, and unambiguous—does the data show a poor programmer or a good tester? If you're working on a project that uses a bug-tracking database, discuss with your manager and the project manager what information will be collected and how it will be used so that there won't be any surprises.

Politics aside, using the bug database as a source for metrics is a super-efficient means to gauge a project's status and your own progress. All the information is there, it's just a matter of pulling it out of the database and arranging it into a useful format. The remainder of this chapter will discuss some of the common metrics that you'll see used in software projects and explain how they're generated and interpreted. Of course, projects vary greatly, so don't

19

MEASURING YOUR
SUCCESS

assume that these are the only metrics possible. Just when you think you've seen the weirdest possible pie chart, someone will think up another that demonstrates a new and useful view into the project's data.

Metrics That You'll Use in Your Daily Testing

Probably the most frequently used feature of a bug-tracking database that you'll encounter (besides entering bugs) is performing *queries* to obtain specific lists of bugs that you're interested in. Remember, bug databases can potentially have many thousands of bugs stored in them. Manually sorting through such a huge list would be impossible. The beauty of storing bugs in a database is that performing queries becomes a simple task. Figure 19.1 shows a typical query building window with a sample query ready to be entered.

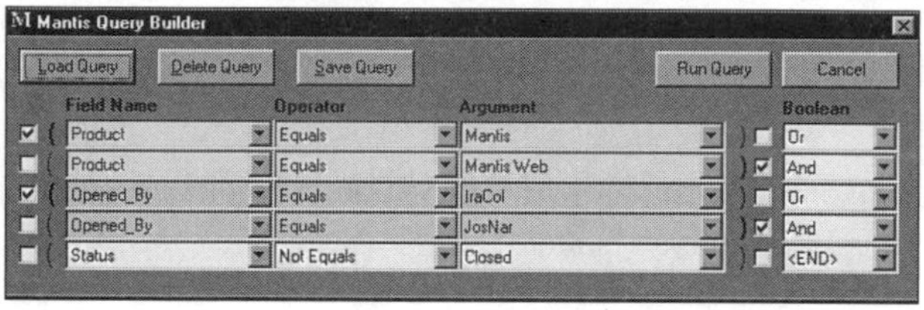

FIGURE 19.1
Most bug-tracking databases have a means to build queries that return the specific information you're looking for. (Mantis bug database images in this chapter courtesy of Dave Ball and HBS International, Inc.)

This bug database's query builder, as with most others, uses standard Boolean ANDs, ORs, and parentheses to construct your specific request. In this example, the tester is looking for a list of all bugs that match the following criteria:

- The software product's name is Mantis OR Mantis Web AND
- The bug was opened by either IraCol OR JosNar AND
- The bug's status is currently Closed

Clicking the Run Query button causes the database to be searched for all the bugs that match these criteria and return a list of bug ID numbers and bug titles for review.

The types of queries you can build are bounded only by the database's fields, the values they can hold, and the database tool you're using. It's possible to answer just about any question you might have regarding your testing and how it relates to the project. For example, here's a list of questions easily answered through queries:

- What are the IDs for the resolved bugs currently assigned to me for closing?
- How many bugs have I entered on this project? In the previous week? Over the last month? Between April 1 and July 31?

- What bugs have I entered against the user interface that were resolved as won't fix?
- How many of my bugs were Severity 1 or Severity 2?
- Of all the bugs I've entered, how many were fixed? How many were deferred? How many were duplicates?

The results of your query will be a list of bugs as shown in the bug-tracking database window in Figure 19.2. All the bugs that matched the criteria in your query are returned in numerical order. The gaps you see between the numbers—for example, the gap between 3238 and 3247—are simply bugs in the database that didn't match the query.

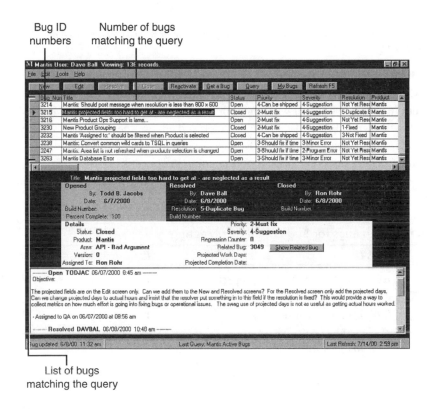

FIGURE 19.2

The results of a query are returned as a list of bugs in the bug database's main window.

Performing queries is a powerful feature of a bug-tracking database and can be very useful in providing the information you need to perform your job and measure your success. Despite their power, though, another step can be taken to make the information even more useful and that's taking the results of a query, or multiple queries, and turning it into printable reports and graphical forms. Figure 19.3 shows the method that this database uses for outputting its query results.

19

MEASURING YOUR SUCCESS

FIGURE 19.3

This bug database allows you to export all the database fields to either a common tab-delimited raw data file or a word processing file.

In Figure 19.2 you saw that the query results list showed the bug ID number, title, status, priority, severity, resolution, and the product name. In many cases that may be all the information you need, but in others you might want more or less detail. By exporting the data using the export window shown in Figure 19.3, you can pick and choose the exact fields you want to save to a file. If you're just interested in the bugs assigned to you, you could export a simple list of bug ID numbers and their titles. If you're going to a meeting to discuss open bugs, you might want to save the bug ID number, its title, priority, severity, and who it's assigned to. Such a list might look like the one in Table 19.1.

TABLE 19.1 Open Bugs for Bug Committee Meeting

Bug#	Bug Title	Pri	Sev	Assigned To
005	Even numbers don't add properly, although odd ones do	1	2	WaltP
023	0 divided by 0 causes crash	1	1	ElP
024	Dead link to deleted topic exists in help file calc.hlp	3	3	BobH
025	Dead link to unknown topic exists in help file wcalc.hlp	3	3	BobH
030	Colors are wrong in 256 color mode but OK in 16 color mode	3	2	MarthaH

Rather than save the query results in word processor format suitable for printing, you can save the data in a raw, tab-delimited form that's easily read into another database, spreadsheet, or charting program. For example, you could create the following generic query:

Product EQUALS Calc-U-Lot AND
Version EQUALS 2.0 AND
Opened By EQUALS Pat

This would list all the bugs against a (fictitious) software product called Calc-U-Lot v2.0 that were opened by someone named Pat. If you then exported the results of this query with the bug severity data field, you could generate a graph such as the one shown in Figure 19.4.

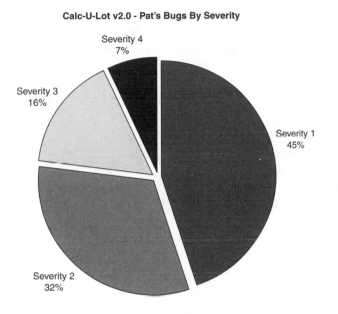

Calc-U-Lot v2.0 - Pat's Bugs By Severity

FIGURE 19.4
A bug-tracking database can be used to create individualized graphs showing the details of your testing.

This pie chart has no bug title or description information, no dates, no resolutions, not even bug ID numbers. What you have is a simple overview of all the bugs that Pat has logged against the Calc-U-Lot v2.0 software project, broken out by severity. Of Pat's bugs, 45 percent are Severity 1, 32 percent are Severity 2, 16 percent are Severity 3, and 7 percent are Severity 4. There are a lot of details behind these numbers, but on the surface you could say that most of the bugs that Pat finds are fairly severe.

Similarly, Figure 19.5 shows another kind of graph generated by a different query that show's Pat's bugs broken out by their resolution. The query to generate this data would be:

> Product EQUALS Calc-U-Lot AND
> Version EQUALS 2.0 AND
> Opened By EQUALS Pat AND
> Status EQUALS Resolved OR Status EQUALS Closed

19

MEASURING YOUR SUCCESS

Exporting the resolution field to a charting program would generate the graph in Figure 19.5 showing that most of Pat's bugs end up getting fixed (a good sign for a tester) and that only a small percentage are resolved as not reproducible, duplicates, deferred, or for whatever reason, not a problem.

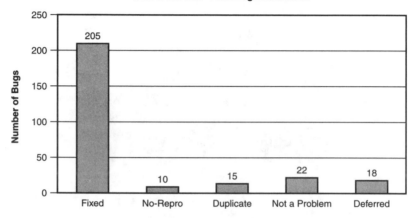

FIGURE 19.5

Different queries can generate different views of the bug data. In this case, you can see how one tester's bugs were resolved.

Once you start testing, you'll find certain metrics that you like to use, or that your team uses, to measure how the testing process is going. You might find that counting your bug finds per day is useful or, as in the previous example, what your "fix ratio" is. The important thing is that by extracting information from the bug database, you can build just about any metric that you want. This leads to the next part of this chapter, which describes a few of the common higher-level metrics that measure how the entire project is doing.

Common Project-Level Metrics

Put on your "big boss" hat and think about the questions that managers mull over their coffee every morning: Is the software project making progress? Will it be ready to release on schedule? What's the risk of it not hitting that date? What's the overall reliability?

Management is fundamentally interested in the overall view of the project—what its quality and reliability level is and whether it's on track to be ready when scheduled. The bug-tracking database is the perfect tool to provide this information.

Think back to Chapter 3, "The Realities of Software Testing," where you learned one of the basic rules of testing—the more bugs you find, the more bugs there are. This concept holds whether you're looking at just a small piece of the software or thousands of modules grouped together. By following this concept, it's easy to create metrics and graphs that can be used to get a view into the software and determine the status of not just the test effort, but the entire project.

NOTE

Most likely it will be the test manager or project manager who builds up these metrics. It's important, however, for you to be familiar with them so that you know how your test effort is affecting the overall project and whether your team is making progress.

Figure 19.6 is a fundamental pie chart that shows a breakout of the bugs found against the Calc-U-Lot v2.0 project. In this chart, the bugs are separated into the major functional areas of the software in which they were found.

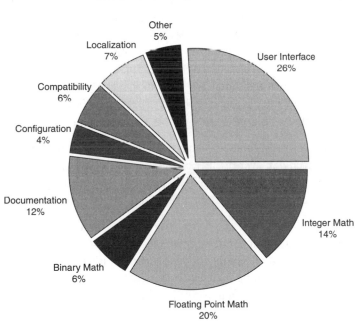

Calc-U-Lot v2.0 - Bugs By Software Area

FIGURE 19.6

A project-level pie chart shows how many bugs were found in each major functional area of the software.

19

MEASURING YOUR SUCCESS

Assume that this graph was generated about halfway through the product development process. By following the rule of "bugs follow bugs," which areas do you think are most likely to still have more bugs and probably need additional testing?

Three areas—the user interface, integer math, and floating-point math—make up 60 percent of all the bugs found. If the test effort to date has been consistent across the entire product, there's a good chance that these three areas are indeed buggy and probably still have more bugs to find.

> **NOTE**
>
> In reaching this conclusion, it's important to consider whether the test effort has been consistent across the product. It's possible that the other areas weren't yet thoroughly tested. This could be the reason for their disproportionately low bug counts. Care should always be taken when generating and interpreting bug data to make sure that all the underlying facts are known.

This data tells you and management a great deal about the project and is a good example of how lots of bug information can be distilled down to something simple and easily understood. This graph is a very common one used by many teams to understand where the bugs are coming from and if there are areas of the project that need more or less testing attention. What this graph doesn't show is timing information. For example, it's possible that the bug find rate for the user interface areas is leveling off and that the find rate for localization is increasing. This is something you can't tell from the graph. For that reason, another basic set of graphs is often used that shows bugs found over time. Figure 19.7 is an example of this type of graph.

In this graph, weekly dates from June 7 through September 6 are shown on the x-axis, and the number of bugs found each day over that period are shown on the y-axis. You can see that at the start of the project, the bug-find rate was low and steadily increased until it became fairly consistent at around 15 bugs per day. Assume that the project schedule is targeting a release date of September 15. By looking at the chart, do you think the software will be ready?

Most rational people wouldn't think so. The graph clearly shows the bug-find rate remaining constant over time with no hint of trending down. Of course, it's possible that the downward spike over the last three days might continue, but that could just be wishful thinking. Until there's a clear trend showing that the number of bugs is declining, there's no reason to think that the software is ready to go.

The clear trend that indicates progress is shown in the graph in Figure 19.8. This project starts out the same as the one in Figure 19.7 but after the bug-find rate peaks in mid July, it starts to trail off, eventually bouncing around one or two per day—an indication that bugs in the software are becoming fewer and more difficult to find.

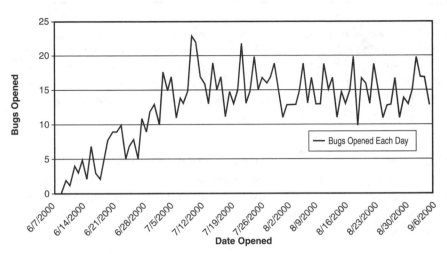

FIGURE 19.7

A graph that shows bugs opened over time can reveal a lot about a software project.

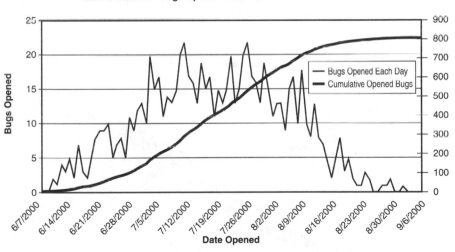

FIGURE 19.8

This graph shows a project that could make its scheduled release date of September 15.

This graph also has an additional line that shows the cumulative bugs found over time. You can see the gentle slope up and then the flattening of the curve indicating the decreasing bug-find rate. A project that makes it to this point is usually in a good position to be released.

> **NOTE**
>
> Be careful how you interpret the data. Consider the graph shown in Figure 19.8. It shows the bug-find rate declining over time. The assumption is that this is due to the product becoming more stable as bugs are found and fixed. But, it could also be due to many of the testers being out of the office because of illness. If the testers aren't testing, there won't be anyone finding bugs and the graph of the bug data will look just like one that says everything's okay.

The simplified graphs shown in these examples have only the calendar dates across the x-axis. In a graph for a real project, it would be important to map not just the dates but also the project's schedule and milestones, such as major releases of the software, the different test phases, and so on. Doing so would help clarify why, for example, the trend line levels out earlier than expected (maybe the end of a test phase has concluded and the testers are waiting for more code to test) or why it climbs almost straight up (a lot of new, previous untested code became available for testing). Again, the chart is just data. It needs to be clarified and thoroughly understood to be successfully used.

One of the most effective bug graphs that reveals the status of a project is shown in Figure 19.9. This graph is similar to the one in Figure 19.8 but adds two more lines, one showing the cumulative resolved bugs and another the cumulative closed bugs, with shading underneath to show the space between them.

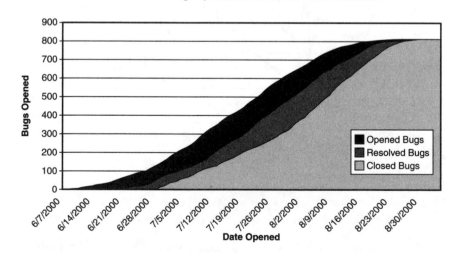

FIGURE 19.9

Is this the be-all-end-all software testing status graph? Maybe, maybe not. It's very effective, though, at communicating the project's status.

The top line is the same one as in Figure 19.8 and represents the bugs opened over time. There's no change here; it's used the same way. The next line down represents the resolved bugs over time—ones that the programmers have fixed or the review committee has determined aren't to be addressed. As the bugs are resolved, this line moves up, hopefully tracking the opened line. There's a gap between the two lines (shown as the black filled area) because the programmers and reviewers often can't resolve the bugs as soon as they're entered by the testers. The bugs usually start to pile up and the gap widens between the two states of the bug's life cycle. Eventually the programmers and project managers catch up and the two lines meet—the number of resolved bugs eventually equaling the number of opened bugs.

REMINDER

> A resolved bug isn't necessarily a fixed bug. Some bugs may be resolved as duplicates, as "won't fix," as by design, and so on.

The third line shows the bugs that are closed over time. Remember, once a bug is resolved it's assigned back to the tester for regression testing to ensure that it's been fixed. If the bug fix checks out, the bug is closed. This line lags the resolved line for the same reason the resolved line lags the opened line—the testers usually can't close bugs as fast as they're resolved because they're still busy testing the rest of the software. Eventually the closed bugs catch up to the resolved and opened bugs and the curves flatten out as fewer and fewer bugs are found, resolved, and closed.

What does this graph tell you? In short, the filled-in areas show how much work is left for the programmers and testers to do. A widening black area means that the programmers are getting further and further behind in fixing bugs. A widening dark gray area means that the testers are having trouble keeping up with the programmer's fixes. If the curves are flattening out and coming together, the project manager is sleeping better at night.

NOTE

> This graph is typically shown using colors. Red indicates opened bugs, yellow indicates resolved bugs, and green indicates closed bugs. A quick glance can tell you the project's status. Lots of red means lots of programmer's work. Lots of yellow means lots of tester's work. Lots of green means the project is getting close to release.

Adding the resolved and closed data lines to the opened data line and putting it all on the same graph provides a comprehensive view of the overall project and helps minimize misinterpretation of the data. A previous note mentioned that a leveling of the bug open rate could mean that the testers were either not finding bugs, or were out sick. The data couldn't tell you which.

Another possibility is that they decided to close out bugs for a few days and forgo new testing. Having all the information on one graph would make it clearer as to what was happening. Think about this and look for a question regarding it in the quiz section for this chapter.

Summary

The individual and project-level metrics presented here are by no means the definitive list. They're merely examples of common metrics used to track and measure software projects. Each project team, test manager, and tester will use the ones that tell them the information they want to know about the software they're developing. To some people, tracking the average bug severity may be important. To others, it may be how quickly bugs are resolved. You may want to know how many bugs you find per day or what your open-to-fix ratio is. The goal of using metrics is to measure your success and your project's success, to know whether everything is running according to plan, and if it's not, what might be done to correct it.

Chapter 20, "Software Quality Assurance," will introduce you to the next evolutionary step, beyond software testing, where metrics are used not just to measure and correct a specific project, but also to improve the overall development process.

Quiz

These quiz questions are provided for your further understanding. See Appendix A, "Answers to Quiz Questions," for the answers—but don't peek!

1. If you were using metrics from the bug-tracking database to measure your progress or success at testing, why would just counting the number of bugs you find per day or computing your average find rate be an insufficient measure?

2. Given your answer to question 1, list a few additional software metrics that could be used to measure more accurately and precisely your personal progress or success at testing.

3. What would a database query look like (any format you want) that would extract all the resolved bugs assigned to Terry for the Calc-U-Lot v3.0 project?

4. If the bug-find rate for a project was decreasing like the one shown in Figure 19.8 and everyone was excited that the project was getting close to releasing, what might be a couple reasons why this wouldn't be true, that the numbers were lying?

The Future

As soon as we started programming, we found out to our surprise that it wasn't as easy to get programs right as we had thought. Debugging had to be discovered. I can remember the exact instant when I realized that a large part of my life from then on was going to be spent in finding mistakes in my own programs.

—Maurice Wilkes, computer pioneer

IN THIS PART

Software Quality Assurance

CHAPTER

20

IN THIS CHAPTER

This book's focus so far has been on its title, *Software Testing*. You've learned how to plan your testing, where to look for bugs, and how to find and report them. Because you're new to the field of software testing, you'll most likely first apply your skills in these areas.

It's important, though, to get a sense of the larger picture so that you can understand how much more needs to be accomplished and how far you can go in your career. This chapter's goal is to give you an overview of the evolutionary steps beyond software testing, to show you what lies ahead, to outline the challenges, and to hopefully motivate you to make improving software quality your ultimate goal.

Highlights of this chapter include

- What it costs to create quality software
- How software testing varies from software quality assurance
- What different ways a software testing or quality group can fit into a project team
- How the software Capability Maturity Model is used
- The ISO 9000 standard

Quality Is Free

Quality is free? Impossible? Nope, it's true. In 1979, Philip Crosby[1] wrote in his book *Quality is Free: The Art of Making Quality Certain*, that indeed it costs nothing extra (actually it costs less) to produce something of high quality versus something of low quality. Given what you've learned so far about software testing and the work involved in finding and fixing bugs, this may seem impossible, but it's not.

Think back to the graph from Chapter 1 (repeated here as Figure 20.1) that showed the cost of finding and fixing bugs over time. The later bugs are found, the more they cost—not just linearly more, but exponentially more.

Now, divide the cost of quality into two categories: the *costs of conformance* and the *costs of nonconformance*. The costs of conformance are all the costs associated with planning and running tests just one time, to make sure that the software does what it's intended to do. If bugs are found and you must spend time isolating, reporting, and regression testing them to assure that they're fixed, the costs of nonconformance go up. These costs, because they are found before the product is released, are classified as *internal failures* and fall mostly on the left side of Figure 20.1.

---

[1] *Philip Crosby, Joseph Juran, and W. Edwards Deming are considered by many to be the "fathers of quality." They've written numerous books on quality assurance and their practices are in use throughout the world. Although their writings aren't specifically about software, their concepts—often in-your-face common sense—are appropriate to all fields. Good reading.*

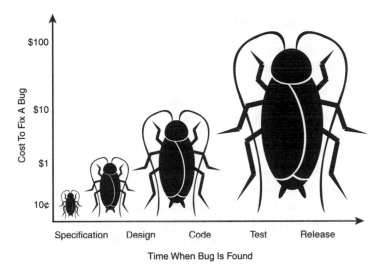

FIGURE 20.1

This graph helps show that the cost of quality is free.

If bugs are missed and make it through to the customers, the result will be costly product support calls, possibly fixing, retesting, and releasing the software, and—in a worst-case scenario—a product recall or lawsuits. The costs to address these *external failures* fall under the costs of nonconformance and are the ones on the right side of Figure 20.1.

In his book, Crosby demonstrates that the costs of conformance plus the costs of nonconformance due to internal failures is less than the costs of nonconformance due to external failures. Stomp out your bugs early, or ideally don't have any in the first place, and your product will cost less than it would otherwise. Quality is free. It's common sense.

Unfortunately, portions of the software industry have been slow to adopt this simple philosophy. A project will often start with good intentions and then as problems crop up and schedule dates are missed, rules and reason go out the window. Regard for higher future costs is written off in favor of getting the job done today. The trend is turning, however. Companies are now realizing that their cost of quality is high, and that it doesn't need to be. Customers are demanding and their competitors are creating better quality software. Realization is setting in that the words Crosby wrote more than 20 years ago for the manufacturing industry apply just as well to the software industry today.

Testing and Quality Assurance in the Workplace

Depending on the company you work for and the project you're working on, you and your peers can have one of several common names that describes your group's function: Software Testing, Software Quality Assurance, Software Quality Control, Software Verification and Validation, Software Integration and Test, or one of many others. Frequently these names are used interchangeably or one is chosen over the others because it sounds more "official"— Software Quality Assurance Engineer versus Software Tester, for example. It's important to realize, though, that these names have deeper meanings and aren't necessarily plug-in replacements for each other. On one hand there's the philosophy that "it's only a name," that what you ultimately do in your job is what counts. On the other hand, your job title or your group's name is what others on the project team see. That label indicates to them how they will work with you and what expectations they will have, what deliverables you will provide to them, and what they will give to you. The following sections define a few of the common software-test-group names and should help clarify the differences among them.

Software Testing

It can't be emphasized enough, so here it is, one more time:

> *The goal of a software tester is to find bugs, find them as early as possible, and make sure they get fixed.*

In this book you've learned about every part of this charter—how to accomplish this goal and the reality and limitations in doing so. Maybe you've realized by now (and if you haven't, that's okay) that software testing can be simply described as an assess, report, and follow-up task. You find bugs, describe them effectively, inform the appropriate people, and track them until they're resolved.

NOTE

The definition of a software tester's job used in this book actually goes a step further than assess, report, and follow-up by tacking on the phrase "and make sure they get fixed." Although there are test groups that would replace this phrase with simply "and report them," I believe that to be an effective tester you need to take personal responsibility for the bugs you find, tracking them through their life cycle, and persuading the appropriate people to get them fixed. The easy way out is to simply stick them in the bug database and hope that someone eventually notices and does something with them, but if that's all there was to testing, you could argue, "Why bother looking for bugs in the first place?"

Being a software tester and working under this charter has a unique and very important characteristic: You *aren't* responsible for the quality of the software! This may sound strange, but it's true. You didn't put the bugs in the software, you had your project manager and the programmers review and approve your test plan, you executed your plan to the letter and despite all that effort, the software still had bugs. It's not your fault!

Think about it. A doctor can't make someone's fever go down by taking her temperature. A meteorologist can't stop a tornado by measuring the wind speed. A software tester can't make a poor-quality product better by finding bugs. Software testers simply report the facts. Even if a tester works hard to get the bugs he finds fixed, his efforts still can't make an inherently poor-quality product better. Quality can't be tested in. Period.

> **NOTE**
>
> Some companies do believe that quality can be tested in. Rather than improve the process they use to create their software, they believe that adding more testers is the solution. They think that more testers finding more bugs will make their product better. Interestingly, these same people would never consider using more thermometers to lower someone's fever.

Ultimately, if you're working in a group named "Software Testing," it will be your test manager's responsibility to make sure that everyone on the project team understands this definition of your role. It's often a point of contention when schedules aren't hit and bugs are missed so it's one that should be made perfectly clear up front, preferably in the project's test plan.

Quality Assurance

Another name frequently given to the group that finds software bugs is "Software Quality Assurance (QA)." Chapter 3 cited the following definition of a person in this role:

> A Software Quality Assurance person's main responsibility is to examine and measure the current software development process and find ways to improve it with a goal of preventing bugs from ever occurring.

Now that you know a lot more about software testing, this definition probably sounds a lot more scary than when you first read it in Chapter 3. A software QA group has a much larger scope and responsibility than a software testing group—or at least they should, according to their job description. In addition to performing some or all of the software testing[2], they're chartered with preventing bugs from ever occurring and assuring that the software is of some

[2]*How much testing a software QA group performs is related to its maturity level. You'll learn more about maturity levels later in this chapter.*

(presumably high) level of quality and reliability. They don't just test and report—their responsibility goes much deeper. You can see why, if your job is to perform software testing (and that's all your time and budget allows), you wouldn't want to casually or arbitrarily assume this more "prestigious" title.

You may be wondering, if software testing alone can't guarantee a product's quality, what a Software QA group would do to achieve it. The answer is having nearly full control over the project, instituting standards and methodologies, carefully and methodically monitoring and evaluating the software development process, suggesting solutions to the problems they find, performing some of the testing (or overseeing it), and having the authority to decide when the product is ready to release. It may be an oversimplification to say that it's like having a project manager who's primary goal is "no bugs" as opposed to keeping the product on schedule or under budget, but it's a pretty good description.

You'll learn later in this chapter that moving from software testing to software quality assurance is a gradual process, sort of achieving increasing levels of maturity. It's not a single-step function—yesterday you were a tester and today you're a QAer.

Actually, some of the skills you've learned in this book can be considered software QA skills depending on where you draw the line on bug prevention and where the separation occurs between an internal failure and an external failure. If the goal of software QA is to prevent bugs, you could argue that performing static testing on the product spec, design documents, and code (Chapters 4 and 6) is a type of software QA because you're preventing bugs from occurring. Bugs found this way never make it through to later be found by the testers testing the finished software.

Total Quality Management

You may have heard of a quality approach known as Total Quality Management (TQM) or Total Quality Control (TQC). The basic philosophy behind this approach is that having a centralized quality assurance group that's responsible for quality isn't feasible because the people doing the work—writing the code or creating the widgets—aren't responsible for quality and therefore won't try to achieve it. To create quality products, a quality culture needs to be instituted from management on down so that everyone shares the responsibility for quality.

Although TQM/TQC has great implications to the mission of an existing Quality Assurance group, it doesn't eliminate the need for software testing. Quite to the contrary, the software testing role in such an environment is more clearly defined. Despite the best efforts of any process, software is still created by people, and people make mistakes. There's still a need for a group to concentrate on looking for bugs. They may not find many, but that's a good thing!

Other Names for Software Testing Groups

Depending on where you work, your test group may use one of many other names to identify itself. Software Quality Control (SQC) is one that's frequently used. This name stems from the manufacturing industry where QC inspectors sample products taken off the manufacturing line, test them, and, if they fail, have the authority to shut down the line or the entire factory. Few, if any, software test groups have this authority—even ones that call themselves Software QC.

Software Verification and Validation is also commonly used to describe a software test organization. This name is one that actually works pretty well. Although it's a bit wordy, it states exactly what the test group is responsible for and what they do. Look back to Chapter 3 for the definitions of verification and validation. It's even possible to have two groups, one for verification and one for validation.

Integration and Test, Build and Test, Configuration Management and Test, Test and Lab Management, and other compound unrelated names are often a sign of a problem. Many times the software test group takes on roles (voluntarily or not) that are unrelated to testing. For example, it's not uncommon for a test group to own the job of configuration management or building the product. The problem with this is twofold:

- It takes away resources that should be used for testing the product.
- The test group's goal is ultimately to break things, not to make things, and owning the software's build process creates a conflict of interest.

It's best to let the programmers or a separate team build the software. Testing should concentrate on finding bugs.

Test Management and Organizational Structures

Besides a test group's name and its assumed responsibilities, there's another attribute that greatly affects what it does and how it works with the project team. That attribute is where it fits in the company's overall management structure. A number of organizational structures are possible, each having its own positives and negatives. Some are claimed to be generally better than others, but what's better for one may not necessarily be better for another. If you work for any length of time in software testing, you'll be exposed to many of them. Here are a few common examples.

Figure 20.2 shows a structure often used by small (fewer than 10 or so people) development teams. In this structure, the test group reports to the Development Manager, the person managing the work of the programmers. Given what you've learned about software testing, this should raise a red flag of warning to you—the people writing the code and the people finding bugs in that code reporting to the same person has the potential for big problems.

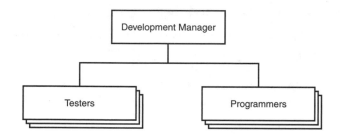

FIGURE 20.2
The organizational structure for a small project often has the test team reporting to the development manager.

There's the inevitable conflict of interest. The Development Manager's goal is to have his team develop software. Testers reporting bugs just hinder that process. Testers doing their job well on one side make the programmers look bad on the other. If the manager gives more resources and funding to the testers, they'll probably find more bugs, but the more bugs they find, the more they'll crimp the manager's goals of making software.

Despite these negatives, this structure can work well if the development manager is very experienced and realizes that his goal isn't just to create software, but to create quality software. Such a manager would value the testers as equals to the programmers. This is also a very good organization for communications flow. There are minimal layers of management and the testers and programmers can very efficiently work together.

Figure 20.3 shows another common organizational structure where both the test group and the development group report to the manager of the project. In this arrangement, the test group often has its own lead or manager whose interest and attention is focused on the test team and their work. This independence is a great advantage when critical decisions are made regarding the software's quality. The test team's voice is equal to the voices of the programmers and other groups contributing to the product.

The downside, however, is that the project manager is making the final decision on quality. This may be fine, and in many industries and types of software, it's perfectly acceptable. In the development of high-risk or mission-critical systems, however, it's sometimes beneficial to have the voice of quality heard at a higher level. The organization shown in Figure 20.4 represents such a structure.

In this organization, the teams responsible for software quality report directly to senior management, independent and on equal reporting levels to the individual projects. The level of authority is often at the quality assurance level, not just the testing level. The independence that this group holds allows them to set standards and guidelines, measure the results, and adopt processes that span multiple projects. Information regarding poor quality (and good quality) goes straight to the top.

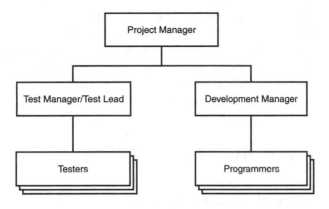

FIGURE 20.3

In an organization where the test team reports to the project manager, there's some independence of the testers from the programmers.

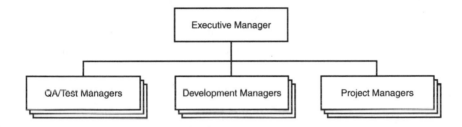

FIGURE 20.4

A quality assurance or test group that reports to executive management has the most independence, the most authority, and the most responsibility.

Of course, with this authority comes an equal measure of responsibility and restraint. Just because the group is independent from the projects doesn't mean they can set unreasonable and difficult-to-achieve quality goals if the projects and users of the software don't demand it. A corporate quality standard that works well on database software might not work well when applied to a computer game. To be effective, this independent quality organization must find ways to work with all the projects they deal with and temper their enthusiasm for quality with the practicality of releasing software. They must also strive to maintain a close working relationship with the programmers and other team members. As the lines of communication grow further apart, this gets more difficult to do.

20

Keep in mind that these three organizational structures are just simplified examples of the many types possible and that the positives and negatives discussed for each can vary widely. In software development and testing, one size doesn't necessarily fit all, and what works for one team may not work for another. There are, however, some common metrics that can be used to measure, and guidelines that can be followed, that have been proven to work across different projects and teams for improving their quality levels. In the next two sections, you'll learn a little about them and how they're used.

Capability Maturity Model (CMM)

The Capability Maturity Model[3] for Software (CMM or SW-CMM) is an industry-standard model for defining and measuring the maturity of a software company's development process and for providing direction on what they can do to improve their software quality. It was developed by the software development community along with the Software Engineering Institute (SEI) and Carnegie Mellon University, under direction of the U.S. Department of Defense.

What makes CMM special is that it's generic and applies equally well to any size software company—from the largest in the world to the single-person consultant. Its five levels (see Figure 20.5) provide a simple means to assess a company's software development maturity and determine the key practices they could adopt to move up to the next level of maturity.

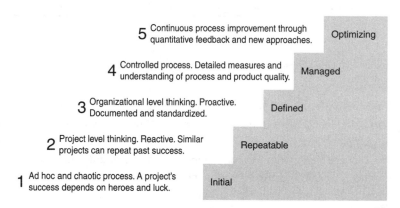

CMM Software Maturity Levels

5 Continuous process improvement through quantitative feedback and new approaches. — Optimizing

4 Controlled process. Detailed measures and understanding of process and product quality. — Managed

3 Organizational level thinking. Proactive. Documented and standardized. — Defined

2 Project level thinking. Reactive. Similar projects can repeat past success. — Repeatable

1 Ad hoc and chaotic process. A project's success depends on heroes and luck. — Initial

FIGURE 20.5
The Software Capability Maturity Model is used to assess a software company's maturity at software development.

---

[3] *CMM, Capability Maturity Model, and Carnegie Mellon are registered in the U.S. Patent and Trademark Office.*

As you read on and learn what each of the five levels entails, think about the following: If you take the entire universe of software companies today, most are at Maturity Level 1, many are at Maturity Level 2, a few are at Maturity Level 3, a handful are at Maturity Level 4, and an elite couple are at Maturity Level 5. Here are descriptions of the five CMM Maturity Levels:

- **Level 1: Initial.** The software development processes at this level are ad hoc and often chaotic. The project's success depends on heroes and luck. There are no general practices for planning, monitoring, or controlling the process. It's impossible to predict the time and cost to develop the software. The test process is just as ad hoc as the rest of the process.

- **Level 2: Repeatable.** This maturity level is best described as project-level thinking. Basic project management processes are in place to track the cost, schedule, functionality, and quality of the project. Lessons learned from previous similar projects are applied. There's a sense of discipline. Basic software testing practices, such as test plans and test cases, are used.

- **Level 3: Defined.** Organizational, not just project specific, thinking comes into play at this level. Common management and engineering activities are standardized and documented. These standards are adapted and approved for use on different projects. The rules aren't thrown out when things get stressful. Test documents and plans are reviewed and approved before testing begins. The test group is independent from the developers. The test results are used to determine when the software is ready.

- **Level 4: Managed.** At this maturity level, the organization's process is under statistical control. Product quality is specified quantitatively beforehand (for example, this product won't release until it has fewer than 0.5 defects per 1,000 lines of code) and the software isn't released until that goal is met. Details of the development process and the software's quality are collected over the project's development, and adjustments are made to correct deviations and to keep the project on plan.

- **Level 5: Optimizing.** This level is called *Optimizing* (not "optimized") because it's continually improving from Level 4. New technologies and processes are attempted, the results are measured, and both incremental and revolutionary changes are instituted to achieve even better quality levels. Just when everyone thinks the best has been obtained, the crank is turned one more time, and the next level of improvement is obtained.

Do any of these levels sound like the process used at a software development company you know? It's scary to think that a great deal of software is developed at Level 1—but it's often not surprising after you use it. Would you want to cross a bridge that was developed at Level 1, ride an elevator, fly on a plane? Probably not. Eventually—hopefully—consumers will demand higher quality software and you'll see companies start to move up in their software development maturity.

> **NOTE**
>
> It's important to realize that it's not a software tester's role to champion a company's move up in software development maturity. That needs to be done at a corporate level, instituted from the top down. When you begin a new testing job, you should assess where the company and your new team is in the different maturity levels. Knowing what level they operate in, or what level they're striving for, will help you set your expectations and give you a better understanding of what they expect from you.

For more information on the Capability Maturity Model, visit the Software Engineering Institute's Web site at www.sei.cmu.edu/cmm.

ISO 9000

Another popular set of standards related to software quality is the International Organization for Standardization's (ISO) 9000. ISO is an international standards organization that sets standards for everything from nuts and bolts to, in the case of ISO 9000, quality management and quality assurance.

You may have heard of ISO 9000 or noticed it in advertisements for a company's products or services. Often it's a little logo or note next to the company name. It's a big deal to become ISO 9000 certified, and a company that has achieved it wants to make that fact known to its customers—especially if its competitors aren't certified.

ISO 9000 is a family of standards on quality management and quality assurance that defines a basic set of good practices that will help a company consistently deliver products (or services) that meet their customer's quality requirements. It doesn't matter if the company is run out of a garage or is a multi-billion-dollar corporation, is making software, fishing lures, or is delivering pizza. Good management practices apply equally to all of them.

ISO 9000 works well for two reasons:

- It targets the development process, not the product. It's concerned about the way an organization goes about its work, not the results of the work. It doesn't attempt to define the quality levels of the widgets coming off the assembly line or the software on the CD. As you've learned, quality is relative and subjective. A company's goal should be to create the level of quality that its customers want. Having a quality development process will help achieve that.

- ISO 9000 dictates only what the process requirements are, not how they are to be achieved. For example, the standard says that a software team should plan and perform product design reviews (see Chapters 4 and 6), but it doesn't say how that requirement should be accomplished. Performing design reviews is a good exercise that a responsible design team should do (which is why it's in ISO 9000), but exactly how the design review is to be organized and run is up to the individual team creating the product. ISO 9000 tells you what to do but not how to do it.

NOTE

A company receiving ISO 9000 certification indicates that it has achieved a specified level of quality control in its development process. This doesn't mean that its products have achieved a specified level of quality—although it's probably a safe bet that its products are of better quality than a company's that hasn't been ISO 9000 certified.

For this reason, especially in the European Union but becoming more frequent in the U.S., customers are expecting their suppliers to be ISO 9000 certified. If two suppliers are competing for the same contract, the one with ISO 9000 certification will have the competitive edge.

The sections of the ISO 9000 standard that deal with software are ISO 9001 and ISO 9000-3. ISO 9001 is for businesses that design, develop, produce, install, and service products. ISO 9000-3 is for businesses that develop, supply, install, and maintain computer software.

It's impossible to detail all the ISO 9000 requirements for software in this chapter, but the following list will give you an idea of what types of criteria the standard contains. It will also, hopefully, make you feel a little better, knowing that there's an international initiative to help companies create a better software development process and to help them build better quality software.

Some of the requirements in ISO 9000-3 include

- Develop detailed quality plans and procedures to control configuration management, product verification and validation (testing), nonconformance (bugs), and corrective actions (fixes).
- Prepare and receive approval for a software development plan that includes a definition of the project, a list of the project's objectives, a project schedule, a product specification, a description of how the project is organized, a discussion of risks and assumptions, and strategies for controlling it.

20

- Communicate the specification in terms that make it easy for the customer to understand and to validate during testing.
- Plan, develop, document, and perform software design review procedures.
- Develop procedures that control software design changes made over the product's life cycle.
- Develop and document software test plans.
- Develop methods to test whether the software meets the customer's requirements.
- Perform software validation and acceptance tests.
- Maintain records of the test results.
- Control how software bugs are investigated and resolved.
- Prove that the product is ready before it's released.
- Develop procedures to control the software's release process.
- Identify and define what quality information should be collected.
- Use statistical techniques to analyze the software development process.
- Use statistical techniques to evaluate product quality.

These requirements should all sound pretty fundamental and common sense to you by now. You may even be wondering how a software company could even create software without having these processes in place. It's amazing that it's even possible, but it does explain why much of the software on the market is so full of bugs. Hopefully, over time, competition and customer demand will compel more companies in the software industry to adopt ISO 9000 as the means by which they do business.

If you're interested in learning more about the ISO 9000 standards for your own information or if your company is pursuing certification, check out the following Web sites:

- International Organization for Standardization (ISO), www.iso.ch
- American Society for Quality (ASQ), www.asq.org
- American National Standards Institute (ANSI), www.ansi.org

Summary

One of Murphy's laws states that there's never enough time to do something right, but there's always enough time to do it over— sounds like a CMM Level 1 company, doesn't it? Forget about Murphy and think Philip Crosby. He was right when he declared that quality really is free. It's just a matter of the software development team following a process, taking their time, being disciplined, and attempting to do it right the first time.

Of course, despite everyone's best efforts, mistakes will still be made, and bugs will still occur. The goal of software quality assurance, though, is to make sure that they are truly mistakes and aren't caused by fundamental problems in the development process. Software testing will always be necessary even in the best run organizations, but if everything runs perfectly, you might be reduced to saying, "Nope, I didn't find any bugs today, hopefully maybe tomorrow."

You've almost completed this book and your tour of software testing. There's one more chapter to cover where you'll learn how to gain more experience in software testing and where to look for more information.

Quiz

These quiz questions are provided for your further understanding. See Appendix A, "Answers to Quiz Questions," for the answers—but don't peek!

1. Why are there testing costs associated with the costs of conformance?
2. **True or False:** The test team is responsible for quality.
3. Why would being called a QA Engineer be a difficult title to live up to?
4. Why is it good for a test or quality assurance group to report independently to senior management?
5. If a company complied with the ISO 9000-3 standard for software, what CMM level do you think they would be in and why?

Your Career as a Software Tester

IN THIS CHAPTER

You're now down to the final chapter of software testing. Well, okay, maybe the final chapter of the book *Software Testing*, but definitely not of the job. Your work in that area has only just begun.

You probably began reading this book with little knowledge of what software testing is all about. You've likely experienced the minor little annoyances and the occasional crashes of the software you use on your computer at home or at work. You've seen and heard news stories of major software bugs and you know about the infamous Y2K bug, which, after all the last-minute testing and preparation, didn't bite as hard as expected.

Hopefully you've now been enlightened and understand why these bugs can still happen despite the best efforts of the people behind the software. You've learned about the test planning process, where to look for bugs, and how to report them. You now understand the difficult decision-making process that's involved in determining which bugs to fix and which ones to defer, and you've seen the graphs that show a product that's ready to release and one that still has a long way to go.

Above all else, you should now understand that software testing is a complex and difficult job. To be successful at it requires discipline, training, and experience. Simply sitting down, pounding the keys, and shouting over the wall to the programmer when you see something odd won't cut it. Software is too important. Businesses have failed, careers have been ruined, and people have died because of software bugs. Your job as a software tester is to find those bugs, efficiently and professionally, before they make it out the door.

This final chapter will give you pointers to more information about software testing, explain a few of the possible career options, and leave you with an important message about software quality. Highlights of this chapter include

- The career path options available for software testers
- Where to look for a testing job
- How to get more hands-on experience at finding bugs
- Where to learn more about software testing
- The Computer User's Bill of Rights

Your Job as a Software Tester

One serious misconception about software testing is that it's only an entry-level position in the software industry. This erroneous belief persists because of the ignorance of what software testing is and what it involves—mainly due to the number of companies still developing software without any real process. They don't yet know that they need software testers of all skill levels to create great software. But, as more emphasis is put on creating software of higher and higher quality, the value of software testing as a career is becoming understood.

Because of this increased awareness, the opportunities are there for the taking. Software testers with just a couple years of experience are highly sought after. Testers who can also program and perform white-box testing or develop automated tests are even more in demand. And, if you've been through a few product development cycles and can lead a small team of other testers, you're in a highly marketable position. It's truly a job-hunter's market for software testers.

Here's a breakout of various software testing positions and their descriptions. Keep in mind, as you learned in Chapter 20, "Software Quality Assurance," the names vary and may not mean exactly what the job really is, but ultimately most software testing jobs fall into these categories.

- **Software test technician.** This is often a true entry-level test position. You would be responsible for setting up test hardware and software configurations, running simple test scripts or test automation, and possibly working with beta sites to isolate and reproduce bugs. Some work can become mundane and repetitive, but being a test technician is a good way to become introduced to software testing.

- **Software tester or software test engineer.** Most companies have several levels of software testers based on experience and expertise. An entry-level tester may perform the duties of technician, working their way up to running more advanced and complex tests. As you progress, you'll write your own test cases and test procedures and might attend design and specification reviews. You'll perform testing and isolate, reproduce, and report the bugs you find. If you have programming abilities, you'll write test automation or testing tools and work closely with the programmers as you perform white-box testing.

- **Software test lead.** A test lead is responsible for the testing of a major portion of a software project or sometimes an entire small project. They often generate the test plan for their areas and oversee the testing performed by other testers. They're frequently involved in collecting metrics for their products and presenting them to management. They usually also perform the duties of a software tester.

- **Software test manager.** A test manager oversees the testing for an entire project or multiple projects. The test leads report to them. They work with the project managers and development managers to set schedules, priorities, and goals. They're responsible for providing the appropriate testing resources—people, equipment, space, and so on—for their projects. They set the tone and strategy for the testing their teams perform.

Finding a Software Testing Position

So where do you look for a software testing job? The answer is the same places you would look for a programming job—with any business or company that develops software.

- **Use the Internet.** A quick search done using several job search engines just before this book went to print found more than 1,000 open software testing positions at companies all around the country. Many of these positions were for entry-level testers. There were jobs testing music software, interactive TV, networking, medical equipment, Web sites, and more. You name it.

- **Look through newspapers and magazines.** As with the Internet, most large city newspapers list numerous software testing jobs every weekend in their high-tech or computer help wanted ads. Computing and programming magazines are also a good source for job ads.

- **Simply call and ask.** Do you like a certain technology or a specific software application, or are you interested in a particular area of computing? Look up the company or companies writing that software, give them a call or send them your résumé. Often there are open software testing jobs that never make it to the help wanted ads. Resourceful testers grab them before anyone knows they're available.

- **Look into internships and co-ops.** If you're in college, take a summer or a semester as an intern or co-op at a software company as a software tester. Most provide great positions where you'll actually be contributing to the success of a real product as you gain experience in the field. If you work hard, you might be offered a full-time position after you graduate.

- **Take temporary jobs.** Many software companies hire software testers under temporary contracts to help run test scripts as a product nears completion. The jobs may last just one month or several months, but you'll gain valuable experience and can take on more difficult jobs each time, learning as you go. Some software testers love to work this way because it gives them the opportunity to work at different companies and try their hand testing very different software.

Gaining Hands-On Experience

Software testing is just like most other computer topics—you can read about it all day, but until you actually try the things you've read about, it's difficult to comprehend. For this reason, one of the best ways to learn software testing is to try it yourself, on your own computer with your own software.

Choose a program you're familiar with and enjoy using or one that you've never used before. Read the manual and the help files as though they were the product specification. Put together a test plan, design the test cases, and look for bugs. Use a spreadsheet or word processor to log them and report what you find to the software company that wrote the application (almost all software companies have a means for reporting problems, usually through their Web site). You'll be surprised what you find, and maybe the company will, too.

With a little experience at this type of testing, you could sign up to be a *beta tester* for new software products. As you learned in Chapter 15, "Bug Bashes and Beta Testing," beta testers receive copies of the software before the general public does. You'll have an opportunity to see

Your Career as a Software Tester

CHAPTER 21

339

21

YOUR CAREER AS
A SOFTWARE
TESTER

and use software that's not quite finished, find bugs that were missed by the company's internal software testers, and, based on what you find, possibly have an impact on the product's design. Every software company has its own system for administering beta tests. Search their Web site for "beta tester" or call them and ask to talk with someone about becoming a beta tester.

> **NOTE**
>
> Be careful if you use beta software on your home or work PC. By its nature, beta software isn't ready for public release and is full of bugs. Some of those bugs can cause serious problems with your computer and existing software, including frequent crashes and loss of data. Make backups of anything important before you run beta software.

Becoming a usability test subject (see Chapter 11, "Usability Testing") is another way to gain some hands-on experience at software testing. Most large software companies making personal computer software have usability labs or contract out to independent usability labs in their area. If you're interested in testing user interfaces, make some phone calls and inquire about becoming a subject for software usability testing. Often you'll be asked to fill out a form to measure your experience and familiarity with certain types of software. As projects go to usability testing, your profile will be reviewed to see if you're the type of person they're looking for; depending on the product being tested, they may need absolute beginners all the way to experts. If you're a match, you'll be called in to try out features in a new product or even a prototype of a new product. The people administering the test will watch what you do, record your actions, and observe how you react to the software. They may invite you back to try out changes they make based on your findings and you'll often be compensated for your time—usually with free software.

Formal Training Opportunities

With the realization that software testing is an important field of study, many colleges and universities have begun to offer classes on the subject. If you're currently in an engineering or computer degree program, it would be well worth your time to enroll in one of these classes. Even if your plans are to become a programmer or engineer, gaining a better knowledge of software testing can help you perform your job even better.

Many community and technical colleges are now offering day and evening classes on software testing and the use of popular software testing tools. Some even award associate degrees and certificates in software testing.

Another option for training is to attend professional software testing conferences. Held throughout the year and in various parts of the U.S. and even the world, these conferences provide an opportunity for you to hear speakers from across the testing industry. Class material spans the entire range from very basic to very advanced and technical. The best part of these conferences is having the opportunity to meet and talk with fellow software testers, sharing ideas, war stories, and solutions. The following list represents some of the more popular conferences, but definitely not all of them. Presence or absence doesn't reflect an endorsement or an opinion.

- **International Conference and Exposition on Testing Computer Software (TCS),** sponsored by the U.S. Professional Development Institute (www.uspdi.org). TCS features international speakers, presentations of current software testing best practices by experienced professionals, opportunities to share lessons and experiences with your peers, and a vendor show of products and services.

- **International Quality Week,** sponsored by Software Research, Inc. (www.soft.com). The mission of the Quality Week and Quality Week Europe Conferences is to "bring advanced technology R&D work relating to software quality, testing and process, contemporary software quality and testing needs, and knowledge and experience from the software quality industry together in a balanced technical forum."

- **International Software Testing Conference (ISTC),** sponsored by the Quality Assurance Institute (www.qaiusa.com). ISTC is a weeklong conference featuring expert speakers from across the software testing and quality assurance industry. Topics range from basic software testing to test automation to testing specific new technologies.

- **Software Testing Analysis & Review (STAR),** sponsored by Software Quality Engineering (www.sqe.com/stareast and www.sqe.com/starwest). The STAR conferences are focused exclusively on software testing and software engineering. They provide classes, tutorials, and discussions by software testing experts and hold an exposition . where test tool, technology, and service companies demonstrate their products.

- **International Conference on Software Quality (ICSQ),** sponsored by the Software Division of the American Society for Quality (www.asq-software.org). ICSQ, like the other conferences, provides an opportunity to share testing ideas and methods with other software testing and quality assurance professionals.

- **International Conference on Software Testing (ICSTEST),** sponsored by Software Quality Systems (www.icstest.com). ICSTEST is an international testing conference held in Germany. It's a forum for presentations, tutorials, discussions, and exchange of experiences on software testing.

Your Career as a Software Tester

CHAPTER 21

341

21

YOUR CAREER AS
A SOFTWARE
TESTER

- **The Second World Congress for Software Quality (2WCSQ)** (www.juse.or.jp/
e-renmei/2WCSQMAIN.htm). 2WCSQ is a worldwide conference on software quality with
members from more than 27 countries. The year 2000 conference was held in Japan.

Internet Links

The Internet has a wealth of material on software testing. You could always do a search for
"software testing" or "software test," but here's a list of popular Web sites dedicated to software testing and software bugs that will get you started:

- BugNet (www.bugnet.com) publicizes bugs found in commercial software and points you
to the appropriate fixes.

- Software Testing Hotlist (www.io.com/~wazmo/qa) lists dozens of pointers to software
testing–related Web sites and articles.

- Software Testing Online Resources (www.mtsu.edu/~storm) is the self-proclaimed
"nexus of Software Testing Online Resources...designed to be a 'first-stop' on the Web
for software testing researchers and practitioners."

- QA Forums (www.qaforums.com) provide ongoing discussions of software testing, automated testing, test management, test tools, and many other topics.

- The newsgroup comp.software.testing and its FAQ (frequently asked questions) document at www.faqs.org/faqs/software-eng/testing-faq provide lots of ongoing discussions by testers and test managers regarding tools, techniques, and projects.

- The newsgroup comp.risks describes and analyzes recent software failures.

- The Risks Digest (catless.ncl.ac.uk/Risks/) is a forum on risks to the public in computers and related systems.

Professional Organizations

Several professional nonprofit organizations are dedicated to software, software testing, and
software quality assurance that may be of interest to you. Their Web sites provide details on
their specific area of coverage:

- The American Society for Quality (ASQ) at www.asq.org and its software division at
www.asq-software.org sponsor the National Quality Forum annually in October
(national quality month). They publish journals and articles on quality and administer the
Certified Quality Engineer (CQE) and the Certified Software Quality Engineer (CSQE)
designation.

- The Association of Computing Machinery (ACM) at www.acm.org and its Special
Interest Group on Software Engineering (SIGSOFT) at www.acm.org/sigsoft has more
than 80,000 members in educational and scientific computing. The software engineering

interest group publishes a bimonthly newsletter with a popular forum titled "Risks to the Public," which details recent serious software bugs.

- The Society for Software Quality (SSQ) at www.ssq.org lists its vision as "To be recognized as the Society for those interested in promoting 'quality' as a universal goal for software."

Further Reading

Numerous books are available on the topics of software testing and software quality assurance. Each has its own audience and approach. Some are very technical, whereas others are very process and managerial oriented. Your best bet to find something that interests you is to visit a large bookstore, university library, or favorite online bookstore and look for titles by Boris Beizer, Rex Black, Bill Hetzel, Cem Kaner, Edward Kit, Glen Myers, and William Perry.

If you're interested in learning more about general product quality assurance techniques, look for titles by Philip Crosby, W. Edwards Deming, and Joseph Juran.

The following Sams Publishing titles are a sampling of some books that you might want to look at to improve your understanding of computers and programming. These books were specifically chosen to get you up to speed quickly and easily and are very appropriate reading for the novice software tester:

- *Sams Teach Yourself Beginning Programming in 24 Hours* is a great introduction to the basics of programming. You won't become a white-box tester just by reading this book, but you will gain a better insight into how software is written—which will help you design better test cases.

- *Sams Teach Yourself HTML in 24 Hours*, *Sams Teach Yourself Visual Basic in 24 Hours*, *Sams Teach Yourself Java in 24 Hours*, and *Sams Teach Yourself C++ in 24 Hours* are a good next step once you've mastered the basics of programming.

- If your goal is to be a serious white-box tester, *Sams Teach Yourself Visual Basic in 21 Days*, *Sams Teach Yourself Java in 21 Days*, *Sams Teach Yourself C in 21 Days*, and *Sams Teach Yourself C++ in 21 Days* will teach you the details of programming in specific languages.

- *Sams Teach Yourself Upgrading and Fixing PCs in 24 Hours* will teach you the basics of adding new hardware and peripherals to your PC—a very important topic for a software tester, especially if you're interested in configuration testing.

- *Internationalization with Visual Basic*

> **NOTE**
>
> To keep up with the latest in programming titles, regularly check out Macmillan Computer Publishing's Web site at www.mcp.com.

Summary

It seems appropriate to close out this book with a mantra that sums up what you should hope to achieve through your work as a software tester. Frequently throughout this book, qualifiers such as "depending on your company or your project team" and "based on your industry" were used when describing development processes, testing techniques, and quality levels. The use of such qualifiers makes it impossible to universally define a common goal for software quality. The qualifiers are necessary, though, because unfortunately, at least so far, the definition of software quality "depends."

In 1998, Dr. Clare-Marie Karat, a psychologist and user interface designer at IBM's Thomas J. Watson Research Center in Hawthorne, NY, proposed a computer user's bill of rights. This bill of rights sets a minimum quality bar, a minimum set of expectations that computer users should have the rights to with the software they use. The computer industry has a long way to go to achieve this level of quality, but with your work as a software tester, you can help to make it a reality.

The Computer User's Bill of Rights (reprinted with Dr. Karat's permission)[1]:

1. **Perspective.** The user is always right. If there's a problem with the use of the system, the system is the problem, not the user.
2. **Installation.** The user has the right to easily install and uninstall software and hardware systems without negative consequences.
3. **Compliance.** The user has the right to a system that performs exactly as promised.
4. **Instruction.** The user has the right to easy-to-use instructions (user guides, online or contextual help, error messages) for understanding and utilizing a system to achieve desired goals and recover efficiently and gracefully from problem situations.
5. **Control.** The user has the right to be in control of the system and to be able to get the system to respond to a request for attention.
6. **Feedback.** The user has the right to a system that provides clear, understandable, and accurate information regarding the task it's performing and the progress toward completion.

---

[1] *Published with permission from IBM Corporation.*

7. **Dependencies.** The user has the right to be clearly informed about all systems requirements for successfully using software or hardware.

8. **Scope.** The user has the right to know the limits of the system's capabilities.

9. **Assistance.** The user has the right to communicate with the technology provider and receive a thoughtful and helpful response when raising concerns.

10. **Usability.** The user should be the master of software and hardware technology, not vice versa. Products should be natural and intuitive to use.

Quiz

These quiz questions are provided for your further understanding. See Appendix A, "Answers to Quiz Questions," for the answers—but don't peek!

1. When looking for a software testing position on the Internet, what keywords should you use in your search?

2. Name two ways that you can become involved in testing computer software before it is released to the public.

3. What's the goal of a software tester?

Answers to Quiz Questions

Chapter 1

1. *In the Year 2000 bug example, did Dave do anything wrong?*

   Not if the product spec and design goals for the software never stated that the product should work beyond year 2000. A software tester should have tested for and found the bug. The team could then decide whether to fix it.

2. ***True or False:*** *It's important what term your company or team calls a problem in its software.*

   False. It's not important, but the term used often reflects the personality of the team and how they approach the finding, reporting, and fixing of the problems.

3. *What's wrong with just testing that a program works as expected?*

   At most, that's only half the testing problem. Users don't always follow the rules, and testers need to prove out what happens when they don't. Also, if testers don't approach their testing with a gotta-break-it attitude, they will miss bugs.

4. *How much more does it cost to fix a bug found after the product is released than it does from the very start of the project?*

   From 10 to 100 times or even higher!

5. *What's the goal of a software tester?*

   The goal of a software tester is to find bugs, find them as early as possible, and make sure they get fixed.

6. ***True or False:*** *A good tester relentlessly strives for perfection.*

   False. A good tester knows when perfection isn't attainable and when "good enough" is reached.

7. *Give several reasons why the product specification is usually the largest source of bugs in a software product.*

   Often a spec isn't even written—remember, if you can't say it, you can't do it. Other reasons are that the spec exists but it isn't thorough, it's constantly changing, or it's not communicated to the rest of the development team.

Chapter 2

1. *Name several tasks that should be performed before a programmer starts writing the first line of code.*

   The development team needs to understand the customer requirements and define the features in a product spec. A detailed schedule should be created so team members know what work has been completed and what work remains to be done. The software should be architected and designed, and the test team should start planning their work.

2. *What disadvantage is there to having a formal, locked-down specification?*

If the market changes because of the release of a competitor's product or changing customer needs, there's no flexibility to adjust the software.

3. *What is the best feature of the big-bang model of software development?*

It's simple. Period.

4. *When using the code-and-fix model, how do you know when the software is ready to release?*

There's no real exit criteria for the code-and-fix process except for when someone, or the schedule, says that it's time to stop.

5. *Why can the waterfall method be difficult to use?*

Just like with salmon, it's difficult to swim upstream. Each step is a discrete, standalone process that follows the one before it. If you get to the end and find that something should have happened further up, it's too late to go back.

6. *Why would a software tester like the spiral model best?*

They're involved very early in the development process and have the opportunity to find problems early, saving the project time and money.

Chapter 3

1. *Given that it's impossible to test a program completely, what information do you think should be considered when deciding whether it's time to stop testing?*

There is no correct answer for when to stop testing. Each project is different. Examples of the information that might go into the decision would be: Are lots of bugs still being found? Is the team satisfied with the number and types of tests that have been run? Have the reported bugs been evaluated to decide which ones to fix and which ones not to fix? Has the product been validated against the user's requirements?

2. *Start the Windows Calculator. Type **5,000-5=** (the comma is important). Look at the result. Is this a bug? Why or why not?*

The answer you get is 0, not 4095 as you would expect. The reason is that the , (comma) was automatically converted to a . (decimal point). What you calculated was 5.000-5=0, not 5,000-5=4995. To determine if this is a bug, verify this operation against the product specification. It might state that commas are to be converted to decimal points. You should also validate this "feature" against the user requirements. Find out if most users want this to occur or if it would be confusing.

3. *If you were testing a simulation game such as a flight simulator or a city simulator, what do you think would be more important to test—its accuracy or its precision?*

The purpose of a simulation game is to put the player into an artificial environment that mimics a real-world scenario. Flying a flight simulator should look and feel like flying a real plane. Running a city simulator should reflect what happens in a real city. What's most important is how accurately the simulator reflects reality. Does the plane fly like a Boeing 757 or Piper Cub? Does the skyline of the city look like the city it represents? After the software has accuracy, precision can follow. If you think about the advancement of simulation games over the years, this is exactly what has happened.

4. *Is it possible to have a high-quality and low-reliability product? What might an example be?*

Yes, but it depends on the customer's expectations for quality. Many people buy high-performance sports cars that are considered to be high quality for their acceleration and speed, their style, and their fit and finish. Often these same cars are notoriously unreliable, frequently breaking down and being expensive to repair. Their owners don't consider this poor reliability to be an aspect of quality.

5. *Why is it impossible to test a program completely?*

With any software other than the smallest and simplest program, there are too many inputs, too many outputs, and too many path combinations to fully test. Also, software specs can be subjective and be interpreted in different ways.

6. *If you were testing a feature of your software on Monday and finding a new bug every hour, at what rate would you expect to find bugs on Tuesday?*

Two axioms come into play here. The first—that the number of bugs remaining is proportional to the number of bugs you've already found—means that you won't come in on Tuesday and miraculously find the software to be perfect. The pesticide paradox tells you that if you continue to run the same tests over and over that you eventually won't find new and different bugs until you add more tests. Given these two axioms, you will probably continue to find bugs at the same rate or slightly less.

Chapter 4

1. *Can a software tester perform white-box testing on a specification?*

Yes, if the tester is involved with the process used in defining the specification. He could attend the focus groups, usability studies, and marketing meetings to understand the underlying process being used to design the features and the overall product. There is a risk, though, that this information could bias the tester into assuming that the spec is correct.

2. *Cite a few example of Mac or Windows standards or guidelines.*

   On the Mac, deleted files go to the Trash Can. In Windows, they go to the Recycle Bin.

   Pressing F1 always displays Help for the software.

   The File menu is always the far-left menu choice in Windows.

   Selecting Help, About displays the software's copyright, licensing, and version information.

   Ctrl+X performs a cut, Ctrl+C performs a copy, and Ctrl+V performs a paste.

3. *Explain what's wrong with this specification statement: When the user selects the Compact Memory option, the program will compress the mailing list data as small as possible using a Huffman-sparse-matrix approach.*

   It uses the phrase *as small as possible*. This is impossible to test because it's not quantifiable and not precise. The spec should state exactly what level of compression will take place.

   The statement also isn't code-free. It explains how the feature will work on the algorithm level. This doesn't belong in a requirements document. The user doesn't care how the compaction occurs, just that it does.

4. *Explain what a tester should worry about with this line from a spec: The software will allow up to 100 million simultaneous connections, although no more than 1 million will normally be used.*

   Testability. It doesn't matter that typical usage is only 1 million connections. If the specification states that 100 million are possible, the 100 million must be tested. The tester needs to find a way to test something this large or get the spec writer to reduce the maximum possible number to something closer to what's typical.

Chapter 5

1. ***True or False:*** *You can perform dynamic black-box testing without a product specification or requirements document.*

   True. The technique is called *exploratory testing*, and you essentially use the software as though it's the product spec. It's not an ideal process, but can work okay in a pinch. The largest risk is that you won't know if a feature is missing.

2. *If you're testing a program's ability to print to a printer, what generic test-to-fail test cases might be appropriate?*

   You could attempt to print with no paper and with jammed paper. You could take the printer offline, unplug its power, and disconnect its printer cable. You could try printing with low ink or toner, maybe even with a missing cartridge. To identify all the possibilities, you could look in the printer's operator's manual and see what errors it supports and attempt to create all of them.

3. *Start up Windows WordPad and select Print from the File menu. What boundary conditions exist for the Print Range feature?*

If you select the Pages option, the From and To fields are enabled. The obvious boundary conditions would be 0 and 99999, the smallest and largest values that the fields will hold. It would be wise to also test internal boundary conditions such as 254, 255, 256 and 1023, 1024, and 1025. There's also another internal boundary condition. Try asking it to print pages 1 through 8 of a 6-page document. Notice that in this case, the software has to stop printing at page 6 because it's out of data, not because it was told to stop at this page. It's a different, internal boundary. See if you can think of more.

4. *Assume that you have a 10-character-wide ZIP code text box. What equivalence partitions would you create for this text box?*

You should have at least these equivalence partitions, although you may think of more:

- Valid 5-digit ZIP codes. Valid means that they're numeric digits, not that they are existing, in-use ZIP codes—although that could be another partition.
- Valid 9-digit (9 digits with a dash) ZIP codes
- Short 5-digit. Have only 4 numbers, for example.
- Short 9-digit.
- Long 5-digit. Have 8 digits without a dash, for example. Hmm, is this the same as a short 9-digit partition?
- Long 9-digit. It may not be possible to type in more than 9 digits and a dash, but you should try.
- 10 digits, no dash. This is a little different than a long 9-digit partition.
- The dash in the wrong place.
- More than one dash.
- Non-digit and non-dash entries.

5. ***True or False:*** *Visiting all the states that a program has assures that you've also traversed all the transitions among them.*

False. Think of visiting 50 different cities spread out across the entire U.S. You could plan a trip that would take you to each city, but it would be impossible for you to travel all the roads that connect to all the cities—that would be all the roads in the entire country.

6. *There are many different ways to draw state transition diagrams, but there are three things that they all show. What are they?*

   - Each unique state that the software can be in.

   - The input or conditions that make it move from one state to the next.

   - Conditions, variables, or output that's produced when a state is entered or exited.

7. *What are some of the initial state variables for the Windows Calculator?*

   The initial displayed value and the internal partial result are set to 0. The memory register (MC, MR, MS, and M+ buttons) is set to 0. The memory system Clipboard contents (where data goes when you cut, copy, and paste) is left unchanged.

   Another initial state variable is where the Calculator appears onscreen when it's started. Open up several copies of the Calculator and notice that the location isn't always the same (at least on Windows 95/98). As an exercise in exploratory testing, see if you can figure out what the rules are for where the Calculator opens.

8. *What actions do you perform on software when attempting to expose race condition bugs?*

   You try doing multiple things at the same time. They could be related, like printing to two printers at the same time from the same application. Or, they could be unrelated, like pressing keys while a computation is taking place. What you want to do is force a situation where the software is competing (racing) with itself to perform some function.

9. ***True or False:*** *It's an unfair test to perform stress testing at the same time you perform load testing.*

   False. No test is ever unfair. Your job is to find bugs.

Chapter 6

1. *Name several advantages to performing static white-box testing.*

   Static white-box testing finds bugs early in the development cycle, making them less time-consuming and less costly to fix. The software testers can gain information about how the software works, what potential weaknesses and risky areas exist, and can build a better working relationship with the programmers. Project status can be communicated to all team members who participate in the testing.

2. ***True or False:*** *Static white-box testing can find missing items as well as problems.*

   True. Missing items are arguably more important than normal problems and can be found through static white-box testing. When the code is checked against published standards and guidelines and carefully analyzed in formal reviews, missing items become obvious.

3. *What key element makes formal reviews work?*

Process. Having a process that's followed is what makes the difference between a formal review and two pal programmers glancing over each other's code.

4. *Besides being more formal, what's the big difference between inspections and other types of reviews?*

The key difference is that with inspections, a person other than the original author of the code is the presenter. This obliges another person to fully understand the software being inspected. It's much more effective than having others simply review the software for bugs.

5. *If a programmer was told that he could name his variables with only eight characters and the first character had to be capitalized, would that be a standard or a guideline?*

That would be a standard. If he was allowed to name them with no less than eight characters, but shorter was preferred, that would be a guideline.

6. *Should you adopt the code review checklist from this chapter as your team's standard to verify its code?*

No! It's provided as a generic example only. There are some good test cases in it that you should consider when you test your code, but you should research and read about other published standards before adopting your own.

Chapter 7

1. *Why does knowing how the software works influence how and what you should test?*

If you test only with a black-box view of the software, you won't know if your test cases adequately cover all the parts of the software nor if some of the cases are redundant. An experienced black-box tester can design a fairly efficient suite of tests for a program but he can't know how good that suite is without some white-box knowledge.

2. *What's the difference between dynamic white-box testing and debugging?*

Both processes overlap, but the goal of dynamic white-box testing is to find bugs and the goal of debugging is to fix them. The overlap occurs in the area of isolating exactly where and why the bug occurs.

3. *What are two reasons that testing in a big-bang software development model is nearly impossible? How can these be addressed?*

With the software delivered to you in one big piece, it's difficult, if not impossible, to figure out why a bug occurs—the needle-in-a-haystack problem. The second reason is that there are so many bugs, some hide others. You'll grab one and shout "gotcha" only to discover that the software is still failing.

Methodically integrating and testing the modules as they are built allows you to find and fix bugs before they start to become hidden or pile on top of each other.

4. ***True or False:*** *If your product development is in a hurry, you can skip module testing and proceed directly to integration testing.*

   False! Unless, of course, your product is a module.

5. *What's the difference between a test stub and a test driver?*

   A test stub is used in top-down testing. It stubs out, or substitutes itself, for a low-level module. It looks and acts to the higher-level code being tested just like the original low-level module.

   A test driver is the opposite of a stub and is used in bottom-up testing. It's test code that replaces higher-level software to more efficiently exercise a low-level module.

6. ***True or False:*** *Always design your black-box test cases first.*

   True. Design your test cases based on what you believe the software is supposed to do. Then use white-box techniques to check them and make them most efficient.

7. *Of the three code coverage measures described, which one is the best? Why?*

   Condition coverage is the best because it also incorporates branch coverage and statement coverage. It assures you that all the conditions within decision logic, such as if-then statements, are verified, as well as all branches from those statements and the lines of code.

8. *What's the biggest problem of white-box testing, either static or dynamic?*

   You can easily become biased. You might look at the code and say, "Oh, I see, I don't need to test that case, the code handles it properly." In reality, you were blinded by the light and eliminated necessary test cases. Be careful!

Chapter 8

1. *What's the difference between a component and a peripheral?*

   Generally, a component is a hardware device internal to a PC. A peripheral is external to the PC. The lines can become blurry, though, depending on the type of hardware.

2. *How can you tell if a bug you find is a general problem or a specific configuration problem?*

   Rerun the exact same steps that revealed the bug on several different configurations. If the problem doesn't occur on those, it's very likely a configuration bug. If it occurs on the different configurations, it's likely a general problem. Be careful, though. It could be a configuration problem across an entire equivalence class. For example, it's possible that the bug shows up only on laser printers, but not inkjet printers.

3. *How could you guarantee that your software would never have a configuration problem?*

   This is sort of a trick question. You'd need to ship the hardware and software together as one package, the software would only work on that hardware, and the hardware would have to be completely sealed, not having a single interface to the outside world.

4. ***True or False:*** *A cloned sound card doesn't need to be considered as one of the configurations to test.*

   It depends. A cloned hardware device is internally identical to another but has a different name and possibly a different case. Often they are 100 percent functionally equivalent, but sometimes the device drivers are different, allowing one to support more or different features than the other.

5. *In addition to age and popularity, what other criteria might you use to equivalence partition hardware for configuration testing?*

   Region or country is a possibility as some hardware devices such as CD-ROM players only work with CDs in their region. Another might be consumer or business. Some hardware is specific to one, but not the other. Think of others that might apply to your software.

6. *Is it acceptable to release a software product that has configuration bugs?*

   Yes. You'll never be able to fix them all. As in all testing, the process is risk based. You and your team will need to decide what you can fix and what you can't. Leaving in an obscure bug that only appears with a rare piece of hardware is an easy decision. Others won't be as easy.

Chapter 9

1. ***True or False:*** *All software must undergo some level of compatibility testing.*

   False. There will be a few rare, standalone, proprietary first versions of software out there that don't interact with anything. For the other 99 percent of the world, though, some level of compatibility testing will be necessary.

2. ***True or False:*** *Compatibility is a product feature and can have different levels of compliance.*

   True. The level of compatibility that your software has is based on your customers' needs. It may be perfectly fine for a word processor to not be compatible with a competitor's file format or for a new operating system to not support a certain class of gaming software. As a tester, you should provide input to these decisions by determining how much work would be involved in checking that compatibility.

3. *If you're assigned to test compatibility of your product's data file formats, how would you approach the task?*

Research whether your program follows existing standards for its files. If so, test that it meets those standards. Equivalence partition the possible programs that would read and write your program's files. Design test documents with representative samples of the types of data that your program can save and load. Test the transfer of these files between your program and the other programs.

4. *How can you test forward compatibility?*

Testing forward compatibility is tough—after all, how can you test against something that doesn't exist yet? The answer is to make sure that what you're testing is thoroughly and carefully defined to the point that it could be deemed a standard. That standard then becomes the means for assuring that what you're testing is forward compatible.

Chapter 10

1. *What's the difference between translation and localization?*

Translation is concerned only with the language aspects—translating the words. Localization takes into account the customs, conventions, and culture of the region or locale.

2. *Do you need to know the language to be able to test a localized product?*

No, but someone on the test team needs to be fluent. You can test the non–language-specific portions of the software, but knowing a bit of the language will help you be more efficient.

3. *What is text expansion and what common bugs can occur because of it?*

Text expansion occurs when English text is translated into another language. The length of text strings can grow 100 percent or more. Text that used to fit onscreen, in dialog boxes, in buttons, and so on no longer does. It can be truncated or cause other text to roll off. It's even possible to have the software crash because the extra long text no longer fits in the memory set aside for the string and other memory is overwritten.

4. *Identify several areas where extended characters can cause problems.*

The order of sorted or alphabetized words and phrases, conversion between upper- and lowercase, and just general display and printing issues.

5. *Why is it important to keep text strings out of the code?*

Localizing becomes much easier if the person doing the work has to modify only a text file rather than the programming code. It also makes the testing work easier because you'll know that the code didn't change on the localized version of the software.

6. *Name a few types of data formats that could vary from one localized program to another.*

Measurements such as pounds, inches, and gallons. Time in 24-hour or 12-hour format. Currency has recently become important now that many European countries have converted to the Euro. There are many others.

Chapter 11

1. ***True or False:*** *All software has a user interface and therefore must be tested for usability.*

True. Eventually, even the most deeply embedded software is exposed, in some way, to a user. Keep in mind that the UI may be as simple as a switch and a light bulb or as complex as a flight simulator. Even if the software is a single module of code, its interface, in the form of variables and parameters, is exposed to the programmer.

2. *Is user interface design a science or an art?*

It's a little bit of both. Many user interface designs have been thoroughly tested in the labs, been through rigorous studies, only to be complete failures in the marketplace.

3. *If there's no definitive right or wrong user interface, how can it be tested?*

Software testers should check that it meets seven important criteria: That it follows standards and guidelines, that it's intuitive, consistent, flexible, comfortable, correct, and useful.

4. *List some examples of poorly designed or inconsistent UIs in products you're familiar with.*

This answer will vary based on the products you use but think about these: Try setting the time on your car radio's clock—can you do it without using the manual?

A few Windows dialog boxes have the OK button on the left and the Cancel button on the right, whereas others have Cancel on the left and OK on the right. If you get used to one layout and click without looking, you could lose your work!

Did you ever accidentally hang up on someone when you clicked the receiver hook on your phone to use call waiting or conference calling?

And, the best one of all time…is up to you to find!

5. *What four types of disabilities could affect software usability?*

Visual, hearing, motion, and cognitive impairments.

6. *If you're testing software that will be accessibility enabled, what areas do you need to pay close attention to?*

Areas dealing with the keyboard, mouse, sound, and display. If the software was written to a popular platform that supports accessibility, the test effort will be a bit easier than if the accessibility features were programmed entirely from scratch.

Chapter 12

1. *Start up Windows Paint and look for several examples of documentation that should be tested. What did you find?*

   Here are a few examples: There's rollover help—the little pop-up descriptions you get when you hold the cursor over a painting tool. Selecting About from the Help menu displays a window with copyright and licensing information. Pressing F1 starts the online help system where you can read the manual, select from an index, or type in words to search for. There's also function help—for example, if you select Edit Colors from the Colors menu, click the ? in the title bar, and then click one of the colors, you'll get help about choosing and creating colors.

2. *The Windows Paint Help Index contains more than 200 terms from* adding custom colors to zooming. *Would you test that each of these takes you to the correct help topics? What if there were 10,000 indexed terms?*

   Every testing task is a risk-based problem. If you have time to test all the index entries, you might choose to do so. If you can't test them all, you'll have to create equivalence partitions of the ones you think are important to check. You could base your decision on information you get from the programmers on how the index system works. You might talk with the writer to find out how the entries were generated. You might try one of each starting letter, or the 1st, 2nd, 4th, 8th, 16th, … and last. You could even wait until you read Chapter 14, "Automated Testing and Test Tools."

3. *True or False: Testing error messages falls under documentation testing.*

   True. But, it's not just documentation testing. The content of the message needs to be tested as documentation, but forcing the message to appear and assuring that the correct message is displayed is testing the code.

4. *In what three ways does good documentation contribute to the product's overall quality?*

   Improved usability, improved reliability, and lower support costs.

Chapter 13

1. *What basic elements of a Web page can easily be tested with a black-box approach?*

   The static elements that are similar to what's in multimedia CD-ROM software—text, graphics, and hyperlinks.

2. *What is gray-box testing?*

   Gray-box testing is when you can take a peek at the underlying code and use that information to help you test. It's different from white-box testing in that you're usually looking at simple scripting code, not a complex, compiled language such as C++. You're also not examining it to the same level of detail as you would with white-box testing.

3. *Why is gray-box testing possible with Web site testing?*

   Because many Web sites are principally created with easily viewable HTML, a mark-up language, not an executable program.

4. *Why can't you rely on a spell checker to check the spelling on a Web page?*

   Because a spell checker can only check ordinary text. It can't check graphical letters or dynamically generated text.

5. *Name a few areas that you need to consider when performing configuration and compatibility testing of a Web site.*

   The hardware platform, the operating system, the Web browser, browser plug-ins, browser options and settings, video resolution and color depth, text size, and modem speeds.

6. *Which of Jakob Neilsen's 10 common Web site mistakes would cause configuration and compatibility bugs?*

   Gratuitous use of bleeding-edge technology. Existing hardware and software is always susceptible to new technology being run on it for the first time. This was a bit of a trick question—it wasn't mentioned in the chapter, but hopefully you could arrive at the answer by applying what you've learned in Part III of the book.

Chapter 14

1. *Name a few benefits of using software test tools and automation.*

   They can speed up the amount of time it takes to run your test cases. They can make you more efficient by giving you more time for test planning and test case development. They're accurate, precise, and relentless.

2. *What are a few drawbacks or cautions to consider when deciding to use software test tools and automation?*

   Because software can change during the product's development, your test tools will need to change, too. You can fall into a trap of spending too much time designing tools and automation, neglecting actual testing. It's easy to rely on automation too much. There's no substitute for testing the software yourself.

3. *What's the difference between a tool and automation?*

   A test tool will help you test, making it easier for you to perform a manual testing task. Automation is also a tool, but it will run without your intervention. Think power saw and hammer building a house while the carpenter sleeps.

4. *How are viewer tools and injector tools similar and different?*

Both types of tools hook into the software at points not normally accessible to the average user. Viewer tools are non-invasive as they allow you to see only what's happening. Injector tools are invasive—they allow you not only to see what's happening, but also to manipulate it. You can try test cases that might otherwise be difficult or impossible to perform at the normal user level.

5. **True or False:** *An invasive tool is the best type because it operates closest to the software being tested.*

   False. Being invasive or non-invasive doesn't make a tool good or bad. The software being tested and the test case that needs to be performed will dictate the best choice of tool.

6. *What's one of the simplest, but effective, types of test automation?*

   Keystroke and mouse action record and playback are the simplest type of automation that can effectively find bugs.

7. *Name a few features that could be added to test automation you described in question 6 to make it even more effective.*

   Simple programming of steps rather than captured steps. The ability to pause or wait for the software to react to the actions. Some type of simple verification so that the macros know whether a bug has occurred.

8. *What advantages do smart monkeys have over macros and dumb monkeys?*

   They're almost self-aware. They know the software's state table so they know where they are and what they can do.

Chapter 15

1. *Describe the pesticide paradox and how bringing in new people to look at the software helps solve it.*

   The pesticide paradox (described in Chapter 3, "The Realities of Software Testing") is the situation that occurs if you continue to test software with the same tests, or the same people. Eventually, the software seems to build up an immunity to the tests because no new bugs are found. If you change the tests or bring in new testers, you'll find new bugs. The bugs were always there, it's just that the new approach made them visible.

2. *What are a few positives to having a beta test program for your software?*

   It gets lots of additional people looking at the software. It's a good way to find configuration and compatibility problems.

3. *What are a few cautions to consider with a beta test program?*

A beta test is no substitute for an organized, planned, methodical test approach—it's not good at general bug finding. You should know who the beta testers are in regards to their experience level, equipment, and needs to ensure that you get what you expect out of the test.

4. *If you're testing for a small software company, why would it be a good idea to outsource your configuration testing?*

The expense and overhead to stock and manage a configuration testing lab is very high and would likely be prohibitive for a small company or project.

Chapter 16

1. *What's the purpose of a test plan?*

To paraphrase the ANSI/IEEE definition, the purpose of a test plan is to define the scope, approach, resources, and schedule of the testing activities and to identify the items being tested, the features to be tested, the testing tasks to be performed, the personnel responsible for each task, and the risks associated with the plan. In short, to tell and get agreement from the rest of the project team exactly how the heck the test team intends to test the software.

2. *Why is it the process of creating the plan that matters, not the plan itself?*

Because all the issues and questions defined in a test plan either impact or are influenced by other project functional groups or team members. Getting everyone to understand and agree to the contents of the plan is what matters. Privately creating a paper document and putting it on a shelf is not just a waste of time, but also jeopardizes the project.

3. *Why is defining the software's quality and reliability goals an important part of test planning?*

Because left to their own, everyone will have different ideas of what quality and reliability mean to them. Since they're all different, they all can't be achieved.

4. *What are entrance and exit criteria?*

These requirements must be met to move from one testing phase to another. A phase can't be left until its exit criteria are met. A new phase can't be entered until its entrance criteria are met.

5. *Name a few typical testing resources that should be considered when test planning.*

People, equipment, offices and labs, software, outsourcing companies, and miscellaneous supplies.

6. ***True or False:*** *A schedule should be made to meet absolute dates so that there's no question when a testing task or phase is to start and when it's to end.*

   False. Because testing depends so much on other aspects of the project (for example, you can't test something until it's coded), a test schedule is best made relative to the delivery dates.

Chapter 17

1. *What are the four reasons for test case planning?*

   Organization, repeatability, tracking, and proof of testing.

2. *What is ad hoc testing?*

   Ad hoc testing is testing without a plan. It's easy and fun but it's not organized, it's not repeatable, it can't be tracked, and when it's over, there's no proof that it was ever done.

3. *What's the purpose of a test design specification?*

   The purpose of the test design spec is to organize and describe the testing that needs to be performed on a specific feature. It outlines the features to be tested and the approach to be used. It identifies the test cases, but doesn't specify them, and what the pass/fail criteria is.

4. *What is a test case specification?*

   This document defines the actual input values used for testing and the expected outputs. It also lists any special environmental needs or procedure requirements and any interdependencies among test cases.

5. *Other than a traditional document, what means can you use to present your test cases?*

   Tables, matrices, lists, graphical diagrams—whatever means most efficiently presents the test cases to you, other testers, and other members of your product team.

6. *What's the purpose of a test procedure specification?*

   The purpose of the test procedure spec is to identify all the steps required to perform the test cases, including how to set up, start, run, and shut down the test. It also explains what to do in case the test doesn't go as planned.

7. *At what level of detail should test procedures be written?*

   That's a question without a specific answer. It greatly depends on who will be using the procedures. Too little detail makes the test procedures ambiguous and variable. Too much detail can bog down the test process. The level of detail should be set by the industry, the company, the project, and the test team.

Chapter 18

1. *Cite a few reasons that a bug might not be fixed.*

   There's not enough time in the schedule, it's not a bug, it's too risky, it's not worth it, and the bug wasn't reported properly.

2. *What basic principles can you apply to your bug reports to give them the best chance of getting the bug fixed?*

   Log them as soon as possible. Effectively describe the bug, making sure it's minimal, singular, obvious and general, and reproducible. Be nonjudgmental in your approach. Follow the report through its life cycle.

3. *Describe a few techniques for isolating and reproducing a bug.*

   Record what you do and review it carefully. Use white-box test techniques to look for race conditions, boundary conditions, memory leaks, and other similar problems. See if the bug is state related, such as initial state or later state dependent. Consider resource dependencies and even hardware problems as the source of the bug.

4. *Suppose that you're running tests on the Windows Calculator and find that 1+1=2, 2+2=5, 3+3=6, 4+4=9, 5+5=10, and 6+6=13. Write a bug title and bug description that effectively describes this problem.*

   Title: Adding a pair of even numbers gives an answer that's one too much.

   Description:

   Test Case: Simple addition

   Setup Steps: Start Version 1.0 of Calculator

   Repro Steps: Try adding pairs of even number such as 2+2, 4+4, and 10+10. Also try adding pairs of odd numbers such as 3+3, 5+5, and 13+13 and pairs of mixed odd and even numbers such as 1+2, 5+6, and 12+13.

   Expected Result: Correct answer for all pairs—2+2=4, 4+4=8...

   Actual Result: For pairs of even numbers, the answer is one too high—2+2=5, 4+4=9, 10+10=21, and so on.

   Other Info: This wasn't tried exhaustively, but the bug occurred in many instances from 2+2 to 65536. The bug doesn't seem to occur with odd numbers or mixed pairs.

5. *What severity and priority would you give to a misspelling in a company's logo on the software's start-up screen?*

   Probably Severity 3 (minor problem), Priority 2 (must fix before release).

6. *What are the three basic states of a software bug's life cycle and the two common additional states?*

Open, Resolved, and Closed are the basic states. Review and Deferred are two possible other states.

7. *List a few reasons that a database bug-tracking system is so much more useful than a paper-based system.*

   You can see at a glance what a bug's life cycle has been—even if it has been complex. The current status of a bug can be instantly known. Bugs can't be lost or neglected as easily.

Chapter 19

1. *If you were using metrics from the bug-tracking database to measure your progress or success at testing, why would just counting the number of bugs you find per day or computing your average find rate be an insufficient measure?*

   It doesn't tell the entire story. You could be testing the most complex area of the software. Your area could have been written by the most experienced programmer. It could have been written by the least experienced programmer. The code you're testing may have already been tested or may be brand new.

2. *Given your answer to question 1, list a few additional software metrics that could be used to measure more accurately and precisely your personal progress or success at testing.*

   Average number of bugs found per day. Total bugs found so far. Ratio of fixed bugs to all bugs found. Ratio of Severity 1 or Priority 1 bugs to all bugs found. Average time from the Resolved state to the Closed state.

3. *What would a database query look like (any format you want) that would extract all the resolved bugs assigned to Terry for the Calc-U-Lot v3.0 project?*

   Product EQUALS Calc-U-Lot AND

   Version EQUALS 3.0 AND

   Status EQUALS Resolved AND

   Assign TO EQUALS Terry

4. *If the bug-find rate for a project was decreasing like the one shown in Figure 19.8 and everyone was excited that the project was getting close to releasing, what might be a couple reasons why this wouldn't be true, that the numbers were lying?*

   It's possible that the software was released to testing in phases and not all the software was tested yet—it might only be leveling off for the current phase. The testers might be busy regressing and closing bugs and not looking for new ones. It could have been a very warm and sunny week or the testers might be out on vacation.

Chapter 20

1. *Why are there testing costs associated with the costs of conformance?*

   Because no matter how good the development process is, testing still needs to be performed one time to verify the product against the product specification and validate it against the user requirements. If no bugs are found, great, but all the costs associated with planning, developing, and executing the tests contribute to the costs of conformance.

2. ***True or False:*** *The test team is responsible for quality.*

   False! Testing looks for bugs. Testers didn't put the bugs in the product and can't guarantee when they're done testing that no more bugs exist.

3. *Why would being called a QA Engineer be a difficult title to live up to?*

   Because it implies that you are the one guaranteeing the product's quality. Are you ready for that responsibility?

4. *Why is it good for a test or quality assurance group to report independently to senior management?*

   If they report to the development manager or the project manager, there's a conflict of interest between finding bugs and the creation of the software or the meeting of the schedule.

5. *If a company complied with the ISO 9000-3 standard for software, what CMM level do you think they would be in and why?*

   They would probably be at CMM Level 3, possibly touching some of the Level 4 requirements. They aren't at Level 2 because Level 2 is just concerned with the project level. Level 3 deals with the entire organization or company. Level 4 is where statistical control starts to come into play.

Chapter 21

1. *When looking for a software testing position on the Internet, what keywords should you use in your search?*

   Since the job names and descriptions for software testers are variable, you should try looking for software test, software testing, quality assurance, and QA.

2. *Name two ways that you can become involved in testing computer software before it is released to the public.*

   Beta testing and usability testing.

3. *What's the goal of a software tester?*

The goal of a software tester is to find bugs, find them as early as possible, and make sure they get fixed.

INDEX

A

X - Y - Z

Other Related Titles

Sams Teach Yourself Beginning Programming in 24 Hours
Greg Perry
ISBN: 0-672-31355-3
$19.99 U.S./$28.95 CAN

Sams Teach Yourself HTML in 24 Hours, Fourth Edition
Dick Oliver
ISBN: 0-672-31724-9
$19.99 U.S./$29.95 CAN

Sams Teach Yourself Visual Basic 6 in 24 Hours
Greg Perry with Sanjaya Hettihewa
ISBN: 0-672-31533-5
$19.99 U.S./$29.95 CAN

Sams Teach Yourself Java 2 In 24 Hours
Rogers Cadenhead
ISBN: 0-672-31630-7
$19.99 U.S./$29.95 CAN

Sams Teach Yourself C++ in 24 Hours, Second Edition
Jesse Liberty
ISBN: 0-672-31516-5
$19.99 U.S./$29.95 CAN

Sams Teach Yourself Visual Basic 6 in 21 Days
Greg Perry
ISBN: 0-672-31310-3
$29.99 U.S./$42.95 CAN

Sams Teach Yourself C In 21 Days, Fifth Edition
Peter Aitken, Bradley L. Jones
ISBN: 0-672-31766-4
$29.99 U.S./$44.95 CAN

Sams Teach Yourself C++ in 21 Days, Third Edition
Jesse Liberty
ISBN: 0-672-31515-7
$29.99 U.S./$44.95 CAN

Sams Teach Yourself Upgrading and Fixing PCs in 24 Hours, Second Edition
Galen A. Grimes
ISBN: 0-672-31881-4
$19.99 U.S./$29.95 CAN

Sams Teach Yourself Java 2 in 21 Days
Laura LeMay, Rogers Cadenhead
ISBN: 0-672-31638-2
$29.99 U.S./$44.95 CAN

Sams Teach Yourself to Create Web Pages in 24 Hours, Second Edition
Ned Snell
ISBN: 0-672-317168
$24.99 U.S./$37.95 CAN

SAMS
www.samspublishing.com

All prices are subject to change.